Fine WoodWorking *on* Tables and Desks

D0507532

Fine WoodWorking on Tables and Desks

32 articles selected by the editors of *Fine Woodworking* magazine

 The Taunton Press

Cover drawing by Christopher Clapp

©1986 by The·Taunton Press, Inc.

First printing: January 1986
Second printing: February 1987
Third printing: March 1989
Fourth printing: October 1990
International Standard Book Number: 0-918804-44-2
Library of Congress Catalog Card Number: 85-51879
Printed in the United States of America

A FINE WOODWORKING Book

FINE WOODWORKING® is a trademark of The Taunton Press, Inc.,
registered in the U.S. Patent and Trademark Office.

The Taunton Press, Inc.
63 South Main Street
Box 5506
Newtown, Connecticut 06470·5506

Contents

Introduction

How much of our lives do we spend at a table—eating, working or just talking? The important part of a table, naturally, is its top: a horizontal surface at the height we want, convenient for lounging, sitting or standing. The rest of it is apparatus for positioning that tabletop exactly where we want it to be.

If we could have antigravity, we wouldn't bother about making table bases. But since we don't have antigravity, woodworkers have had to devise innumerable ways of joining sticks together, to support the goal of floating the tabletop. In this collection of 32 articles reprinted from the first ten years of *Fine Woodworking* magazine, authors who are also craftsmen tell you all about making tabletops and bases. Sometimes we can plant the tabletop on the boxes and drawers we make for storing our stuff, and then the table becomes a desk. This volume also includes detailed plans for a lap desk, a pigeon-hole desk, and a roll-top desk.

John Kelsey, editor

Round-Top Table
A piece that's subtle and direct

by Kenneth Rower

Here is a table capable of extensive variation in the shape of the legs, treatment of rails and outline of the top. It is straightforwardly built since all the joints are the same and the parts of the square frame are in two groups of four copies each. By altering the length of two rails, it is readily adaptable to rectangular or oval forms, and a rectangular section could be used for the legs. The top is quickly detachable via a locking system of dovetail pins cut on the leg tops and housings cut into the underside of the top.

The example shown here is in Georgia pine, with tapered, chamfered legs, chamfered rails and a 48-in. dia. top. The marriage of round top and square frame is not entirely serene, the difficulty being to make the frame large enough to seem right when viewed straight on, yet small enough not to seem bulky when viewed from a corner. The ideal stock for legs and rails is rift-cut, so that the grain is the same on all faces. A certain amount of heart figure can be included near the upper edges of the rails where it will be obscured by the overhang of the top. But do take the legs from near the edges of a flatsawn plank where the end grain shows the rings at about 45° to the face of the piece.

The thickness of the top should be less than half the thickness of the legs, but somewhere above two-fifths. Many arrangements are possible for the boards in the top. One good plan is to start with a long, thick plank and resaw all the pieces required, and then arrange them in a balanced pattern. Another approach is to use a fairly wide, flatsawn piece in the middle and build out to the edges with rift-sawn and quarter-sawn pieces. Given random stock, it is best to order the pieces to minimize discontinuities at the joints. There is normally no purpose in alternating heart and bark faces of the

boards except to gain a flowing appearance at the ends. Once glued up, the top is likely to curl upward at the edges regardless of the way the boards are laid. What counts most in the end is the appearance of the surface.

To make a top round by hand requires a compass or other coarse handsaw, a heavy spokeshave and an adjustable circular plane. Lay out the circle with a trammel. Saw away most of the waste, then set the top on edge in a bench vise, and work to the line with spokeshave and circular plane, exercising caution on the changing grain between quadrants. The goal is to achieve a fair curve kept pretty square to the top, free of perceptible irregularities. Some tearing is likely, and the edge will need to be sanded with paper wrapped around a thin, flexible stick about 6 in. long.

Frame size derives from the diameter of the top. A ratio of about five to eight is satisfactory if the top is round, but the frame would be somewhat larger under a square top because of the prominent overhang at the corners. Rectangular tops permit considerable variation in overhang without straining the eye. Comfortable rail depth for a table 29 in. high is about 4½ in. The leg section should be between 1¾ in. and 2½ in., assuming a thickness for the top from ¾ in. to 1¼ in.

Tenon thickness accords with leg section and the chosen system of mortising the legs. In this design, mortises are cut equal distances in from the leg faces and open into one another at the back. For tables of ordinary size the tenons should be ½ in. to ⅝ in. thick. Rail thickness, in turn, depends further on the style of the frame. If the rails are to be set flush to the legs, they must be twice as thick as the tenon in order to yield an equal amount of stock in the outer wall of the mortise. But if the rails are set in ¼ in. to create a strong

Close attention to joinery, proportion and grain orientation can make the difference between success and failure in the simple design of the table at left. Removable top is secured by dovetail pins, above, which are engaged in housings.

From *Fine Woodworking* magazine (September 1981) 30:88-89

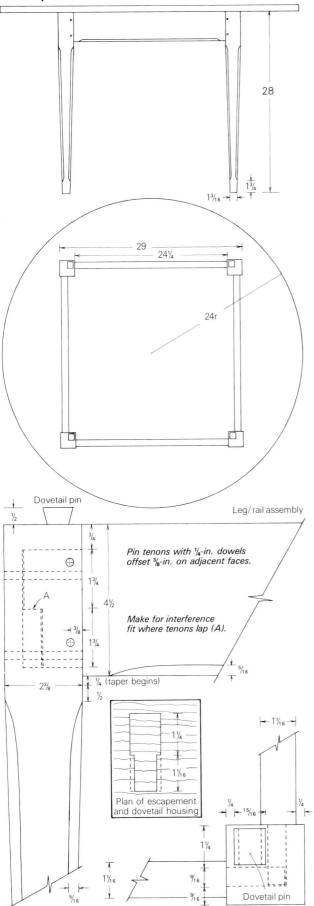

Dovetail pin

Leg/rail assembly

Pin tenons with ¼-in. dowels
offset ⅜-in. on adjacent faces.

Make for interference
fit where tenons lap (A).

¼ (taper begins)

Plan of escapement
and dovetail housing

Dovetail pin

shadow at the joint, they can be thinner by that amount, or the extra wood can be cut away to form an inner shoulder, certainly desirable in the absence of corner blocks. In any case, the mortises should not be cut closer than ¾ in. to the top of the leg, and it is good practice to reduce the mortise a little at the other end, allowing a small shoulder at the bottom of the tenon to conceal any bruising or shrinkage.

Tenons may be haunched or not, according to one's opinion of the relative importance of maintaining the integrity of the mortise, compared with keeping the rail flat and increasing the withdrawal resistance of the tenon. The latter is perhaps more definitely achieved by a pair of tight pins fitted across the joint close to the shoulders. But in the case of a frame with rails flush to the legs and not pinned, haunched tenons are well justified.

Taper in the legs may be scant or bold, inner faces only or all faces. The legs shown here are boldly tapered all faces, each face being reduced by half from a point a little below the joint to the bottom of the leg. This is a satisfactory proportion if the legs are to be chamfered. If they are to be left plain, it is better to use scant taper of about ½ in. for the inner faces, or ¼ in. on all faces. It may be that tapered legs yield a more durable frame than straight legs, since tapered legs are more flexible, and strains at the feet are distributed near the leg bottoms, rather than communicated fully to the joints.

Tapers and chamfers on the legs, and chamfers on the rails, should be cut after the joints are fitted and little further handling will be required. Stop chamfers can be cut with the drawknife (bevel down), and finished with rapid, firm strokes of the spokeshave. Entrances may need to be corrected with a sharp chisel. Tearing is a frequent danger. Lay out chamfers in pencil, because scribed lines cannot be removed without broadening the chamfer.

The construction of the frame does not preclude the use of turned or specially shaved legs, as long as the inner faces of the legs are flat and square in the area of the joints.

To assemble the frame, join two legs and their rail, repeat with the other legs and their rail and then join the assemblies to each other with the remaining rails. If there is plenty of friction when the joints are tested dry, glue only the first inch or so of the tenon nearest the shoulders since any glue at the back of the mortise will cause trouble if the leg shrinks.

The fastening system between frame and top consists of four dovetail pins cut on the tops of the legs and four housings with escapements cut in the underside of the tabletop. The method for cutting these is described in the article on pages 55-56. When cutting out the legs, leave stock at the top ends for the pins, which should be sawn after the legs are mortised but before the frame is assembled. This fastening system will not interfere with seasonal movement of the top, but when the top shrinks or swells in width, two of the pins will remain partly engaged when the top is slid over to unlock, and you can damage the pins when removing the top. The simplest solution is to lengthen the escapements away from their housings, those on one side accounting for expansion, those on the other for contraction. This method of joining top to frame offers no advantage of strength over the customary use of screws between rails and top. But it does allow quick removal of the top, and it satisfies a certain notion of pure construction. □

Kenneth Rower makes furniture in Newbury, Vt.

Parsons Tables
Building and veneering them

by C. Edward Moore

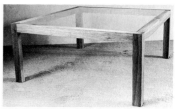

Solid walnut table with recessed glass top. Exposed rail tenons are mitered.

The Parsons table came into existence during the 1930s as a result of a simple drafting technique. Students of John Michele Franc of the Paris division of the Parsons School of Design were taught to block out a cube or rectangular prism and then to design an object within it. At some point the students and Franc decided that such a block form itself could be a design solution. Consequently, the first Parsons table was produced and one of Franc's own designs is in the collection of the Cooper-Hewitt Museum in New York City.

A Parsons table is a rectangular table that appears to be made of stock of one thickness. Simplicity has made these tables a stock item with interior decorators (especially those besieged by clients with visions of "modern eclectic"). They are frequently placed behind a sofa to support a lamp. Large cities, where contemporary design is most likely to flourish, sometimes have small shops specializing in wooden Parsons tables. One also finds wicker, plastic, metal, glass-topped, painted and plastic-laminated Parsons tables. It is possible to adapt this style to obtain a wide variety of results.

It would appear that the easiest way to make such a simple item as a Parsons table would be with solid wood, with the skirt outside and around a beautiful solid wood top. I made such a table once, with a beautiful butcher-block walnut center, finished it with much elbow grease, and gave it as a wedding gift. Six months later there was a split (in the table, not the marriage). The violation of grain direction doomed it from the start, despite the valiant efforts of resorcinol glue. Consequently, I am convinced that it is virtually impossible to make a true Parsons table with a solid top and solid rails that will withstand the test of time. A parquet top might be the exception.

Industry has produced a vast assortment of false or floating tops in this style of table to circumvent the problem. Many such tables are laminated or lacquered particle board, designed more for quick sale than for strength or durability. In general, Parsons tables are among the worst-made items available from any source. One eventually concludes that a Parsons table with wood as its visible surface should be veneered over a sturdy base.

Some early thought should be given to the veneer. If you are new to veneering, stick with mahogany, walnut, oriental-wood and other "strong" veneers, and avoid thinner veneers such as rosewood and the burls. If you aren't using any matching, some attention should be given to "loose" versus "tight" sides of the veneer. Flick your finger across the end of a piece of veneer and note from which side little pieces chip. This is the loose side and when possible it should be the glue side rather than the exposed side. Obviously this is of more concern with some veneers than others. I frequently maximize the randomness in the butcher-block patterns I use and violate the principle just stated. Some books ignore this subject and others seem to say little more.

Let's discuss an end table 21 in. wide, 31 in. long and 22 in. high, with stock thickness a 2⅜ in. These are arbitrary dimensions, provided only for ease of discussion. It is best to use a leveler or glide on the bottom of the legs, and to account for it in designing the height of the table. I start with 4/4 poplar, which I plane and laminate in three layers with Titebond glue. (I use Titebond glue for the entire project when making a table this size.) Then I rip, joint and plane the poplar to stock that is 2⅜ in. square. Suitable solid stock could be used for smaller tables.

For the legs, cut four pieces 5/16 in. shorter than the final height of the table, or 21¹¹/₁₆ in. long. I try to add a touch of elegance by beveling the inside of the legs, but this is a matter of personal taste. The next step is to veneer the inside of the legs, before cutting the joints.

It is important that the beveled side of the leg be veneered first, then the two adjoining sides, because this sequence will yield the fewest visible seams. I apply the glue to the leg with a rubber roller or brayer, to get a uniform application. Then I place the veneer on the glue-covered wood and clamp the assembly against a suitable flat surface. Sometimes I roll the veneer with a dry rubber roller before clamping.

Glue spread with a roller seems to dry very quickly, so some haste is required. But use no more glue than is necessary. If

Parsons table appears to be made from stock of constant thickness, a, although it looks best when inside of leg is beveled as shown. Veneer the bevel first, clamping with V-block, then veneer adjoining sides.

2⅜"   1⅜"   45°

Ed Moore is an associate professor of mathematics at the U.S. Naval Academy in Annapolis, Md. His work is usually on display at Elizabeth Interiors in Annapolis.

From *Fine Woodworking* magazine (Summer 1978) 11:70-73

you apply too much glue it will either seep through the porous veneer or form dry pockets, leaving you with either a sandwich of leg and clamping bench, or a lumpy surface. To avoid making a sandwich, cover the bench with a plastic film such as "Glad Wrap" (but not waxed paper, because it can mess up finishes). The plastic forms a moisture barrier, so the clamping time must be increased and after removing the clamps the wood should be allowed to sit undisturbed overnight, until the moisture dissipates.

It takes a little care to trim the veneer at the bevel. Place the veneered side down on a piece of scrap wood and insert a piece of waste veneer between the stock and cutting tool. I find a serrated veneer knife most convenient. Cut carefully and then plane or sand off the little lip of veneer that remains. A slip or split here can lead to a very ugly repair. Next veneer the adjacent inside faces in the same way.

With three of the five sides veneered, one may start cutting and fitting the joints at the top of the leg. Cut a ½-in. shoulder 2⅟₁₆ in. from the top of the leg on the inside faces, leaving a 1⅞-in. square cross section. Then cut open mortises ½ in. wide and ¾ in. long, and ½ in. from the outside. I use a router mounted under a table. This is a lot of wood to remove in a single pass, and it is best to drill out some of the waste first. Extreme care must be taken to have the fences fit snugly and to control the feed carefully.

The end and side rails are each 2¼ in. shorter than the respective outside dimensions of the table, so you need two pieces 18¾ in. long and two pieces 28¾ in. long. For the top I use ⅝-in. imported 11-ply birch plywood. To accommodate it, it is necessary to cut a rabbet ½ in. wide and ⅛ in. deep into the inner edge of the side and end rails. For balanced construction, you must completely veneer the rails. Cover the 1¾-in. inside face first, then the bottom of these four pieces. Each end of each rail gets a tenon ¾ in. long, ½ in. thick and ½ in. from the outside edge. I crosscut the shoulders on the radial-arm saw (using a stop block for uniformity) and rip the other cuts on a band saw (using a rip fence). A dry fit of a rail and a leg shows two things: One, you need a ½-in. miter on the inside shoulder, so cut it; and two, the rail is ⁵⁄₁₆ in. plus the veneer thickness higher than the top of the leg. Cut a dado ⁵⁄₁₆ in. deep across the top of each end of each rail, 2 in. or 2½ in. from the end. Adjust this cut to make the resulting surface flush with the top of the leg when the joint is in place. This will accommodate a cap, to prevent end grain from telegraphing through the veneer.

When everything fits, glue up the two end assemblies. Then dry-clamp the two side rails in place to get a precise measurement for the plywood top. Be sure the plywood has no hollow spots, and veneer its bottom side to balance the construction. With 11-ply stock, as opposed to 5-ply or 7-ply, this balance may be more cosmetic than actual. Now glue up the two end assemblies, side rails and top. By breaking the gluing into these segments you are more likely to get square corners and parallel legs. Sometimes I glue a cross-rail to the underside of the top, between the long sides of the table. If the table is so large that the 5/8-ply seems too thin I glue another layer of plywood, of a size to fit tightly between the rails, to the underside. I always use glue blocks between the top and rails, as insurance, and a 3-in. mitered brace at each corner. The brace solidifies the leg construction when it is glued to the top and screwed into the adjoining rails.

I cap the corners with ⅜-in. poplar that is 2 in. wide and

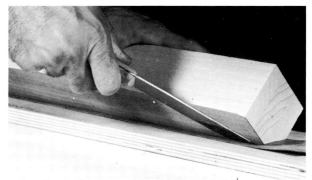

When the glue has set, use a serrated veneer knife, or a veneer saw, to trim the excess veneer and plane flush.

With some of the waste drilled out, a two-flute straight bit in the router table is used to mortise the legs.

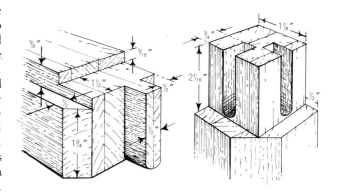

Typical leg-rail joint is dimensioned above, and fits together as shown below. End caps strengthen joint and keep grain from telegraphing through veneer.

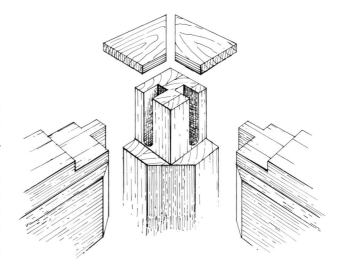

mitered to cross the corner. After these eight pieces are glued in place it is best to let the table sit idle for a day or so while the glue cures. Then hand-plane to true up the surfaces at the corners. Now the only exposed end grain is on the bottom of the legs. Capping avoids the telegraphing of end grain, which one can see on old pieces where uncapped dovetailed corners are veneered. This is the "ring around the collar" of veneer work and should be avoided. Also, running the caps back onto the rails strengthens the joints.

The outer surfaces of the table will be veneered in the order of ends, sides and top. Now the advantage gained by veneering the inside of the legs and the underside of the rails while they were accessible becomes apparent. Matching veneer patterns is the dominant consideration in determining the overall appearance of the table, but the details are best left up to each maker and the wood he is using. I like the crispness of

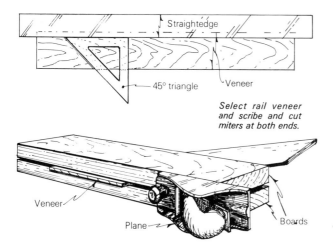

Select rail veneer and scribe and cut miters at both ends.

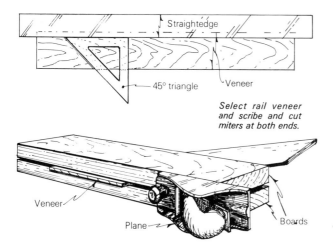

Sandwich the veneer between two boards to plane the miter clean and true.

mitered corners that meet exactly, and the drawings above show how I do it.

First, I veneer the ends of the table. Cut overlong strips for the rails and legs, at least a half-inch wider than dimension *a*. Choose a strip to cover an end rail and overlap ¼ in. of veneer with the long metal ruler. Find the finished length (21 in., at the 10-in. and 31-in. marks), and use a plastic drafting triangle to scribe the miters. Then cut them along a metal straightedge—I use a Stanley utility knife with a new blade, or a deluxe musical instrument maker's knife.

Sandwich each veneer between two boards with the mitered edge protruding ¹⁄₁₆ in., and use a shoulder or block plane to clean off the irregularities left by the knife. If you don't square up the cuts, the joints will open when you sand or scrape the finished surface.

Now cut a miter at one end of each leg piece, and join the three pieces of veneer together to form an overlarge *U*. Check each joint and get it perfect before taping tightly across the joints with several strips of masking tape. Then turn the veneer face down and apply a little glue with the joints cocked slightly open. Rub the glue into the joint with your finger, flatten out the veneer, and roll. Place a piece of tape across the glue line to equalize the tension of the tape on the other side. Avoid getting glue on the front. Place this veneer on a

flat surface and prevent the joint from buckling by applying a little weight (such as a plane) while the glue sets. The result should be a U-shaped piece that, when carefully placed, has joints crossing the interior and exterior corners exactly and appropriately.

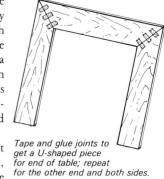

Tape and glue joints to get a U-shaped piece for end of table; repeat for the other end and both sides.

Leave the tape on what will be the outside surface, but remove it from the inside and put the veneer face down on the bench, with the corresponding end of the table on top of it. Manipulate the arrangement until the corners do line up just right, and mark the position. Then turn the table over, remove all but one piece of tape from the veneer (take care not to break the joint), and apply glue to the table end.

When you glue, keep in mind that too much glue makes it difficult to clamp the veneer in place without drifting, and that clamping force applied even slightly askew can pull the joints apart. After spreading glue on the wood, place the veneer exactly in place and lay smooth 4/4 maple cauls across the rail and along the legs. First put bar clamps along the top side of the rail (anchoring them to the bench or to the other end of the table), and C-clamps along the bottom side of the rail. Then C-clamps with protective blocks go down both legs. Before tightening them down hard, I check and recheck the positioning to make sure nothing has drifted.

After removing the clamps and boards, carefully peel off the tape to avoid tearing up patches of veneer. Lacquer thinner will soften the tape and remove its traces. Trim, and repeat this process at the other end and on the sides. I clean up the edges of the veneer with a router and a three-flute carbide bit with ball-bearing guide. Be wary of grain directions. I pass the router in the opposite direction of normal feed so that it nibbles off the excess veneer. This prevents wholesale splitting, which can be disastrous if there is an area of nonadhesion at the edge. Trim the inside corners with a knife. Before moving on, feather (gently flick as if to lift) the trimmed edge with your finger to detect spots that did not adhere—the remedy is a little glue. Be very careful when you remove the clamp boards since there always seems to be a spot or two where glue comes through. Use a cabinet scraper to remove such debris from the clamping boards before using them again. And repeat the whole process on the other three sides

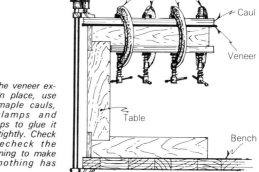

With the veneer exactly in place, use hard maple cauls, bar clamps and C-clamps to glue it down tightly. Check and recheck the positioning to make sure nothing has drifted.

Left, finished table in walnut veneer has butcher-block center field and crisply mitered corners. Veneered construction can be enhanced by geometric marquetry, center. Solid oak table, right, has ceramic-tile top and will be used for plants.

of the table. Now you are ready to veneer the top.

Although innumerable veneer patterns might be used, my most popular tabletop is walnut veneer in a butcher-block pattern, set inside a veneer border of width *a* (here 2⅜ in.) which adds to the illusion of constant dimension. Randomness and variety count more than pattern matching in achieving an attractive top.

Begin by laying out the border directly on the plywood tabletop and draw in the miters from the outside corner to the center field. Measure the center field—on this 21-in. by 31-in. table, it is 16¼-in. wide and 26¼-in. long. Use eight strips 2½2 in. wide or ten strips 1⅝ in. wide. To obtain strips of uniform width and with good edges, pass the edge of a 30-in. piece of veneer across the jointer (or past a sharp router bit). Then cut a strip about ⅛ in. larger than needed. Cut a good second edge on the router table with a rip fence and a three-flute carbide bit. Tape and glue the joints one at a time, as before, cut the field to length and carefully plane across the edge to square it. The center field is done.

The four mitered joints of the border can be most difficult. Veneer matching, joint tightness and corner alignment are crucial. Start by jointing one edge of a 3-in. strip of veneer, and miter one end so the jointed edge is inside.

Fit this jointed edge and the mitered corner along one edge of the center field, tack it in place with tape, then scribe and cut the miter at the other end. Cut it the merest hair fat, so the knife-work can be planed clean, then tape tightly in place, turn over and rub glue into the joint.

Prepare the next strip the same way, with a jointed inside edge and a miter at one end, and fit it along an adjacent edge of the tabletop. Tuck the uncut end under the extended miter of the side already taped. Tack down with tape, then use the first miter as a guide to scribe and cut the new piece—again, allow a tiny bit extra and plane it clean. Tape and glue, and continue around the tabletop. If the miters drawn on the plywood table-

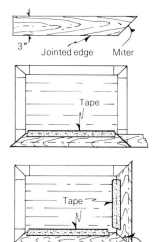

To fit the top border, scribe each miter from the real table, not from the drafting triangle.

top are not precisely 45°, prejudice your miter cuts in the veneer accordingly.

When the top is completely taped and glued together, remove the tape from the side that will be attached to the table. Remove all but a few strategic pieces from the exposed side, and place the veneers face down on the bench. Align the table on the veneer and mark the corner positions—a red pencil is easiest to see. Turn the table over again, roll a thin but uniform layer of Titebond glue onto it with a rubber roller (brayer), and move quickly because one side of the surface may dry before you finish spreading the glue. Carefully align the top on the table and clamp with care. I sometimes press the veneer down with a clean rubber roller before placing the clamping boards, and check the alignment again. Then cover with as many clamps as will fit. If the table is simply too big to be clamped, you will have to use contact cement—another problem altogether, and a course I do not recommend, whenever it can be avoided.

After trimming the edge, feather it with your finger to locate spots that didn't adhere and reglue them. Then pass your fingers lightly over the surface and listen carefully. At a bad spot it will sound almost as if you are passing over loose newspaper instead of solid material. When you suspect an area, tap it with your finger and again the sound will tell you if the veneer is not stuck down. Make a small slit with a razor blade, with the grain, inject a little glue with a syringe, and roll. Immediately wipe with a moist cloth to remove all exterior glue traces. The moisture in the glue and from the cloth will swell the slit back tight. Rub dry with a different cloth and roll again with a clean roller; clamp if necessary.

Don't use steel wool on bare veneer; it invariably snags and requires difficult repair. Never throw away any veneer scraps; you never know when a sliver will be needed for a repair. An oil finish, if necessary on, for example, rosewood, should not be allowed to saturate an area. If oils penetrate deeply, they may break down glues, especially contact cements. First test your finish on a sample. Satin urethane varnish over a light application and immediate rub-off of Watco oil have worked well on my walnut tables with butcher-block centers. Don't forget to stain the underside of the top if you used a dark veneer. Always apply finish to the underside to seal the wood and prevent warpage. The faint smile of surprise on the face of someone who runs a hand underneath a side or end rail and discovers a solid, finished surface is usually amplified when curiosity leads him to peek and discover that it is actually veneered. Somehow this justifies the extra effort and thorough approach we have taken. □

Making 50 Tables
Jigs and fixtures do the job

by Peter Pennypacker

Could you build one of these tables in eight hours for $225? Joe Tracy and Peter Pennypacker did. Using the production methods described in this article, they made 50 of them.

After years of throwing countless pots, a potter friend surprised me when I asked if he was still challenged by his work. "I'm finding new enjoyment in pottery by simplifying the steps," he said, "streamlining the process, enjoying the exactness of efficiency."

Not long ago, I found out what he meant when I helped a fellow woodworker with a furnituremaking operation entirely new to me—a limited production run. Until that time, I had built only one-of-a-kind furniture, all commissioned by clients after lengthy discussions about how a certain design should look. I'd found one-off work gratifying and certainly instructive, since I often had to experiment with new tools, techniques and materials to satisfy my customers' demands.

Competence and speed came with practice, but my work still consumed enormous amounts of time, and with the time came a large price tag. I began to feel that some of my pieces assumed a more exaggerated posture than handcrafted, functional furniture ought to have. I became uneasy with the preciousness I was bestowing upon single works. I was anxious to find more efficient work patterns, and to repeat some of my favorite pieces, applying the refined technique and clarity of vision I'd learned from the first tries.

I was eager to try a production run. I had seen fine examples of production-run furniture from the more discerning manufacturers—much of it slippery-looking stuff from Italy—so I knew it could be done well. But did it take a factory? Joe Tracy provided the answer. He had just contracted to build 50 oak restaurant tables and needed help. A woodworker trained at the Rochester Institute of Technology, Tracy specializes in one-of-a-kind furniture, but he has also done a fair amount of production work. He has a natural ability for designing and engineering jigs and fixtures for the process.

Working with Tracy, I learned that in a moderate-size, well-organized shop with good though not prohibitively expensive machines, limited production is an enjoyable—and profitable—way to work. Jigs that favor choreographing repeated movements into concise, economical patterns produce a great quantity of work with minimum effort. And with just two of us working, there was always a variety of tasks to choose from, relieving tedium and making the process relaxing and rewarding. With careful planning and Tracy's simple, effective jigs, we were able to produce each table, from raw lumber to final finish, in a little less than eight hours. Henry Ford and the Puritan Ethic hummed over our shoulders.

The 50 tables were for the newly rebuilt Jordan Pond House restaurant, a historic landmark in Acadia National Park, near Tracy's home/shop on Maine's Mt. Desert Island. When the Pond House was nearing completion, Tracy had

From *Fine Woodworking* magazine (January 1984) 44:32-37

taken the rather bold step of designing and building an unsolicited prototype dining table that he thought would harmonize with the restaurant's contemporary decor. The Acadia Corporation overseeing the work was impressed with his initiative, but not convinced his design would hold up to commercial abuse.

Undaunted, Tracy built another prototype. Though sturdier, his second design was still a beauty—a delicate, flared leg-and-apron piece that shows the influence of James Krenov, with whom he had worked for six months in Sweden during 1972. The table's white oak top was supported by red oak aprons joined to the legs with floating tenons, a joint that's strong and readily made with Tracy's equipment.

This time the design was approved, and Tracy was asked to quote prices for four sizes of tables. Working out a time/cost sheet, he outlined each construction step on paper, drawing on his experience to calculate how long each would take and adding a 10% safety margin for potentially troublesome operations. To figure labor costs, Tracy multiplied the total number of hours by his $20 hourly shop rate, which, for this job, included our hourly wages plus shop overhead—the mortgage, power and heat bills, machine loans and maintenance, and incidentals. To this figure, he added the prices of lumber, lacquer and varnish, glue, screws, abrasives, and $150 to rent a truck to haul the finished tables to Pond House.

The price came to $225 per table, a figure within 5% of what a big Maine furniture company had quoted for a somewhat heavier-handed design. Because he was a local craftsman, the Acadia Corporation gave Tracy the job. The risk of making the prototype had paid off.

Tracy's 30-ft. by 40-ft. shop, on the ground floor of his house, seemed too small to hold the hundreds of parts we would be making. His equipment includes an old but accurate 10-in. tablesaw, a drill press, an ancient 34-in. bandsaw, a real prize of a machine called a Steton Combinata (planer, jointer, mortiser and knife grinder), a 1-in. spindle shaper, and a beast of a stroke sander that impressed us by speedily sanding the tabletops. Despite his limited floor space, Tracy's big machines are spaced well apart to allow plenty of swing plus room to dolly parts from one machine to another.

While Tracy designed and built the production jigs, I began thickness-planing and cutting to width and length 1700 bd. ft. of red and white oak. Milling the lumber was pretty tiresome—the only shortcut we could take was to rip stock to width first, bypassing the task of facing warped or twisted wide boards on the jointer. Following Tracy's detailed cutting list, I crosscut each part to rough length, then to final length, using stop blocks on the tablesaw miter gauge to ensure consistency. Cutting the longest pieces first and using the offcuts for shorter components minimized waste.

Before working with Tracy, my experience with jigs and fixtures had been limited to the occasional stop block or router template. I hadn't felt the need to construct jigs for single pieces. Tracy was soon to enlighten me on jigs and fixtures. Old woodworking texts suggest that a jig clamps the work and guides a cutting or shaping tool to produce identically shaped parts, independent of the operator's skill. A fixture, on the other hand, merely holds or positions the work, leaving the tool to be guided by other means. Tracy put it more concisely: a jig is portable, a fixture attaches firmly to the

Tracy's table design adapted readily to jig and fixture work.

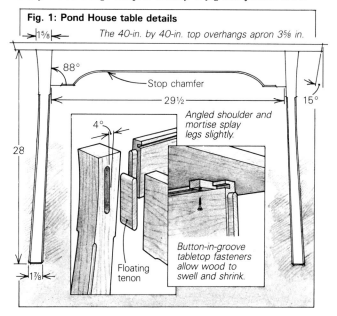

Fig. 1: Pond House table details

1⅝

The 40-in. by 40-in. top overhangs apron 3⅝ in.

88°

Stop chamfer

29½

15°

28

4°

Angled shoulder and mortise splay legs slightly.

Floating tenon

1⅞

Button-in-groove tabletop fasteners allow wood to swell and shrink.

machine or tool. Either way, the purpose is to increase the accuracy, safety and consistency of machine work.

Jigging is most useful when you must make many identical parts, as in our table job, but there are good reasons for jigs when fewer pieces are required. Safety is probably the best one, especially if you're making small, odd-shaped or hard-to-hold pieces, which are liable to be hurled or kicked back when fed past a whirring cutter. A well-designed jig will solidly grip the stock, so you can feed it with your hands well away from the danger zone. A jig also promotes an orderly work rhythm that lessens the chance of an accident. In addition, the consistency of jigged parts all but excludes the inaccuracies that would otherwise have to be corrected at assembly.

Obviously, there's a break-even point. Sometimes too few parts are needed, or they're so complicated that you'd spend more time devising the jig than you would making the pieces by hand. Yet even in this case, Tracy, like other woodworkers who derive as much satisfaction from process as from prod-

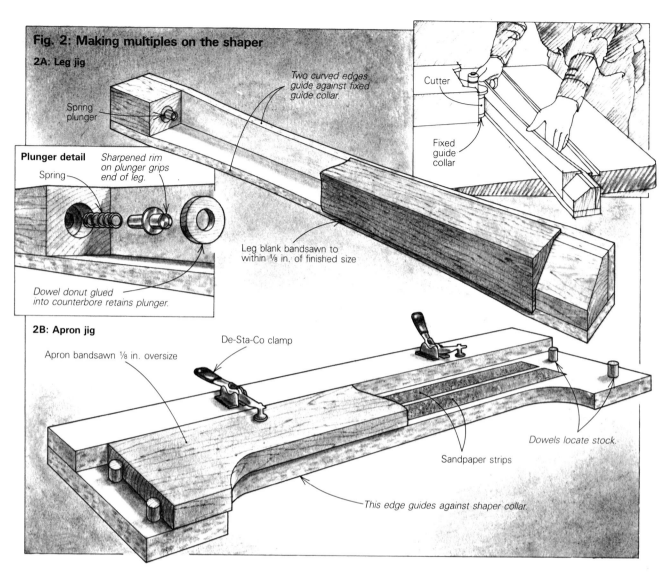

Fig. 2: Making multiples on the shaper

2A: Leg jig

Spring plunger

Two curved edges guide against fixed guide collar.

Cutter

Fixed guide collar

Plunger detail

Spring

Sharpened rim on plunger grips end of leg.

Dowel donut glued into counterbore retains plunger.

Leg blank bandsawn to within ⅛ in. of finished size.

2B: Apron jig

De-Sta-Co clamp

Apron bandsawn ⅛ in. oversize

Dowels locate stock.

Sandpaper strips

This edge guides against shaper collar.

uct, will sometimes go ahead with the jig anyway. He designs much of his furniture with repeat commissions in mind, reasoning that a jig hung on the wall is a lasting resource that will save him the trouble of rethinking the problem months later when another job arrives.

Tracy's jigs for straight or angular parts are usually guided by a fence clamped or screwed to the machine table. Jigs for curved pieces are fed past a single-point guide—the fixed collar on his shaper or a router pilot bearing. Whether straight or curved, Tracy's jigs have some common features, the most important of which is a way to position and clamp the wood so that it won't slip or fly out under the stress of cutting. Blocks, fences or pins can be arranged so that blanks go into the jig only in the correct position. Quick-action toggle clamps (available from De-Sta-Co, PO Box 2800, Troy, Mich. 48007) are best for anchoring the blank, though screw hold-down clamps do a good, if slower, job. If a jig has no flat surface for mounting clamps, the blank can be held between blocks by a spring plunger, as in figure 2A. As extra insurance against slippage, Tracy glues strips of sandpaper to the jig's supporting surfaces.

Controlling a jig is vital, so Tracy puts handles on his, or makes them big enough so there's plenty of material to hold on to. Also, so it can be aligned with the machine's guiding

fence or collar before the blank engages the cutter, he extends each jig at least 3 in. beyond each end of the blank. Most of the jigs we used were made of ¾-in. medium-density fiberboard, with pine fences and stop blocks glued and screwed in place. Fiberboard, also called Baraboard, is ideal for jigs—it is dimensionally stable, can be accurately shaped, and won't wear out when repeatedly passed by fences and guide collars. Plywood also makes decent jig stock, if its interplies are free of voids. Applying lacquer or spray graphite to the edge of a jig eases its passage.

For the table job, Tracy designed the shaper jigs illustrated in figure 2. Even though his shaper has a 1-in. spindle and plenty of power, shaping the raw blank in a single pass would have provoked chattering or a dangerous kickback. To avoid this, we used the jigs as templates, marking out the curves and bandsawing off most of the waste to within ⅛ in. or so of the finished profile. The pieces could then be shaped safely and smoothly in one pass by running the jig against the fixed guide collar attached to the shaper. To make the legs, I first bandsawed the waste off all the blanks. Next, with a blank in the jig, I shaped one curved side, then flipped the jig 90° to shape the other. The aprons were similarly shaped, using a version of the jig shown in figure 2B for each of the four different length aprons (for the four different size tables).

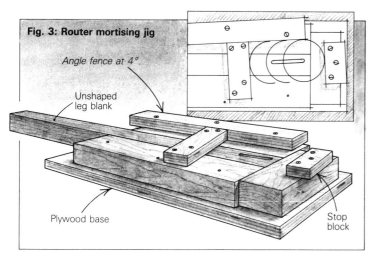

Fig. 3: Router mortising jig

Angle fence at 4°

Unshaped leg blank

Plywood base

Stop block

To mill angled mortises in 200 legs, Tracy bolted a 4° ramp to his Steton Combinata. A mirror taped to the machine lets him view the action.

If production work is to proceed apace, like parts should be stacked together to be machined as units of work. These table aprons, which have been shaped, mortised and grooved, await assembly. The box contains the floating tenons that will join aprons to legs.

I had never used a shaper of this size before, and I was a little intimidated by its size and power. With only small amounts of wood to remove, however, the process was smooth and free of kickbacks. By the end of the job, shaper work felt safe. Shops not equipped with spindle shapers could adapt these jigs to routers, using ¼-in. tempered Masonite templates to guide a bit's pilot bearing. A 2-HP router driving industrial-quality ½-in. shank bits would do the job. Even with a powerful router the counterforces developed in a heavy cut make precise control difficult, so first bandsaw the waste to within ¹⁄₁₆ in. of the finished surface.

As our job progressed, I began to understand why so much factory production furniture is so lifeless. Churning out chairs or tables by the thousands, a big furniture plant would squander its profit on the extra steps and special tooling that distinctive designs require. Tracy proved to me that a re-sourceful small-shop craftsman needn't be similarly con-strained. To accentuate the sweep of each table's flared legs, for example, Tracy splayed them slightly by cutting 88° shoulders on the ends of the aprons and milling the leg mor-tises at a 4° angle, as shown in the construction detail in figure 1. The operation added one jig, but without this refine-ment the tables would have looked just ordinary.

I cut the 88° shoulders (before shaping them) on the ta-blesaw miter gauge fitted with a stop block. To mill the mor-tises in the shaped legs, we bolted a 4° ramp to the Combi-nata's mortising table and cut all the mortises on one side of all the legs before reversing it to mortise the other side. After milling 400 mortises on this machine, I can only sing its praises. It made what could have been a time-consuming chore a concise process that took about two minutes per leg. If you don't have a slot-mortiser—and most of us don't—you could dowel the legs, or use the router jig shown in figure 3.

As material went from rough to final size, the pieces be-came stacks of multiples, crisscrossed on dollies, sorted by size or function. Parts were processed as units of work, the entire pile passing through one operation before moving on to the next. This saved us hours of redundant set-up time, and is the key difference between production and one-of-a-kind work, where, at best, you're more likely to carry individual parts through a series of steps to completion or, at worst, move them around the shop in chaotic bundles.

Tracy varies the order of events according to the job. He shapes parts before cutting joints, as long as the part isn't so odd-shaped that it can't then be accurately fixed in the joint-cutting machine. Sometimes, though, a mortise or a tenon offers a handy way to hold the part in the shaping jig, so it makes more sense to cut joints first. Sanding should come

Gluing up tabletops can be a slow, frustrating job. To speed it along and minimize sanding later, Tracy aligned the surfaces of the clamped-up boards with the pressure of a hydraulic jack, above. He fabricated a Plexiglas ramp, left, to allow the curved edge of each leg to feed uniformly against the router's chamfering bit.

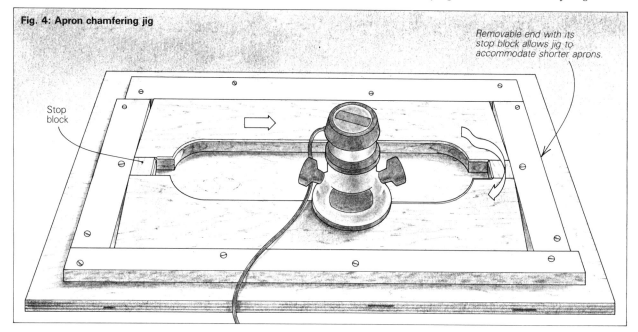

Fig. 4: Apron chamfering jig

Removable end with its stop block allows jig to accommodate shorter aprons.

Stop block

---

after joint-cutting. That way, you can manhandle pieces without fear of damaging them and you won't ruin the accuracy of your joinery by knocking off the crisp reference edges.

Next we began the detail work that makes the Pond House tables look more like one-of-a-kind custom work than the fruit of a production run. First, I stop-chamfered the four edges of each leg. Because two sides of each leg are curved, feeding them over a flat router base would produce an uneven, tapered chamfer. We solved this problem with a Plexiglas ramp clamped to the router base. It kept the leg edges in uniform contact with a 45° chamfer bit. The jig shown in figure 4 speeded the stop-chamfering of the aprons.

We had several hundred boards to pick from for gluing up the 50 tops. Finicky grain- and color-matching could have eaten up weeks, so Tracy set a reasonable minimum standard and sorted the boards accordingly. To eliminate the usual pounding and cursing, and to minimize having to sand boards whose surfaces were misaligned, we suspended a hydraulic pump on a long pipe anchored to a ceiling beam. We rolled our glue-up table under this setup and used the jack's pressure—distributed by a 2x4 batten—to force the boards into the same plane. Spreading the glue with a 3-in. paint

roller, we could glue up a top in three minutes.

In a crowded restaurant, the squared corner of a dining table can be a leg-jabbing, purse-snagging menace. Tracy eliminated this hazard by rounding the corners and undercutting the tabletop edges by 15°. The tops were first sized on the tablesaw, with the arbor set to cut the 15° undercut, then the corners were rounded with a saber saw set to the undercut angle. We used one of the router methods illustrated in figure 5 to clean the rounded corners. The top edges of each tabletop were eased with a roundover bit whose pilot bearing Tracy modified with a brass bushing.

By now we had 450 table parts neatly stacked around the shop. We were ready to glue up the bases, which went faster than I expected. I swabbed glue in both leg and apron mortises, inserted a floating tenon, and drew the joints up with leather-padded bar clamps. After 30 minutes in clamps, the table bases were stacked, to await touch-up sanding. Tracy, meanwhile, sanded the tops on the stroke sander. To pinpoint irregularities, he positioned a fluorescent light behind the sander, throwing oblique, shadow-making light across each top.

Finally, we were ready to spray-finish the tops and bases. While I carried out the last barrel of chips and sawdust, Tracy tacked up plastic sheeting to create a makeshift spray booth

Fig. 5: Edging the tabletops

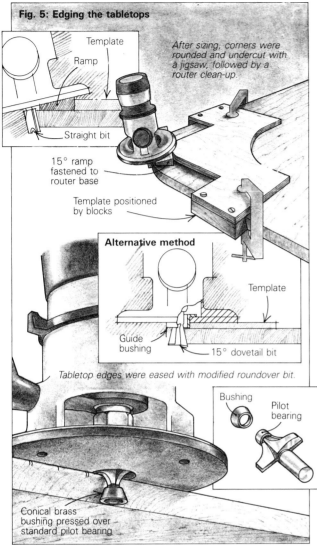

Template

Ramp

After sizing, corners were rounded and undercut with a jigsaw, followed by a router clean-up.

Straight bit

15° ramp fastened to router base

Template positioned by blocks

Alternative method

Template

Guide bushing

15° dovetail bit

Tabletop edges were eased with modified roundover bit.

Bushing

Pilot bearing

Conical brass bushing pressed over standard pilot bearing

Fig. 6: Cutting buttons in one pass

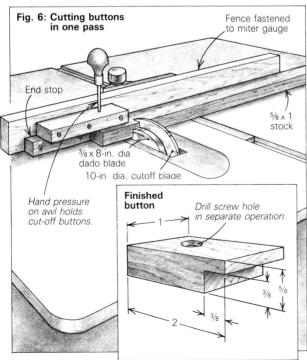

Fence fastened to miter gauge

End stop

⅝ x 1 stock

³⁄₈ x 8-in. dia dado blade

10-in. dia. cutoff blade

Hand pressure on awl holds cut-off buttons.

Finished button

Drill screw hole in separate operation.

1

⅝

³⁄₈

³⁄₈

2

Fig. 7: Carrying handle and drying rack

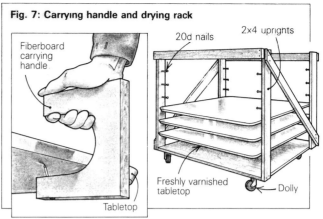

Fiberboard carrying handle

20d nails

2x4 uprights

Freshly varnished tabletop

Dolly

Tabletop

in the corner of the shop, ventilated by the exhaust fan. His spraying equipment consists of a good-quality gun with a separate pressure feed tank and 1½-HP compressor.

Since the tabletops would see heavy commercial use, they needed a tough, water- and alcohol-resistant film. Tracy chose a natural resin varnish, Rock Hard (write H. Behlen & Bros., Rt. 30 N., Amsterdam, N.Y. 12010 for local distributors). The bases received a nitrocellulose lacquer, tinted to match the tops. Each top and base took three coats of finish. Since lacquer dries almost immediately, we stacked the bases as they were sprayed. Rock Hard, however, is a slow-setter. As we sprayed the tops, we grabbed them with the shopmade carrying handles shown in figure 7, and stacked them in a 2x4 rack bristling with 20d nails to allow air movement between the tops. When the last coat was dry, we buffed the tops to a flat sheen on the stroke sander, using fine Scotch-Brite pads glued to an old belt.

When we delivered the tables to Pond House, we fastened the tops to the aprons with wooden buttons let into mortises, as shown in figure 6. Tracy's final touch was to brand his logo into each table apron. I remember that the day was beautiful. Spring was in the air and the island sparkled. We had done it.

The tables have seen two seasons of hard use, and apart from a few dings and dents, they show little sign of wear. Tracy keeps extra parts on hand in case they're needed and the jigs stand ready for another run. The tables were so well-received that the Acadia Corporation ordered additional furnishings, including display cabinets for the restaurant gift shop, cash register stands, and several large *shoji*-style folding screens papered in birch bark, a material much in vogue when Pond House was first built.

This production run led me to agree with Tracy's philosophy. Mass production needn't compromise the quality of a piece of furniture. The production prototype can be as vital a design vehicle as any one-off piece. Imagination and skill must remain paramount—properly developed designs and techniques can produce high-quality multiples. Efficiency helps create comfortable and competitive work patterns. Many small shops are more than capable of completing a job like this, which will pay the bills during many lean months of custom furnituremaking. □

Peter Pennypacker lives in Sullivan, Maine. Photos by the author.

Lion's-Paw Pedestal Table

Classic piece combines turning, carving and veneering

by Roger Schroeder

Oak furniture didn't originate in America. But the period from 1850 to 1930 in this country saw a profusion of solid oak furniture, paneling and molding, most of it finding its way into middle-class homes. Peculiar to this period was the widespread use of quartersawn oak lumber and oak veneer. Quartersawing produces very attractive grain patterns and makes for more dimensionally stable boards, although, unfortunately, the veneer is becoming increasingly difficult to find in this country.

The oak pedestal table shown here and owned by Lee Sachs and Joy Kleinsasser of Kings Park, N.Y., was probably made at the end of the American oak period when solid oak tops gave way to plywood. What particularly impresses me about this piece is the exceptional quality of its veneers and the unusual character of its carving. Though its paws are rather typical and stylized, the lions' heads lack the marauding eyes and predacious fangs of rampant beasts. In fact, with their soft features and toothless jaws, they seem almost friendly. The faces of the four lions and the pleasing proportions of the pedestal distinguish this table from many others of its kind and make it a worthy model for reproduction.

It's not an easy matter to reconstruct hypothetically a complex piece of furniture, but this table so intrigued me that I couldn't resist the temptation. What follows, based on a careful study of the original, is my account of how this table was made, or rather how I would make it. With but two exceptions—the joinery of the staves that compose the pedestal and the design of the expansion slides—my description is faithful to the original. I've altered the actual construction in these two instances because a contemporary craftsman working in a home shop can improve upon these existing features.

Traditionally, pedestals of this size were coopered from eight planks to form a hollow octagon. A solid column would require much more lumber, have an unmanageable mass, especially for turning, and be liable to develop deep checks from tangential shrinkage. To make the central column (figure 2, page 16), rip eight pieces of 6/4 quartersawn oak to precise 4½-in. widths and crosscut the pieces to a rough length of 25½ in. Set your saw arbor at 22½° and bevel each stave on both edges, taking care not to diminish the finished width of 4½ in. from toe to toe. Next, slot each beveled edge to receive a ¼-in. by ¾-in. spline, which you should rip from solid stock or plywood.

Dry-assemble the staves and splines and draw the column together with three or four band clamps to make certain that all the joints will close tightly when the glue is applied. Disassemble and reassemble using a glue with moderate to long open time, like plastic resin glue.

When the glue is set and you've scraped away the excess, you want to prepare the stock for the applied collars, one of which is 4½ in. wide and located about midway on the pedestal while the other is 2½ in. wide and located at its foot. Cut eight pieces of your oak to a length of 8 in. and bevel both edges so that the heel-to-heel width, on their inside faces, is the same as the toe-to-toe width on the outside faces of the column staves. Crosscut the collar staves to length, 4½ in. for the central collar and 2½ in. for the foot collar. Hot hide glue is best for applying these because of its strong initial tack and slow curing time. All eight pieces for each collar should be applied at once and then clamped with deep-engagement bar clamps from opposite sides.

Now cap both ends with ¾-in. plywood plates so the blank can be mounted on the lathe. The plates should be flush with the outside of the pedestal and secured with white or yellow glue. Find the centers in each plate and mount the blank between centers on your lathe. Round the stock at a low speed, and then make the decorative cuts shown in figure 1, though it's a good idea first to make the parting cuts top and bottom that will define the finished length of the column.

With the turning done, you have the choice of veneering the unrelieved cylindrical surfaces while the stock is still in the lathe. If you do, the veneer can be trimmed at the several coves with a sharp skew chisel in scrape position. If you find the grain attractive as is, then there's no need to add veneer, and you're ready to deepen the parting cuts top and bottom so you can finish these cuts with a backsaw. The end-grain surface at the top should be square, as two supporting plates will lie across it.

Each leg and attached head is laminated from ten pieces of ⅝-in. oak, glued face to face. But I see no reason why thicker stock, 6/4 oak for example, can't be used, providing the final thickness is the same as the original. The grain for the legs runs horizontally, so edge-gluing pairs of boards that make up the head portion of the blank may be necessary to avoid using 12-in. wide lumber and having lots of waste.

A careful look at the head shows that the three outer boards on each side were sawn to shape and then glued to the leg and head like cheeks. Presawing these cheek pieces will save carving time. The paws, since they are also 2 in. wider on each side than the leg, can be treated in the same way.

Before shaping the blanks further, you need to bore two holes in the end-grain surface of each where the leg and head will abut the pedestal. On a centerline from top to bottom, bore a hole 3 in. down from the top, ⅜ in. in diameter and 1 in. deep to accommodate a tapered locating pin. Then bore another hole 6 in. down from the top and 5⁄16 in. in diameter for a ⅜-in. by 4-in. hanger bolt, which will secure the leg to the pedestal. Next, contour the inside surface of the leg to conform to the circumference of the pedestal. Pencil the arc on the leg blank and waste most of the wood by cutting a series of kerfs on your table saw, lowering the blade appropriately as you get closer to the outside of the arc. Clean up the rough contour with a Surform, half-round rasps and files.

Remove as much stock as possible on the band saw and

From *Fine Woodworking* magazine (November 1980) 25:74-77

This quartersawn oak table was made toward the end of the American oak period, probably in the 1920s. Reproducing it involves a challenging range of procedures. The lions' heads, arms and paws are carved from laminated stock. The pedestal is coopered and turned. And the top, aprons and parts of the pedestal are veneered. Scale drawings appear on the following pages.

Fig. 1: Side elevation

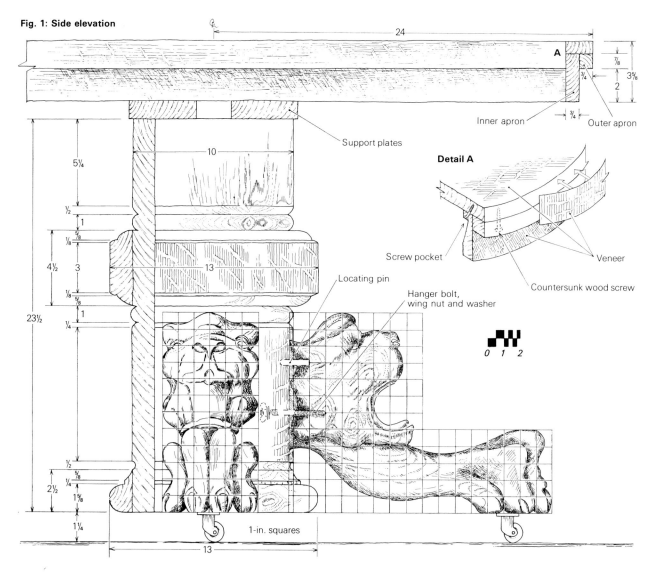

24

A

⅞

3⅝

2

¾

Inner apron

¾

Outer apron

Support plates

10

5¼

½

1

⅝

⅛

Detail A

Veneer

Screw pocket

Countersunk wood screw

4½

3

13

⅛

⅝

1

¼

Locating pin

Hanger bolt,
wing nut and washer

23½

0 1 2

½

⅝

2½

¼

1⅝

1¼

13

1-in. squares

Fig. 2: Section of pedestal blank and plan view of leg

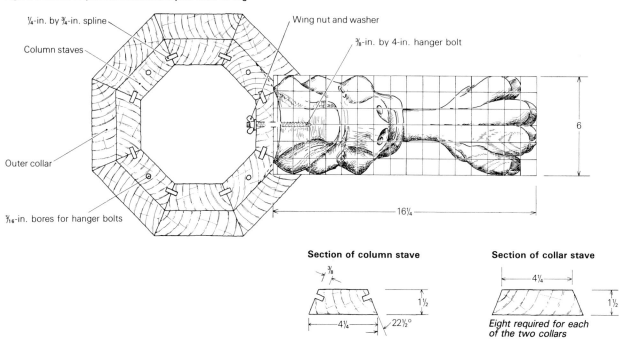

¼-in. by ¾-in. spline

Column staves

Wing nut and washer

⅜-in. by 4-in. hanger bolt

Outer collar

6

⁵⁄₁₆-in. bores for hanger bolts

16¼

Section of column stave

⅜

1½

4¼

22½°

Section of collar stave

4¼

1½

*Eight required for each
of the two collars*

Drawings: Christopher Clapp

Fig. 3: Expansion slide assembly

To cut dovetail housings, first plow ¾-in. wide and ½-in. deep grooves down the center of slide; then using a standard ½-in. dovetail cutter and an appropriate setting on your router fence, form the inward angle on both sides of the groove.

Cut the dovetail keys from one long piece of stock after passing it through your table saw with the blade set at the proper angle and to the proper depth. Experimentation is necessary to get the precise settings. Then crosscut the keys to length.

All four 3-in. keys are screwed in their housings in fixed central rail. 1-in. keys are screwed into the ends of moving slides.

Fig. 4: Bottom view of tabletop

Inner apron
Outer apron
Table expansion slides
Grain direction of plywood core
Countersunk screw holes are plugged or the entire under-edge can be veneered.
⅜-in. by 4-in. hanger bolts, four required
Support plates
Apron support bracket
Locating pin, three required

Direction of slide

32

Three countersunk wood screws secure tabletop to slide from underneath.

Direction of slide

Central rail is bolted to support plates. Bolt heads must be countersunk.

Slide rail
Slide rail
Stationary rail

Detail A: Apron bracket

Bracket is attached with countersunk wood screws.

then begin carving the heads and paws, paying close attention to those anatomical details that determine the friendliness or ferocity of the lions. You'll find #5 and #7 gouges are good for much of the preliminary carving, while the sharper details can be executed with a *V*-tool.

If you choose to make an expanding top with leaves, the legs must be attached to the pedestal so that the separation in the top is diagonal to the legs. This gives greater support when the top is lengthened. Secure the legs to the pedestal with the hanger bolts bored for previously, running the machine threads run through the column and fastening with wing nuts and washers (figure 2).

Next the table-slide support plates (figure 4) are attached to the top of the pedestal with four ⅜-in. by 4-in. hanger bolts and secured with hex nuts and washers. Affixed on top of these are the tabletop expansion slides, which will permit the addition of two 15-in. wide leaves, making for a 78-in. long table surface. It's easiest to purchase these expansion slides commercially (available by mail order from Craftsman Wood Service, 1735 W. Cortland Ct., Addison, Ill. 60101), but if you choose to make your own, the necessary operations can be performed as described in figure 3.

I recommend using ¾-in. lumbercore plywood for making the tabletop (and leaves) and veneering it on both sides with ⅛₂₈-in. quarter-sliced veneer, reserving the most attractively figured pieces for bookmatching or slipmatching on the top. If you divide the top to accept leaves, you should fit the three locating pins before sawing the top to shape. When you've

rough-sawn the circular top, you can true it to a perfect circle by attaching your router to a trammel anchored with a wood screw to the bottom of the tabletop and trimming with a 1-in. straight-face bit.

The top has two aprons, one that fits flush with the edge to give the appearance of a thicker top and another that fits inside this one. The outer apron, ⅞ in. by ¾ in. in section, is fastened to the top with countersunk wood screws and glue. You can kerf-bend this piece, steam-bend it or make it from bent laminations. Once it's trimmed flush with the table edge, veneer the entire edge with quarter-sliced oak.

The inner apron, ¾ in. thick and 2¾ in. wide, fits snugly against the outer apron and can be steam-bent or made from bent laminations. It too should be veneered. The top is attached to the inner apron by means of wood screws set in angled screw pockets (figure 1, detail A). The leaves, should you choose to add them, must be treated in the same manner.

The kind of finish I recommend (a filler and light oak stain are optional) is several applications of satin varnish or lacquer, with each coat rubbed down with 4/0 steel wool. For resistance to alcohol and other liquids, the top will need at least four coats, more if you want to deepen the tone of the wood. More coats need not mean more gloss if you take care to rub properly between coats and give the final application a light buff with steel wool and a lamb's-wool wheel. □

Roger Schroeder, of Amityville, N.Y., is a teacher, writer and amateur woodworker.

The Laminated Wood Ribbon
A built-up joint with sculptural possibilities

by James Rannefeld

Visual lightness and the illusion of mass without weight make the laminated wood ribbon a compelling method for sculptural furniture. 'Inspiration Bench' (top of page) is made of 33 pieces of oak accented with padauk. 'Signature' (above) illustrates another application of this method. The drawing (facing page) shows how short-grain is cross-laminated for strength.

A great deal has been said about the vanishing line between sculpture and furniture, part of a larger dialogue about the indistinction between art and craft. The stack lamination techniques pioneered by Wendell Castle have contributed substantially to this discussion, resulting in forms more closely related to sculpture than to traditional furniture.

The laminated joint I'll describe here (actually a finger or box joint) is a natural outgrowth of Castle's early bricklay lamination techniques. It differs from traditional joinery in that the joint is made *during* the lamination process, rather than being cut into prepared stock. This joint makes the solid wood ribbon possible, freeing the contemporary woodworker from many of the constraints imposed by traditional rectilinear furniture construction.

The laminated wood ribbon has the assets of mass, without being massive—a common criticism of stack-laminated furniture. It can also be light and delicate, without seeming weak or fragile. As an alternative to bent plywood, the laminated-joint technique requires less initial setup time, with little or no specialized tooling or forms, and allows better use of lower grades of wood. And it's truly versatile—as easily used to wrap a set of drawers, doors or tambours as to define a spare, flowing table form or a bench.

The laminated ribbon is made by face-gluing many individual strips of wood that have been roughly bandsawn to shape. It's not unusual for a small, relatively simple bench to involve 33 or more bandsawn pieces, and a complicated project such as the "Signature" bench/console (above) might require more than a hundred.

Construction begins with two templates—one for each alternating layer. I make my templates out of Masonite from a full-size sketch of the profile, taking care to fair their shape as close to the finished profile of the piece as I can, to conserve wood and to minimize shaping work later. For a recurved foot, such as that of "Inspiration Bench" (top of page), I make a series of templates, one for each layer, from a full-size drawing of the parabola.

Bandsawing curves from flat, straight-grained boards (usually 1 in. or 1¼ in. thick) inevitably leaves weak, short-grain areas. Templates must be arranged so that any short grain is cross-laminated by long grain in the next layer. This usually

Hardly a surface goes unclamped when a wood ribbon is glued up. Rannefeld assembles at a pace that allows the glue's natural tack to keep parts from sliding. Particleboard cauls spread clamping pressure and align the faces of the outermost laminae. Once the ribbon has cured, Rannefeld works it over with body grinders, sculpting by hand and eye to the final shape. He uses a small drum sander to get inside the tight spots.

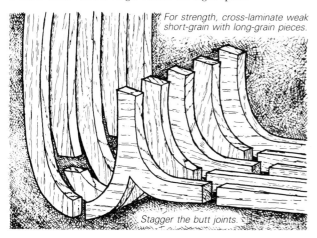

For strength, cross-laminate weak short-grain with long-grain pieces.

Stagger the butt joints.

results in an odd number of laminations in the finished piece, much as a sheet of plywood is made up of an odd number of veneers. In New Mexico's arid climate, such cross-grain constructions have held up well, but in areas where the seasonal moisture gradient is higher, they might crack. To avoid this problem, orient the layers so that the grain runs at a slight bias instead of at right angles.

When laying out pieces to be bandsawn, the shapes can be nested and ganged on individual boards to best utilize random width and length stock. Often I am able to use lower grades of lumber, at considerable savings, by working around natural flaws in the wood. Wood for lamination must be of uniform thickness, and should be free from obvious ridges from the planer. Flat surfaces, where the laminae butt together, for example, or where a table's legs meet the floor, are best cut square on a radial-arm saw.

Before laminating, it's a good idea to make cauls the shape of the finished project. This speeds glue-up and aligns the layers. Wax or varnish the cauls so that they won't stick to the work. Obviously, glue-up is the most critical operation, and the most difficult, since the glue (I use Titebond) acts as a lubricant, encouraging the laminae to slip out of alignment. You could use dowels or tacks to hold the layers in place, but I prefer to lay up the stack one by one, working as quickly as possible but at a rate that allows the glue to grab, holding one layer in place before the next one goes on. Timing is important here. As the glue slowly cures, it becomes increasingly tacky, and with a little bit of care you get a feel for the speed at which layers can be stacked without causing lower layers to slip. In cold weather I sometimes bring in a small electric heater to expedite things.

Spare no clamps—especially in complex, staggered layering. Spacing clamps closely will straighten out slightly bowed or wound pieces and will flatten minute irregularities between boards.

When the clamps are removed 24 hours later, the piece can be attacked with a variety of sculpting and sanding tools to shape it to the desired form and surface. My favorite tools for removing wood quickly are 7-in. and 4-in. body grinders. I also have a pneumatic sculptors' gouge that comes in handy for wasting large amounts of wood quickly.

I use a drum sander on a flexible shaft to give shape and clarity to the form, followed by electric and pneumatic finish sanders, and then a smaller drum sander for hard-to-reach places such as tight inside curves.

I finish my laminated work with a 3:1 mixture of Watco exterior Danish oil and polyurethane. This mixture gives a satiny finish, looks and repairs like an oil finish, yet resists water and alcohol like polyurethane.

My most recent explorations of the ribbon have shown me that these forms have even wider applications than I had first imagined. It is the laminated joint that gives us the ability to realize complex, even convoluted forms in solid wood, without the intimidating technology associated with laminated veneer construction. And it is the ribbon that sets our imaginations free. □

James Rannefeld sculpts fanciful ribbons and contemporary furniture in Taos, New Mexico. Photos by the author.

All three Shaker round stands are made of cherry and finished in clear varnish. Stand at left (The Shaker Museum, Old Chatham, N. Y.) is subject of this article; center stand (Metropolitan Museum of Art) has tapered Sheraton-style convex legs dovetailed into urn-shaped pedestal; right, top of early 19th-century stand (The American Museum in Britain, Bath, England) is 16 in. in diameter.

Shaker Round Stand
Three legs are dovetailed to turned pedestal

by John Kassay

Round stand is a name given by Shakers to the pedestal, tripod candle stand. These stands were derived from the English Queen Anne and Sheraton styles. American cabinetmakers made them less ornate and Shaker cabinetmakers further simplified the stands in line and form, in accordance with their religious doctrines.

The stands shown here were all made in the first half of the 19th century, when the Shaker sect was at its peak. They were used to furnish the retiring rooms of the Shakers' communal dwellings, which often housed 100 or more people. Today, these graceful stands make lovely accent tables. To duplicate the one shown, you need about 7 board feet of cherry.

Construction of the stand should start with the legs (A in measured drawing). Draw a full-size pattern of the leg, including the dovetail pin, on a piece of thin cardboard and carefully cut it out. Mill the stock for the legs to the required 3/4-in. thickness and position the pattern on the wood with the grain of the leg in the longest direction, as in the front-view drawing. Trace the pattern three times and then separate the legs with rough cuts; make no attempt to cut to size. The ends of the blank that will form the dovetail and the bottom of the foot are now cut precisely to length and per-

John Kassay is the author of The Book of Shaker Furniture *(Univ. of Mass. Press, Box 429, Amherst, Mass. 01004).*

pendicular to each other. Sandwich the legs together and firmly nail two scrap pieces of 1/4-in. plywood on these end surfaces. This assembly is now sawn to final shape and sanded as a single unit. Separate the legs, lay out the dovetail pins very precisely and cut the shoulders and sides with a dovetail saw. Of course they can be cut on the table saw, but that makes the operation less personal. Clean up with a chisel.

To make the pedestal (B), turn a piece of cherry, 2-1/8 in. square and 20-3/4 in. long, to a 2-in. cylinder. Lay out the pedestal with its upper end at the tailstock. To make an exact reproduction of the original stand, mark pencil lines along the cylinder at 1-in. intervals to locate parting tool cuts at the diameters shown. The experienced turner, like the craftsman who made the original, will find it sufficient to part the smallest and largest diameters. Remove the excess wood with a gouge. Then rough- and medium-sand the pedestal.

A tenon, 1 in. in diameter and 11/16 in. long, is established on the upper end of the pedestal to hold the disc (C). On the original table, wood threads fasten the pedestal to the disc. If you have a 1-in. wood threading tap-and-die set, by all means use it. Otherwise, the tenon is simply glued into a hole in the disc. At the lower end of the pedestal, turn an absolutely straight cylinder, 1-7/8 in. in diameter and 3-1/2 in. long. This is where the legs will be dovetailed to the pedestal. Finish sanding the pedestal while it is in the lathe. Be sure to

From *Fine Woodworking* magazine (Winter 1977) 9:68-70

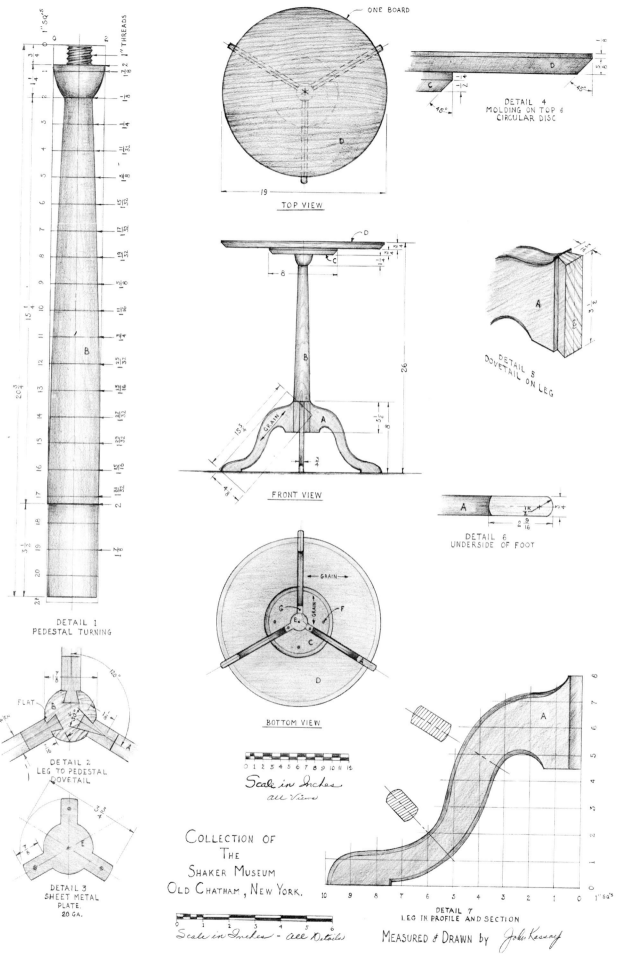

ONE BOARD

TOP VIEW

DETAIL 4
MOLDING ON TOP &
CIRCULAR DISC

DETAIL 5
DOVETAIL ON LEG

FRONT VIEW

DETAIL 6
UNDERSIDE OF FOOT

DETAIL 1
PEDESTAL TURNING

GRAIN

BOTTOM VIEW

DETAIL 2
LEG TO PEDESTAL
DOVETAIL

DETAIL 3
SHEET METAL
PLATE.
20 GA.

0 1 2 3 4 5 6 7 8 9 10 11 12
Scale in Inches
all Views

COLLECTION OF
THE
SHAKER MUSEUM
OLD CHATHAM, NEW YORK.

0 1 2 3 4 5 6
Scale in Inches - All Details

DETAIL 7
LEG IN PROFILE AND SECTION

MEASURED & DRAWN BY John Kassay

Tables and Desks 21

dampen the wood to raise the grain, and sand along the pedestal with the lathe turned off in order to remove any circular scratches.

Choose the most attractive grain pattern on the pedestal and locate one leg here. The other legs will be located 120° right and left from this point (detail 2). Index the legs to the pedestal with pairs of identification marks. Lines establishing the center of each leg are drawn on the bottom of the pedestal and extend along the sides. Then parallel lines 3/8 in. from these center lines are drawn on each side. To enable the legs to seat properly against the pedestal, absolutely flat surfaces must be cut within these outer lines. Cut a series of kerfs with a backsaw and pare away the excess wood with a sharp chisel. Redraw the center lines on these flat surfaces, using the center lines on the bottom as a guide. Draw lines 3/16 in. on each side of these center lines to indicate the thickness of the dovetail pins, 3/8 in., at their shoulders. Hold each leg in position against the bottom of the pedestal, and trace the outline of each dovetail pin (three lines for each) on the bottom of the pedestal. These three lines, along with the two parallel lines on the flats, determine the material to be removed to produce the dovetail sockets. With a brace and a 5/16 auger bit, bore a series of holes along the center line of one leg. Count the number of brace revolutions to gauge the depth. The waste wood is removed with wood chisels. Patience along with much trial fitting is now necessary. Make certain right from the start that the leg is being committed perfectly straight; do not force the leg in place. These dovetail sockets may be produced using a router, a dovetail bit and a home-designed jig for supporting the router while the piece is still in the lathe. On the other hand, by the time you have tooled up, you could be gluing up. After the legs are fitted to the pedestal, they are disassembled and a spokeshave and abrasive paper are used to form the curves on the upper and lower edges, as shown in section in detail 7.

Plane stock for the circular disc (C) to the finished 3/4-in. thickness. Mount it on a lathe faceplate and turn to the indicated diameter and chamfer. Finish-sand while the disc is on the lathe and bore a 1-in. hole on center for the dowel end of the pedestal. Bore and countersink four equally spaced holes for flathead wood screws (F), which fasten the disc to the top.

Fabricate the top (D) from three or four narrow boards that have compatible grain patterns. The circular shape and undercut chamfer can be turned outboard on a lathe, as for C. Both C and D can also be made with a hand router or a homemade circle-cutting jig on the band saw, or cut by hand with a bowsaw or a sabre saw.

Before assembly, the parts of the stand should be rough-, then medium-sanded. Make a jig of plywood to hold the legs and pedestal in an upright position while the glue hardens. Apply glue to both pins and sockets.

The disc is first screwed to the top with its grain 90° to the grain of the top, then glued or threaded to the pedestal.

Shakers often used a thin sheet-iron plate (E) to reinforce and cover the dovetail joint. If your dovetails have been well made, the plate is not necessary.

To finish the stand, raise the grain and fine-sand. Carefully dust. If a stain coat is desired, it should be of a brown shade; apply it before the first varnish coat. Apply three or four coats of clear furniture varnish. The final coat is hand-rubbed with fine (4F) pumice or rottenstone lubricated with lemon oil, and waxed. □

On Mortising
And joining table legs to aprons

by Frank Klausz

There are hundreds of variations on the mortise-and-tenon joint and many different ways to make them. The method and the tools I learned to use as an apprentice in Hungary are different from the English way. The latter method has been described by Ian Kirby, so I will compare his methods with mine, as I explain how I make a kitchen table with mortise-and-tenon joints, out of 3x3 poplar legs with 5/4 pine for the 4-in. apron and for the top.

I disagree with Kirby on the following points: 1) the shape of the mortising chisel; 2) the method of sawing the tenon cheeks; and 3) how to mark out and cut the tenon shoulders.

1) Kirby corrects his chisels so the sides are parallel and square with the back. For me a chisel with parallel sides is a car without a steering wheel. The sides of my chisels are tapered 1° toward the front face as shown in fig. 2. This is better because you can twist it against wild grain to keep the mortise straight. The chisel back has to be straight, the edge sharp and the handle large and square with rounded corners and rounded top, so it can take a beating. The partially square handle is easier to steer and sight up—you can get a good solid grip. To make such a handle I turn it oversize, mount the chisel, then plane the flats.

I have three or four different makes of chisels, old ones, including a German ½-in. stamped D-FLIR Franc Wertheim, a French ⅜-in. stamped Peugeot Freres Agier Pondu, and a Hungarian blacksmith's made from an old file. These chisels were made with tapered sides purposely to do mortising. Besides being able to steer them, the sides rub less, and the clearance helps in levering out the chips.

2) Kirby uses a backsaw for sawing the cheeks of the tenon and he changes the position of the wood several times. I use a bowsaw 30 in. long with 5½ teeth to the inch, a common ripsaw. I don't move the wood; I keep it straight upright in the vise at a comfortable height so I can occasionally check the mortise-gauge line on both sides. Start cutting the corner farther away from you, then come straight back across the end grain and down. Let the saw do the work, don't push it too hard. A beginner should practice with scrap wood, marking the whole length and sawing as far as the wood will allow. You end up with 10 or 20 inches of tenon.

3) Kirby makes the shoulder line with a knife, then saws ¹/₁₆ in. away from it for final paring to the line with a chisel. This method requires a master craftsman and extremely sharp tools, and I beg the beginner to stay away from it. I use a sharp, soft pencil to mark the shoulders. Then I use a bowsaw 23 in. long with 10 teeth to the inch. For a table apron I saw right on the pencil line on the inside of the apron and leave half the line on the outside for a perfect, invisible joint where it shows. If you're making a frame or a door, you have to cut both sides the same, either removing both lines, or leaving half of them. Either way, you avoid the unnecessary and difficult step of chiseling the shoulder.

From *Fine Woodworking* magazine (September 1979) 18:54-57

The completed joint before assembly. Tenon ends are sawn at 45° so they almost meet in the leg mortise.

Making a kitchen table —Start by cutting and planing the legs to size, ready for laying out the joints. Mark the outside corners and line up the legs on the bench. Measure the depth of the apron and mark that distance across all four legs with a square and the sharp, soft pencil. Mark a second line the actual height of the mortise, leaving at the top of each leg an area for the haunch at least one quarter but less than one third of the apron's total width. Turn the legs and mark the other inside of all four legs with the same mortise and haunch lines (fig. 1). The haunch is very important; it keeps the apron from twisting. If this were not a table but a frame where the pieces were all the same size, or if it were small and delicate, it would also be important to leave an extra length of wood beyond the mortise, called the horn. This keeps the wood from splitting during mortising and gluing up.

Set the mortise gauge spurs to the width of the chisel, in my example, ½ in. Draw on the leg the thickness of the apron, ¾ in., setting it in from the edge ¼ in. Then move the fence on the mortise gauge so the spurs are in the center of the apron lines and mark the mortise. This sets the apron in from the outside of the leg. If you want a Parsons table, which has legs flush with its apron, you draw the apron outline flush with the outside face of the leg and set the gauge fence to center the mortise in that apron outline.

Find a good solid spot on the bench and clamp the wood down, ready for chiseling. Here my method is similar to Kirby's, except i would also chop out for the haunch. Start from the completed mortise and go toward the end of the wood, chopping straight down but not too deep. Then come in on the line from the end. If you are a beginner and the inside of the mortise seems too rough, you could smooth it out with a patternmaker's rasp, Nicholson No. 50. Make sure you don't round any edges.

Now to saw the tenons. Put the four apron pieces on the bench, mark the good side (the outside, which will show) and the bottom edge, and square the shoulder lines all around. Make neat, skinny pencil lines. Mark the haunch and from the actual width of the mortise, reset the mortise gauge and mark the tenon in the center of the apron ends (fig. 3). Also mark a scrap for a try piece. Put the try piece upright in the vise, saw in from the far corner then saw all the way down. Saw the shoulders, then try it in the mortise to see how snug or loose it is. The important fit is the width, not the thickness. How snug should it be? My father taught me, if you use

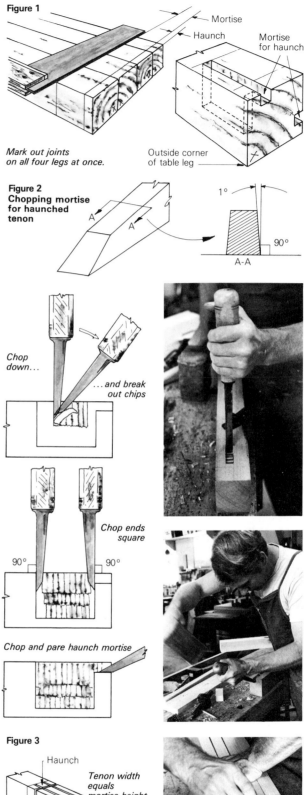

Figure 1

Mortise

Haunch

Mortise for haunch

Outside corner of table leg

Mark out joints on all four legs at once.

**Figure 2
Chopping mortise for haunched tenon**

A

A

A-A

1°

90°

Chop down...

...and break out chips

Chop ends square

90°   90°

Chop and pare haunch mortise

Figure 3

Haunch

Tenon width equals mortise height

Shoulder line

Tenon thickness equals mortise width

Lay all four aprons on bench, square across for shoulder lines, then gauge mortise width on each apron.

Clamp a pair of aprons upright in the vise to saw the tenon cheeks. Start sawing on the end grain, at the far side, then lower the saw so it cuts straight across and down to the shoulder line. Move to the side and saw the haunches together.

Glue legs and short aprons in pairs before gluing long aprons.

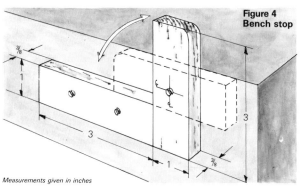

Figure 4
Bench stop

Measurements given in inches

your mallet to bang it together it is too tight, if you use your hat it is too loose, so find the middle way and push it together by hand. If your scrap piece is too tight, cut away the mortise-gauge mark; if it is too loose, leave the line on. Make another try piece until you get it right—practice makes the master.

Put one pair of aprons upright in the vise at a time, and saw down all four cheek lines—one apron steadies the other and it saves time. Move around and cut down the top of the apron to the haunch, both pieces at once. Now to cut the shoulders, take the wood out of the vise and put it on the bench. To hold the work I have a special stop, which can be made of any hardwood, cut to the dimensions shown in fig. 4. Cut the haunch and then the shoulders using the 10-tooth bowsaw or any fine saw. Saw right on the line on the inside of the piece, turn it over and saw to leave half the line on the outside, the side that will show. Finally, you cut the end of each tenon at 45° so they can almost meet inside the mortise. Try the joints together. A beginner can use the rasp to correct the tenon if the joints are too tight. A good joint is rough from the chisel and saw, which makes a good gluing surface.

Before gluing, clean all four sides of the leg with a smoothing plane, round off the corners tastefully and sand each side before you rotate the leg to the next. This saves work. Some craftsmen argue about corners. I say you want a crisp straight line, but fine woodwork has no sharp corners, especially the outside corner, which will get kicked and knocked round anyway. Office and children's furniture should be rounded even more. Next clean the apron with a smoothing plane and sand. The table is ready for gluing.

With the mortise-and-tenon joint it is important to put a thin, even coat of glue on the walls of the mortise but not to fill up the mortise. Most beginners use too much glue; on the other hand, most production lines use too little glue because they don't want to fuss with cleaning up afterward. On a big table it is easier to glue the two short ends in pairs, then glue the table together. Clamp with a bar or pipe clamp. Your scrap pieces from cutting off the shoulders are perfect blocks under the clamps so they don't mar the work. Make sure to check if it is square. The best method is to measure from corner to corner; it should be the same. □

Simple bench stop (left) holds work for sawing haunch and tenon shoulders. Flip stop down to get it out of the way.

Frank Klausz, trained as a master cabinetmaker in Hungary, builds and restores furniture in Bedminster, N.J.

Q & A

Gluing mortise and tenon
Put a moderate amount of glue in the mouth of the mortise, and just a little on the beginning of the tenon cheeks. There should not be so much glue that it runs out over the work, bench, and craftsman. A tight joint doesn't allow room for too much glue.
—*Tage Frid*

It is not good practice to put glue on only one surface when gluing two pieces of wood together—it makes for a weak joint. Glue squeezing out is a good sign, in spite of the mess.
—*Simon Watts*

Spline-Mitered Joinery
Concealed strength for fine lines

by Eric Hoag

Some years ago I solved a few design and construction problems with leg-and-apron structures using splined miters. Since then I've applied the technique to a number of projects, and after seeing these pieces exposed for several years to New England's fluctuating humidity, I believe the principles involved are sound. I was looking for a structure that would not be affected, visually or mechanically, by wood movement resulting from end grain butting long grain in the typical leg-and-apron joint. I also wanted to produce an unbroken, sweeping line from the bottom of one leg, up and across the apron, and down the other leg. Finally, I had to have strength in the joinery that would not be obtrusive or detract from the delicate appearance I was after.

The technique I worked out calls for mitering the leg-and-apron joint, which is reinforced with a blind spline, and also for joining the two halves of the legs with a splined miter (or bevel). The procedure I'll describe is for making a table like the one shown below, but you can modify it to build chairs, cabinet bases and other structurally similar pieces.

To establish the curves of the legs and aprons and to proportion the widths and thicknesses of these members, I start with an elevation drawing, fitting the end or side view within a square or rectangle of predetermined dimensions. Since the eight identical leg halves in the table must be uniformly cut, I

The legs and aprons of this white oak table are joined with splined miters. The delicate appearance of the piece belies the inherent strength of its joints. An additional advantage is that the whole assembly can be glued up with a minimal use of clamps.

make a Masonite pattern for these (see photo A, next page). Although adjacent aprons may be different lengths, I make only one pattern, which I lengthen or shorten in the middle (where the line is straight) as required. In proportioning the longer apron, pay close attention to its depth lest it produce, when shortened, a clunky, heavy-looking shorter apron.

Once the patterns are made, I joint and thickness-plane enough material for the four aprons and eight leg halves before tracing the layout lines onto them. Be sure when tracing that the straight edges of the patterns are flush with the jointed edges of the stock. Then bandsaw the inner curved and straight edges of the separate pieces.

Next, cut the miters for the leg-and-apron joints using an accurately set miter gauge in your table saw. The aprons must be mitered to finished length at this point (opposites must be identical), but the legs are left long at the bottom and cut to final length after assembly. Now the bandsawn edges are given a final rough shaping and smoothing to eliminate the need for too much of this kind of work when the pieces are assembled and more unwieldy. Some of the sweat can be taken out of shaping the legs by trimming the straight tapered edges on the table saw using a taper jig and stopping just shy of the curve.

Before cutting the spline slots for the leg-and-apron joints, I study the grain and color of all the pieces and decide which leg halves will go together and which aprons will go with which legs, and I determine the face side of each piece. Then I mark them all accordingly. Once I have this information marked on each piece, I cut the spline slots using a router table and straight-face bit of the appropriate diameter—usually one-third the thickness of the stock. The advantage of the router table is that you can adjust the depth of cut without disturbing the fence setting. This allows you to make a series of progressively deeper cuts when routing these slots—a safer and more accurate way to get good results than cutting to full depth all at once.

I set the fence on the router table to precisely half the thickness of the stock, measuring from the center of the cutter. Also, I project the centerline of the cutter onto the fence, using a square and pencil. With this line as a central reference, I mark on the fence two sets of diagonal lines that will show me where to position the stock for the initial plunge of each cut and where to stop advancing it into the cutter (photo B). The distance between these diagonals (one pair for each orientation of the stock) is determined by the length of the miter involved in the joint. Keep in mind that it's necessary to leave more space at the top of the slot (where the angle is acute) than at the bottom. If you're not careful you could cut all the way through the stock at the tip of the miter.

For spline material I often use plywood, as it allows me to rip a piece the desired length of the splines and to crosscut them to width. Because the router bit leaves the slots rounded at their ends, the splines must be rounded or chamfered to fit (photo C). After dry-fitting all the joints to check for proper tightness and accuracy, I glue each leg-and-apron assembly together. If the joints fit well to begin with, the miters need not be clamped, only forced together by hand and secured with several strips of tape across the joints on both sides. Sometimes unequal stresses exerted by the tapes cause the joints to rock and cure out of square. This can be remedied by tacking three carefully positioned strips of wood on a flat surface at right angles to one another. The three members can be clamped to this U, which will keep them square while the glue sets. Remove the tape as soon as the glue dries or it may pull up bits of wood when you peel it off.

Scrape and sand the area of the joint when the glue has dried; then smooth out any irregularities in the curves where the legs and aprons meet. My preference is to round these inner edges with my router, using a quarter-round bit with a ball-bearing pilot. This rounding also helps with the final shaping, as it eliminates a goodly amount of the edge I have to file and sand to get a finished contour.

Ultimately, these four leg-and-apron assemblies will be joined together with splined miters running almost the entire length of the legs. But before proceeding further, you should provide some means of attaching the tabletop support stringers to the inside of the aprons. I use a pair of stringers, with slotted expansion holes for screws (photo D) to attach the top. These stringers have tenons that are housed in shallow mortises cut into the upper inner faces of the long aprons. It's best to rout these mortises before gluing the separate assemblies into a single unit.

I cut the leg miters (bevels) on the table saw (photo E, next page). First I tilt the arbor to exactly 45°, checking with a combination square, and then lower the blade below the insert. Next I attach a straight wooden auxiliary fence to the saw fence, which I set on the left side of the blade, and with the saw running, I raise the blade slowly so that it just nicks the bottom outside edge of the wooden fence. The setup is checked by making a partial cut into scrap stock. The blade should enter the stock on the edge side, not the face side, and should leave behind a very narrow flat or land on the edge. This is necessary for holding the stock against the fence and keeping the beveled edge from creeping under the fence dur-

A. *Author traces interior curve and taper of half a leg from Masonite pattern. Only one apron pattern is needed, since the line between the curves can be lengthened or shortened as required. Straight side of the pattern must be registered along a jointed edge of the stock.*

B. *Diagonal lines on router-table fence show where to position stock and where to stop the feed for cutting blind spline slots in leg-and-apron miters. There are two pairs of diagonals, one for each orientation of the stock.*

C. *Corners of spline must be rounded or chamfered to fit into the rounded areas at the ends of slot. The slot must be stopped at least ¾ in. short of the miter's toe to prevent the bit from cutting through the edge of the stock.*

D. *Tabletop support stringers are slotted for screws and mortised into the ends of the long aprons. Screw slots allow the top to expand and contract without bowing or cupping. Mortises are routed before table frame is completely assembled.*

Photos: William K. Sacco

E. *Wooden auxiliary fence guides bevel cut on legs. A push stick is used for the last several inches of the cut, and care is taken to keep stock from being burned or gouged by the blade.*

F. *A wide fence on router table is used to guide stock when slotting the miter down the length of the legs. The extra-large fence gives needed support to the leg-and-apron assembly and ensures accuracy in cutting.*

G. *The legs should fit together easily, and the mating surfaces should have no gaps for an ideal interface. When the glue is applied, the joints are assembled by hand, pressed together and secured with clamps and tape at frequent intervals along their length.*

ing the cut. When two leg halves are assembled, these lands will create a small chamfer down the outside corner of the miter. This may be eliminated by planing or filing, or you may choose to increase its width or to round it over. Use a push-stick for the final 6 in. or so of the cut and take care that the work doesn't lurch against the blade as the cut ends, as this will create a gap in the joint.

Though you can cut the grooves for the splines on the table saw, I prefer to use the router table, which I equip with a high fence, angled accurately at 45° (photo F). Cutting the grooves this way allows you to stop them easily, and the high fence gives good support for the stock, ensuring accuracy. I cut the splines from scrap stock planed or resawn to the proper thickness, or I cut them out of plywood. With the splines in place, I dry-fit all four assemblies together (photo G), looking for a fit that is snug, with all joining surfaces in contact. The fit should not be so tight, however, as to require force to get the whole thing together. Use a band clamp around the top and C-clamps or spring clamps on the legs, working from top to bottom to ensure proper glue squeeze-out. Then I reinforce the joints with tape, where possible.

Depending on the piece of furniture you are making, there are additional steps prior to final assembly. A chair or a stool with a drop-in seat will need a groove near the upper inside edge to accommodate the tongue of a frame to support the seat. An inset tabletop will require a rabbet along the top inside edge. Although I've never had to use stretchers with this design, an end table with a shelf may require making some joints to receive the shelf supports. Lastly, in the case of a large piece (or one that will get rough treatment), corner braces may be necessary. Where they are placed will depend on where the increased stresses are expected. I mortise them into the structure, usually across the mitered joint between the leg and apron at an angle that will conceal their presence so they don't detract from the appearance of the curve. These corner braces can be decorative as well as functional in tables with inset or overlapping glass tops.

As I said earlier, I like to cut the legs to final length after assembly, whenever this is feasible. After the glue is cured, the tape removed and the excess glue scraped away, I set the fence on the table saw to the finished length of the legs and make the cuts by running the two long aprons against the fence. Before cutting, however, I wrap some tape around the foot of the leg where the sawblade will exit. This helps keep the wood from chipping out as the blade comes through. □

Eric Hoag is a professional cabinetmaker. He lives in Branford, Conn.

Making the Rule Joint
With hand tools, the process is as important as the product

by Alasdair G.B. Wallace

While inspecting repairs being made to the roof of his village church, the vicar was puzzled to see that an old woodcarver was putting the finishing touches to an elaborately carved angel's face. To the question of why such beauty should be located where nobody would ever see it, the craftsman replied that both he and God knew it was there. I recently was reminded of this story when a customer requested that I sign a butternut chest I had made. It occurred to me that whatever task we undertake, the finished product is in itself the quintessence of the craftman's signature.

In this age of mass production, personal signature has become the exception rather than the rule. The development and improvement of the tools of mass production have lessened the need for skills. Haste has become our byword, convenience our creed. The product has become more important than the process, and in the transition, something of inestimable value has been lost.

Unlike steel or plastic, no two pieces of wood are identical. Species, age, moisture content, cut, grain configuration, knot placement all contribute to the character of each piece and demand individual treatment. The proliferation of plywoods, chipboard and cheap veneers and the abhorrence of faults, knots and unusual grain pattern by those involved in mass production have almost obscured the diversity and beauty of this warm, venerable and versatile medium.

At Rendcomb College in England, my passion for manual processes stemmed from necessity. There were no power tools. A visionary headmaster, when questioned by a student about purchasing a table saw for the workshop, replied that ripping by hand was good for the soul. I still remember many hours of pumping a treadle lathe and hand-planing ¾-in. oak for ¼-in. panels. The sense of pride and accomplishment in the finished product was directly related to the time and effort expended in completing the task.

I continue in the manual tradition today because for me the process continues to be of greater importance than the product. Today's machinist will argue that leaving no traces of the saw, planer and shaper attests to his mastery of the tools and the care with which they were programmed. This is true. But machines, whether television or router, destroy the sensations of wonder, joy and accomplishment. The table saw's wail, the sander's whine, the router's scream deny a subtler, finer music and remove the woodworker from the personality of his medium. To submit to the machine denies the sensuous process so essential to the woodshop, and the work shows no trace of the craftsman, his tools, his labor. Wood is not homogeneous. Why then use a machine that by its very nature seeks to create a uniform product? Beauty lies in diversity, not uniformity. Hear the varying song of the plane as it skims oak, walnut or pine, the crunch of the chisel's edge cutting to the dovetail's line. Savor the perfumes of the crosscut in cherry, maple and elm.

It is important to realize at the outset that the mass-produced product and the handcrafted product do not compete in the same marketplace. Whereas the mass-produced product frequently assumes its market either ignorant or indifferent in terms of design and function—the short-range goal manifest in the stapled-drawer syndrome—the handcrafted product usually assumes a market aware and appreciative of form, function and signature. The onus is on today's craftsmen to educate the public, to demonstrate the superiority of their products. The creations of today's finest artists, such as David Brown, James Purdey, and James Krenov, to name a few, will continue to be prized for their design excellence and for the personal signature they incorporate in an age of anonymous machines.

Two arguments will be posed by those who advocate machines to the exclusion of manual processes. The first is that the machine, once programmed, is labor-economical. One worker operating one or several machines will outperform one manual worker in quantity and uniformity of product. If efficiency is measured solely in these terms, the argument is irrefutable. The human price of such economy, however, exacts a terrible toll.

Equally pervasive is the argument that a relatively unskilled worker can, with the flick of a switch, in-

Wallace's Jacobean table, of oak, open and closed.

From *Fine Woodworking* magazine (September 1979) 18:66-69

itiate a series of complex operations that result in a sophisticated product. This ease is, however, anathema to craftsmanship. The craftsman's skill is acquired through lengthy apprenticeship, exposure to many aspects of the art and hours of exacting labor. Practice may not make perfect, but it probably does result in continued development, both personal and functional.

When deciding whether to purchase hand tools, machines or a combination, the craftsman should bear in mind that anything that can be produced by machine can also be produced by hand. Space is probably of greater concern to the amateur than to the professional. The home workshop simply cannot accommodate all the larger machines—table saw, radial-arm saw, drill press, planer, jointer, lathe, band saw. For most amateurs, table saw and lathe commonly take preference, together with a selection of smaller power tools such as drill, sander or router. Krenov's observation that there is little point in ripping up the rough stock by hand and doing a vast amount of preparatory work with much effort is well taken. His apprenticeship served, he prefers to devote his skills to delicate detail imparted by hand. This is the essence of the craftsman—the judicious use of a few carefully selected machines to rough out the work. Elizabethan craftsmen of necessity employed the same principle: The pit sawyers supplied the boards; the craftsmen smoothed them, shaped them and signed them with their hands.

Of equal concern to most craftsmen is cost. As an amateur I cannot realistically contemplate the cost of a multiplicity of machines that would enable me to perform tasks I can already perform by hand. To submit to the machine would deny me the joy of creating with my hands, and would largely negate the sense of accomplishment. In R.L. Stevenson's words, "to travel hopefully is a better thing than to arrive, and the true success is to labor."

Hence my preference for hand tools. Using my grandfather's Stanley 45 and wooden molding planes, I become part of and continue a tradition as my hands impart to each tool a deeper, richer flesh-print. I select a hand-forged chisel bearing the faint initials H.W. on its worn maple handle. It fits the hand. As I use it, I relish the vision of history, and part of H.W. lives on in me and the works of my hands.

The small oak Jacobean double-dropleaf table shown on the previous page is a recent expression of this manual process. My decision to use rule joints between the tabletop and the leaves is in keeping with the Jacobean tradition. The rule joint satisfies aesthetically for several reasons. In neither the open nor the closed position is the hinge knuckle visible. The decorative character of the open joint enhances the finished

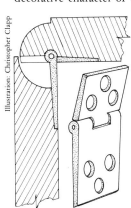

Illustration: Christopher Clapp

product. The closed joint is strong—downward pressure on the open leaf is transmitted to the central tabletop, effectively tightening the joint rather than relying solely on the hinge and screws, as would be the case in butt joints.

The rule joint takes its name from the brass-bound, boxwood rule that until recently graced every carpenter's tool chest. The drawing shows how the rule joint operates. If you think of the rule joint as two concentric circles with the center of

Tools for making rule joints include (clockwise from top) molding plane, Stanley 45, marking gauge and scratch beader with matched cutters. Wallace also uses a rabbet plane, not shown.

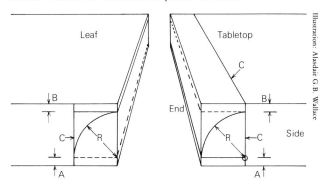

Illustration: Alasdair G.B. Wallace

the hinge pin as their center, you can see that the radius of the leaf arc is very slightly larger than that of the top. In laying out the joint, however, it is more practical to assume a common radius and sand to a perfect fit prior to finishing.

To work the joint you'll need a multiplane or rabbet plane, a small round molding plane or a gouge, and a homemade scratch beader with matched cutters or a matched pair of sanding blocks carved to the precise curve. The cutters or blocks must match precisely, or the finished joint will bind and gap.

Because the dimensions of the joint are determined in part by hinge size, you must obtain the special table hinges required prior to layout. These hinges have leaves of unequal size and are countersunk on the side opposite the knuckle. They are available from Period Furniture Hardware Co., P.O. Box 314, 123 Charles St., Boston, Mass. 02114, or from Ball and Ball, 436 W. Lincoln Hwy., Exton, Pa. 19341, as well as major woodworking supply houses.

Once the top and leaves have been planed to thickness, work on the joint may commence. There are two reasons for leaving the top and leaves oversize at this stage. Construction of each joint reduces the usable width of the finished top by a measurement equal to the radius of the curve. This is critical if a round or oval top is planned. It is also easier to scribe the joint on square stock and work a decorative edge molding after completion of the rule joint.

First, true and square the adjoining edges. All measurements in laying out the joint are taken from these edges and precision here will largely determine the nicety of the final fit.

The drawing above illustrates layout procedure. Distance A is the thickness of hinge to pin center. The lower edges of both tabletop and leaf are scribed to this measurement on sides and ends. Distance B is the depth of the top fillet and is variable, but probably should be no less than 3/16 in. The upper edges of both tabletop and leaf are scribed to this measurement, again on sides and ends. R, the radius of the curve, is the distance between the top line of A and the baseline of B. The top of the table and the sides of table and leaf are scribed to this measurement (line C). Line C is also scribed on the underside of the leaf and on the underside of the tabletop in the hinge area (several inches in from the sides) to help center the pin later. The dotted scribe lines on the drawing may be superfluous if you've already tested the setting of the plane's depth gauge and fence on scrap, but I continue out of habit to use them as safety checks. The point at which A and C intersect gives the hinge center projected to the side of the tabletop. A divider or compass centered at this point facilitates scribing the curve on the sides of top and leaves.

I find it easier to work the tabletop first and test-fit the leaves to it. Small adjustments are thus made in the leaf arc, the concealed section of the joint. The center top portion always retains its true cylindrical section. Use either the Stanley 45 or a rabbet plane to remove fillet B on the tabletop quickly and efficiently. Remove most, but not all, of the waste. The bulk of the remaining waste outside the scribed curve is then removed from the radius with a rabbet plane. The scratch beader completes the shaping, leaving a surface that will require little if any sanding.

The leaf joint is worked in a similar fashion. The Stanley 45 or the rabbet plane is set to measurement A, the hinge thickness, and this material is removed. Most of the material inside the scribed curve can be removed with a rabbet plane, but be careful to remain within scribe lines A and B. On the resulting chamfer, use a molding plane to clean up to just

Wallace uses his grandfather's Stanley 45 to remove the fillet from the tabletop, left. A rabbet plane works just as well. At right, the fillet is cut to just shy of the scribed line.

A series of passes with the rabbet plane wastes the bulk of the curve. The open side of this plane allows the iron to cut right to the shoulder of the fillet. At right is an end view of the roughed curve.

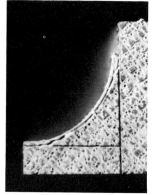

The curve is shaped to the scribed lines with a scratch beader and requires no further finishing. An alternative to scratch beader and matched cutters is a matched pair of sanding blocks carved to the precise curve.

The joint for the leaf is worked much like the joint for the top. The rabbet plane, used to remove the bulk of the material, yields the chamfer, left. The molding plane or the scratch beader cleans up to the line, right.

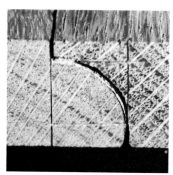

When cleaning up to the line, work the first groove into the chamfer by using your fingers as a fence.

Test-fitting the joint. When closed, leaf and top should form a flat plane.

The assembled top. Hinge is invisible when leaves are up or down.

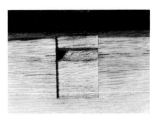

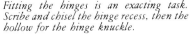

Fitting the hinges is an exacting task. Scribe and chisel the hinge recess, then the hollow for the hinge knuckle.

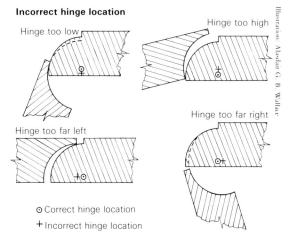

Incorrect hinge location

Hinge too low

Hinge too high

Hinge too far left

Hinge too far right

⊙ Correct hinge location
+ Incorrect hinge location

within the radius. The novice may at first find it difficult to use his fingers as a fence when working the initial groove in the chamfer with the molding plane. Butting a board next to the chamfer as a guide will do the job but will not help you master the convenient traditional technique. Finally, clean up with the scratch beader.

The leaf may now be offered to the tabletop for its initial test-fitting. Clamp the top to the bench edge with enough overhang so the leaf can operate. The leaf should glide evenly and smoothly over its mating surface and form, when in the closed position, a flat plane with the top. The precision with which the scratch-beader cutters were matched becomes apparent during testing. Any roughness during the fitting may be alleviated by judicious sanding of the leaf joint. Shaped blocks to which medium-grit garnet paper has been glued are most effective.

Fitting the hinge is an equally exacting task. I find it easiest to clamp the leaf to the tabletop face-down in the closed position with a strip of paper between to maintain a slight margin as the hinges are screwed tight. Align the center of the hinge pin, knuckle up, on previously scribed line C on the underside of the tabletop, and scribe around the hinge with a sharp knife. Chisel out the recesses thus scribed for the hinge plate and the knuckle.

Once the hinges have been inset flush with the surface, which should automatically locate the pin center at the requisite depth, drill lead holes for each of two diagonally opposed screws closest to the knuckles. These two screws will be used to test the accuracy of the hinge location when the paper and clamps are removed. If you have been precise, you will have a perfect joint.

To test the joint, lightly clamp the tabletop face-up on the bench allowing the necessary overhang while at the same time supporting the leaf horizontally. Sighting along the joint edge while gently lowering the leaf will reveal any inaccuracies. If the joint binds or a gap appears, the hinge location is faulty. The drawings above, which have been exaggerated for clarity, identify the possible faults and their causes. To move the hinge laterally, lengthen the hinge recess at the appropriate end, plug and glue the initial test holes, and redrill for the new position. To move the hinge vertically, either shim the hinge or deepen the recess. Once the fit is satisfactory, the remaining screws should be carefully inserted prior to complete dissassembly for finishing.

Working the traditional rule joint offers a special satis-

faction. Unlike the dovetail or mortise-and-tenon joint, both of which are static, rule and knuckle joints by their very action impart another dimension to the craftsman's art. They play an active, visible, functional role while at the same time contributing aesthetically to the whole. Evidence of the manual process—its diversity, its ingenuity, its minute irregularities and its failures—bespeaks the apprenticeship served and stands as a signature of personal creation. Look for these signs and, having found them, cherish them. In this age of machines they are increasingly rare. □

Alasdair Wallace, of Lakefield, Ontario, teaches high-school English. Woodworking has been his consuming hobby for many years.

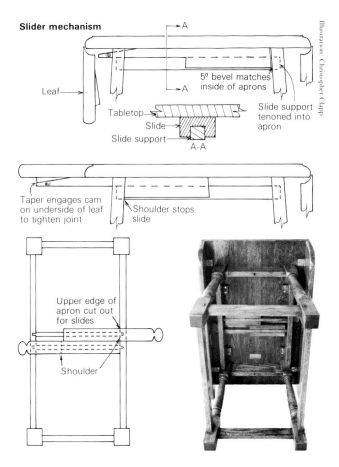

Slider mechanism

A

A

5° bevel matches inside of aprons

Leaf

A-A

Tabletop

Slide

Slide support

Slide support tenoned into apron

Taper engages cam on underside of leaf to tighten joint

Shoulder stops slide

Upper edge of apron cut out for slides

Shoulder

Expanding Tables
500 years of making room to dine

by Alastair A. Stair

In the Middle Ages, when it was customary for the entire household to assemble for meals in the great hall, the usual dining table was of trestle construction, massive boards of oak or elm resting on central supports. Tops were detachable and the entire table was often removed after meals.

"Joyned" or "framed" tables came into general use in England, France and Italy around 1550. As these were not intended to be moved and the frames were of fixed size, a "draw top" was soon introduced. With this simple sliding mechanism the length of the table could be doubled. This style reached a height in Tudor England.

No less ingenious than draw-top tables are those of smaller size, arranged with gate legs and hinged flaps, meeting the need for expanding portable tables as rooms became smaller and special rooms set apart for dining came into general use after the 15th century.

The early tables are in the form of half an octagon or oval, with a flap hinged to the broad side. When not in use the table is pushed up against the wall with the flap folded over the top. The gates swing on oak pin pivots driven through the framing. In some examples a single gate pivoting on the central stretcher supports both flaps.

In the first half of the 18th century gate legs were made with a swing leg (most often cabriole), without stretchers. These tables display a new method of hinging the gates: a true hinge accurately formed in wood, generally of oak or beech, with a stout wire core. Instead of oak pins, metal

---

Alastair A. Stair, a transplanted Englishman, is a New York dealer of 18th-century furniture. All of these tables have passed through his showroom.

screws hold the fixed portion of the top by passing obliquely through the underframe and into its undersurface.

Although the oak, elm and yew gate leg reached its greatest popularity about 1700 (sometimes in very large constructions with 12 legs), such tables were made in country districts until the end of the 18th century. Hardly any two tables are alike. For example, the early makers constructed the edge of the leaf where it is hinged to the table in three ways. One was to make a groove in the tabletop and a tongue in the edge of the leaf. The method generally used was to cut the edge of the leaf in a concave curve, with the reverse on the table edge, so that when the leaf is open the two fit snugly together—a rule joint. The third method has two short tenons on each leaf with corresponding mortises cut into the top of the table. About 1760 the gate-leg was revived in the guise of a small, light "spider-leg" table for the drawing room.

There was no notable advance in methods of enlargement until 1800, when Richard Gillow patented an improvement in the construction of dining tables "calculated to reduce the number of legs, pillar and claws and to facilitate their enlargement and reduction...by attaching wooden or metal sliders (which run in dovetail and square or cylindrical or other grooves) with or without wheels or rollers." These sliders are extended to the length required, and flaps are laid upon them. This is known as a "telescope" table. In 1805 Richard Brown patented a device by which "the two ends of the table frame are connected by pieces of wood, so joined together as to form what are commonly called lazy tongs."

The dining tables of the late 18th and early 19th centuries were generally made in sections held together by brass clips and supported on turned pedestals with three or four splayed

---

Leaves of Tudor-style draw-top table are fixed to raked runners, and center section is located by two horns that fit mortises in cross-rail. The leaves rise as they are pulled outward and the center rises along

with them. When the leaves are just clear the center drops flush. Below, two legs are fixed and two legs pivot from wooden hinges at center of apron in gate-leg table. Early 18th-century tables more commonly had five or six legs. Note rule joint where leaf meets top.

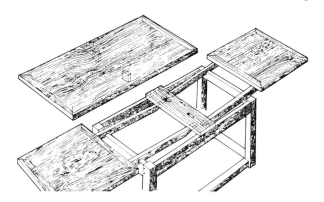

From *Fine Woodworking* magazine (Spring 1977) 6:44-45

Sheraton-style pedestal table extends, on interlocked sliders, to 90 in.

legs. These are referred to in the contemporary literature as "pillar and claws," because the curved legs often end in brass lion paws with casters. These tables were considered more elegant than their predecessors, partly because they have no legs to interfere with comfortable seating. A two-pedestal table can support one or two leaves; a three-pillar table can support more. In this fashion a dining table might stretch to 15 feet.

In the Regency period (1811 to 1820) a desire for ingenious constructions and novel forms encouraged the development of mechanical dining tables. A cabinetmaker named Pococks patented a rectangular table divided at the center into two leaves. When these are pulled away from each other, the extra leaf, stored beneath the top, snaps into place. The ends then push together and clip into place.

The large, circular table was fashionable and ingenious methods were devised for expanding it. Underframings became elaborate with all manner of rollers, sliders and hinges. Some examples have shaped sections added to form an outer border, fixed in position by long bearers and kept rigid by brackets. More commonly, the sections composing the surface were "caused to diverge from a common center (like a star, a pie or a medallion), and the spaces caused thereby filled up by inserting leaves."

About 1835 Johnson and Jeans devised a method by which the pie-type top opens to add sections by twisting or cranking by hand. The spaces are filled with various numbers of spear-shaped leaves. Robert Jupe patented a similar table in 1835. These were made until 1900 and enjoyed a renaissance about 1920 when Schmeig-Kotzian reproduced them, winning first prize at the Chicago World's Fair. But they were too expensive to make, so production ended around 1935. ☐

Gate-leg variation consists of six-legged center table with rectangular flaps supported on swing legs. Semicircular end pieces, each with three legs, have independent existence as wall or side tables.

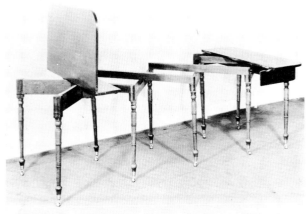

"Lazy-tongs" table folds tightly into apron at right, where hinged flap, left, conceals mechanism. Leaves are stored separately.

Mechanism of rare Johnson and Jeans table (1840) shifts wedges outward when top is rotated upon its pedestal, then leaves are dropped in. Wedges of octagonal table, below, pull out from the center and pointed slabs drop into the spaces, making it round.

Designing for Dining
Dutch pull-out extends table for guests

by Tage Frid

There are several different systems to choose from when making an extension dining table. Some you can purchase ready-made; they are usually quite expensive. Of the ones you can make yourself, I prefer the "Dutch pull-out" dining table. It is both simple and fast to make.

The tabletop consists of two pieces of plywood, both the same size, one mounted right above the other on the base. The lower piece is cut into three sections—two of them are the leaves, and the third is a fixed center piece. The top rests on the center piece and the leaves and is held there by two vertical dowels sitting loosely in guide holes. Thus it is free to move up and down but not from side to side. The leaves are mounted on long tapered slides that allow them to be pulled out from the ends. The slides travel in grooves in the end aprons and in a supporting rail across the center of the table base. As a leaf is extended, the taper makes it rise slowly throughout its travel to the level of the top. As the leaf rises, so does the top, until the leaf is fully extended and clear of the top. Then the top drops down again, flush with the leaf. Before the leaf can be pushed back in the top has to be lifted high enough to clear, then the top settles back down onto the center piece as the leaf travels back to its original position.

I made the table illustrated here 25 years ago, and it took four or five days, including veneering and edging plywood for the top. Once you understand the system, the work is easy and should go very quickly. You'll have to make four slides and only eight mortise-and-tenon joints. Other than wood for the base and the slides, you need hardwood-veneered plywood, two 3/4-in. dowels and edging for the top.

In addition to being easy to make, the leaves store right inside the table and are easy to pull out, even with the table set. If uninvited guests show up just when the food is on the table and you are ready to sit down, and they apologize for interrupting your meal but hint that they haven't eaten yet themselves, before you know it they are invited to join you. With most extension systems you would have to clear the table before you could enlarge it. But with the Dutch pull-out you can pull out the leaves without disturbing the setting at all.

There are several important dimensions you must consider when designing a dining table. Since the seat height of a dining chair is usually about 18 in., the height of the table should be between 29 in. and 31 in. I usually use 30 in.—this seems to be most comfortable for the average person. And since people differ in height more from the hip down than from the seat up, the distance from the floor to the bottom of the table apron should be at least 24 in., so that someone's long legs or fat legs aren't the legs holding up the table. In the length, I like to allow 24 in. for each person, so no one feels squeezed in. I try to place the legs so that no one ends up with a table leg between his or her own. (The easiest way to avoid that situation is to make a pedestal or trestle table.)

A place setting—dishes, glasses, and so on—is about 14 in. deep. So the minimum width of the table must be 30 in., or else you may drink the wine of the person across from you. Whenever possible, I make dining tables 42 in. wide, to leave space in the center for food, wine, flowers and condiments.

Leaves of Dutch pull-out store right inside table and can be extended from either or both ends without disturbing dishes.

34 Fine Woodworking

From *Fine Woodworking* magazine (Winter 1977) 9:34-37

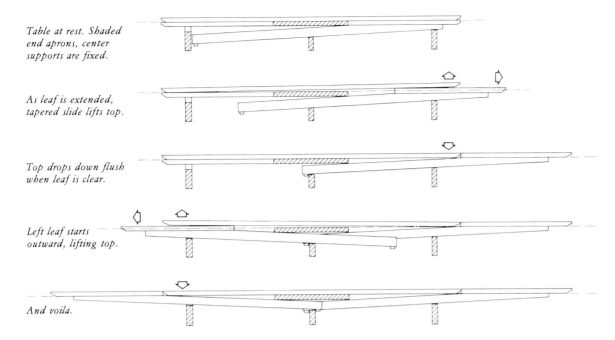

Table at rest. Shaded end aprons, center supports are fixed.

As leaf is extended, tapered slide lifts top.

Top drops down flush when leaf is clear.

Left leaf starts outward, lifting top.

And voila.

The table shown here was designed for a very small room and is only 32-1/4 in. wide, about the minimum.

For the last 12 years I have belonged to a gourmet club made up of seven men who cook for each other once a month during the winter. We have five good meals for ourselves, and at the last dinner of the season, two of us cook and the wives are invited. I feel that half the success of a meal is a result of how it is presented, and how comfortable each person is.

There is nothing worse than being seated near one end of a long, straight table and trying to talk with someone on the same side at the other end. If you want to see the person, you have to lean in so far that you might get gravy on your ear. The most logical shape for a table is round or oval, so everyone can see each other. And with a round table, each person uses less space because the chairs and elbows are out in a bigger circumference. A simple Dutch pull-out cannot be used on a round table, although complex systems using the same idea have been thought of. But a Dutch pull-out will work for a table with curved sides, though the overhang between the top and the leaf will not be the same all the way around (which I don't mind). I prefer to curve the sides slightly.

In designing a Dutch pull-out, remember that the less overhang there is between base and top, the bigger the leaves can be. This is because each leaf must travel its full length outward before it can clear the top. The tail end of the slide to which the leaf is attached of course travels the exact same distance. But the slide can't go any further than the inside length between the apron and the center support, less about an inch for the stop. Therefore, when you have chosen the length of the closed table, you can decide how much the top will overhang the base and calculate the length of the leaves. Or you can decide the length of the leaves and figure the overhang. One determines the other.

The measurements given in the drawings were taken from the old table in the photographs, and I will use these dimensions to explain the system. But you will want to use your own dimensions and make the table to suit your own dining area.

When my table is closed it is 50-1/2 in. long. I decided the top should overhang the base by 4 in. all around. Since the apron is 7/8 in. thick, the aprons and overhangs at both ends

Partly open view from below shows system of slides, stops.

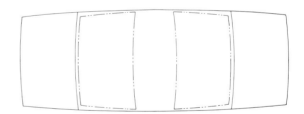

System works with curved sides, although overhang is uneven.

Table has beveled edge and careful rounding where leg joins apron.

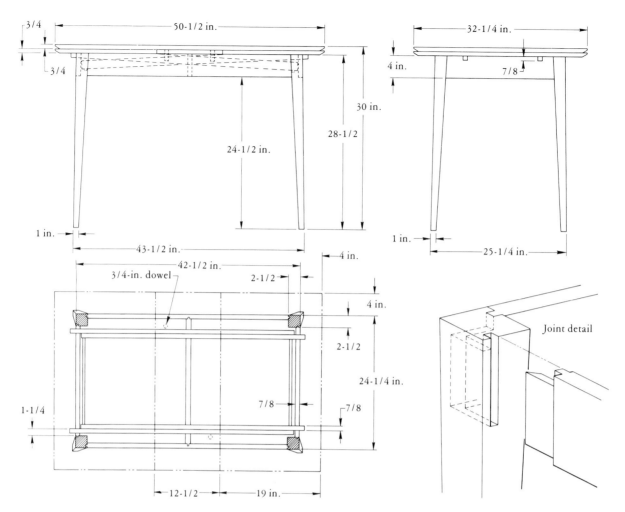

Joint detail

add up to 9-3/4 in. Deduct that from 50-1/2 in. and you get 40-3/4 in., the inside length of the base. Divide that in half (20-3/8 in.) and deduct 1-3/8 in. for the stop and half the thickness of the center support, and you get 19 in. for each leaf. Thus the table will extend 38 in., its open length will be the sum of the leaves and top, or 88-1/2 in., and the width of the center piece will be the difference between the leaves and the top, or 12-1/2 in.

If I had started with both the open and closed lengths, I would follow the same calculation in reverse to find the overhang. Since my table measures 50-1/2 in. closed and 88-1/2 in. open, simple subtraction gives 38 in. for the combined length of the leaves. Add the thickness of the two aprons (1-3/4 in.), both stops and the center support (2-3/4 in.) and you get 42-1/2 in. Deducting this from the length of the top gives 8 in. So the top would be allowed to overhang the base by 4 in. at each end.

The table base consists of four tapered legs joined to an apron that is 4 in. deep. I used haunched tenon joints in the legs. If the tenon came up through the leg in a slip joint, you would have to clamp across the cheeks when you glue the pieces together. By leaving the leg solid on top this is not necessary; you need clamps only in the direction that will pull the tenon into the mortise. To get as much strength as possible, I let the two mortises meet and cut the ends of the tenons to 45°, but left a 1/8-in. space between them for expansion. Use a tongue and groove to join the center support across the base. This piece will guide the slides and serve as a place to run the stops against to keep the leaves from falling out.

Because the tabletop is loose and the slides are glued and screwed to the leaves, the top and leaves must either be made out of plywood or be made using frame-and-panel construction. If you use plywood, you should get a top grade. You can buy it already veneered, or veneer it yourself, or you can paint it, stencil it or finish it however you like. I veneered the top and leaves together, so the grain would follow when the table is open, applied solid wood edging and beveled it. There are two reasons to bevel it. First, if the table gets used a lot, there might be a little play in the dowels and the beveled edge will help to hide discrepancies; second, when the leaves slide down, they will slide more easily.

The success of your table will depend on your accuracy in laying out and cutting the four slides. Be sure that the wood you use is straight. I usually cut the slides oversize and leave them for a few days to give them a chance to warp. Then I joint and thickness-plane them to size, in this case 7/8 in. thick and 1-1/2 in. wide. Their length is the inside measurement of the base (40-3/4 in.) plus the 7/8-in. thickness of the apron plus the 4-in. overhang, or 45-5/8 in. The slides will be trimmed shorter later, for looks, but they have to be full length now, for measuring.

The ends of the slides that hold the leaves must be cut at an angle so that they will wedge the leaves up to the level of the tabletop as they are being extended. On this table, the top and leaves are 3/4 in. thick. Thus each leaf must rise 3/4 in. when it has traveled 19 in., its full extension. From one end of one of the slides, measure down 19 in. and square the line off. Then make a point 3/4 in. over on the same end. A line connecting this point with the edge of the 19-in. mark will give the angle at which to cut the slides.

To be sure that all the slides will have the same angle and be cut exactly the same, you should construct a jig. Square a piece of plywood about 6 in. wide and a foot longer than the angled portion. Place the slide over the plywood with both marks (the ends of the line you have drawn) just touching the bottom edge of the plywood. Then trace the end and the other side of the slide and bandsaw out the shape.

With the table-saw fence still at the same setting you used to cut the plywood jig to width, insert the slide into the jig and make the cut. Use the same setup for all four slides and you can be sure they will all turn out the same.

The slides run in slots in the end aprons and the parallel center support. One pair of slides travels inside the other pair, and the two run side by side in the slots in the center support. To lay out these grooves, mark lines on top of the apron at both ends, 1-1/4 in. from the inside edge of all four legs. With a long straightedge, transfer these lines to the center support. Mark the thickness of the slide to the *outside* of the table from these lines on one apron, and to the *inside* of the table from the lines on the other. On the center support, mark the thickness of a slide to *both* sides of the center line.

The grooves on the end aprons must be the same depth as the slide at that point, so that the leaf will clear the apron as it is extended. To find this depth, measure in 4 in. from the tapered end of the slide and cut the groove to the exact depth of the slide at this point, in this case 7/8 in.

To find the depth of the grooves in the center support, first mark its location onto the slides, in this case 25-1/4 in. from the tapered end, or half of the length of the closed table. Then push the tapered side down flat and measure the depth at the marked point, in this case 1-7/8 in. This is the minimum depth that will allow the leaf to rise 3/4 in. in its travel; the grooves may be cut a little deeper if you wish.

Now that all the measurements and cuts have been made, the tapered ends of the slides can be trimmed. I wanted the closed slides to extend 1 in. beyond the apron, so I cut off 3 in.

To assemble the table, place the slides in the grooves with the angled sides up. Put the leaves in position (don't forget that you just trimmed 3 in. off the end of each slide), and glue and screw the slides to the leaves. To locate the stops, extend the leaves 19 in. and mark where the slides pass through the center support. Then screw on the stops at this point.

The central plywood piece is screwed to the base above the central support. It prevents the leaves from falling down when they are pulled out and locates the tabletop. Drill two 3/4-in. holes in the central plywood piece between the slides and the apron; these are the guide holes for the top.

Now push the leaves in and locate the top in its correct position. Clamp it down to the leaves and mark the location of the guide holes on the underside of the top. Then drill and glue two 3/4-in. dowels into these holes. The dowels should be about 2-1/4 in. long, since the top has to move up a full 3/4 in. while the leaves are being extended.

When you push the leaves back in you have to lift the tabletop. To prevent scratches from the tabletop's sliding on the leaves, I glued two strips of felt to the bottom of the top. Use hot hide glue or rubber cement. ☐

Tage Frid is the author of Joinery: Tools and Techniques *and* Shaping, Veneering, Finishing *(The Taunton Press).*

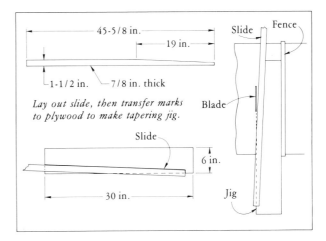

Lay out slide, then transfer marks to plywood to make tapering jig.

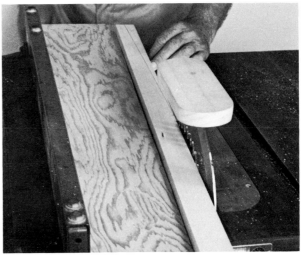

Ripping the taper: Jig guarantees four identical slides.

Push taper flat to measure depth of slot at center support line.

Slots for slides are cut in aprons, center support.

Dining table choices

I plan to build an oak dining table and haven't decided on the refectory (trestle) style or the conventional four-leg type. Are there inherent advantages or disadvantages to either design? I have oak boards of varying widths. Should I make the tabletop from a few wide boards, with a greater tendency for cupping, or use a large number of narrower boards, with more glue joints? I want to use breadboard ends on the top. How can I cut the tongues and grooves accurately? —Brent J. Stojkov, Concord, Calif.

Trestle tables offer more seating space for top size because there are no table legs to interfere with chair legs and diners' knees. Place the trestles at least 14 in. in from each end of the top so people sitting at the head and foot won't bang their knees. Another advantage is that trestle tables are easy to make knock-down by through mortising the uprights to receive the tenoned stretcher (see pages 40-43 and 44-46).

I prefer tabletops glued up from an odd number of boards 5 in. to 8 in. wide. The top will not cup if you secure it on both sides to the horizontal members atop the uprights.

I have little use for breadboard ends and cannot recommend that you use them. Inevitably you get unsightly gaps and projections as the top expands and contracts with the seasons. This movement degrades the glueline, and eventually your breadboard will fall off, unless the tabletop is tenoned into it and provisions are made in the joinery to accommodate the cross-grain movement of the top. If you are determined, you can cut the tongues on the top with a dado blade in your table saw and then groove the breadboards also with the dado blade. But before you go to this added trouble, ask yourself why you're doing it. —Simon Watts

Cupped table leaves

I have a walnut drop-leaf table and the leaves have moderately cupped. Is there any way to remedy this situation? —John Smoot, Baton Rouge, La.

I have had some success in unwarping wide boards from antique tables using the following method: On a sunny, dry day, soak the concave side of the board with water and lay it in the grass, convex side up. Let it dry for a while.

Alternatively, wet the concave surfaces of two cupped boards, clamp the wet sides together and set them in a dry shop. Monitor their progress every half hour or so. If the boards were sawn from compression wood, or are wide planks rift-sawn from near the pith, this procedure will have only temporary effects, or it will not straighten the wood at all. If the procedure works, coat both sides of the wood with the same finish to equalize moisture exchange and keep the wood from warping again. —Jim Richey

Battens make leaves cup

I recently built a gate-leg drop-leaf table of walnut. To the undersides of the leaves I attached a system of battens with screws and glue for added strength. I finished the undersides with Watco, and also applied some to the tops. After a week, I applied a mixture of tung oil and polyurethane to the top surfaces but not to the bottoms. About two weeks later the leaves began to cup outward; now they are severely warped. How can I overcome the warping problem and straighten out the leaves? —Dan Hayes, Elkhart, Ind.

The battens that are screwed and glued to the undersides of the leaves keep the wood from moving. Pretty soon the leaves will split. The best thing is to start over. Don't put any supports on the undersides of the leaves, and whatever the finish you may use on the top, treat the undersides of the leaves exactly the same way. —Tage Frid

Gate-Leg Table
A contemporary version

by Paul Buckley

Gate-leg tables are by no means new. They were popular in colonial America where settlers sometimes ate, slept and lived in one-room houses. Multi-functional furniture that uses space efficiently was highly desirable under such crowded conditions.

Our needs today are typically much different, yet many modern interiors lack usable living space. The increase in apartments, condominiums and smaller homes has again caused multi-functional and folding furniture to become very popular.

Sensing this need for more efficient furniture, I set out to design a table that would belong esthetically in a contemporary environment and be completely functional, yet conveniently small when not in use. After one year of designing and experimenting, I was satisfied that this table fulfilled all my criteria.

In this article I include the methods used to construct the table and solutions to problems inherent in the design. The dimensions are from my table, which was designed specifically for my personal needs and taste. I encourage each craftsman to evaluate this design in the light of his or her own needs, feelings and creative abilities. Changes can be made in any part of the design as long as you realize the table has two natural limitations. The height of the table determines the length of each drop leaf. And the gate legs, to maintain stability, must be at least six inches wide or apart when closed.

Wood selection is no great problem. It is safe to assume that any hardwood is suitable. I used white oak because it is stable and has strong grain pattern, which I felt was desirable in this simple design. Because some shaping is involved, it is also advisable to use a wood you are familiar with.

I have found that the most logical sequence of construction is to build the gate-leg frames, then the table frame and finally the leaves. The entire table is made from 7/8-inch thick stock. In cutting the leg parts, remember to allow 2-1/2 inches extra for tenons for the horizontal crosspieces. Next, lay out and cut 1/2-inch mortise joints, and tenons to fit. Care must be taken in assembling the members to ensure a square leg frame. After clamping, measure the diagonals and re-square if necessary. This step will avoid problems later in the table frame assembly. Before shaping the legs, drill and position the dowels the legs will pivot on. Then shape and sand each leg until you get finished surfaces.

Frame construction begins with cutting all members to length and width. Lay out the dovetails (which I chose because of their strength and simple beauty). First cut the pins on the frame side members, where pressure will be

From *Fine Woodworking* magazine (Summer 1976) 3:42-43

exerted if wracking of the frame occurs. Then cut the tails on the top and bottom members.

After the jointing is completed, dry-clamp the frame into position. This step will help avoid confusion while laying out the side handles, bottom frame cutouts and the 1/2-inch diameter holes for the gate legs. The hinges have to be routed into position before the frame is assembled. (I found these drop-leaf hinges in the catalogs of The Woodworkers' Store, 21801 Industrial Blvd., Rogers, Minn. 55374 and Craftsman Wood Service, 1735 W. Cortland Ct., Addison, Ill. 60101.)

It is easier to sand the interior surfaces before assembly because the legs will interfere with any later attempts.

Assembling the frame is simple if your dovetails fit well and the gate legs are square. The legs must be in position before final assembly.

The tops are simple laminations with tongue and groove breadboard ends. A few tips may be helpful. To ensure that the wood of each leaf matches up, laminate one large top and then crosscut into two pieces. Remember that wood expands. The width of the leaves is determined by the season of the year that you fit the top to the frame. Leave a larger gap if you build the table in the winter. You may still have to adjust the leaves for summer humidity. A slight friction fit holds the leaf closed against the bottom of the frame when the table is folded. This fit is accomplished by planing the breadboard end and moving the adjustable hinges until the desired pressure is attained.

To allow the leaves to expand and contract, I secured each breadboard with three 2-inch #12 roundhead wood screws set into 1/2-inch diameter counterbored holes that were later plugged. When drilling the shank clearance holes, I elongated the outer two holes, creating a slot in which the fixing screws could slide. The pilot holes for all screws were drilled normally. By using this method you can securely fix the tabletop to the breadboard ends, but also allow the outer edges to move freely.

Because I used only one breadboard on each leaf, an additional method to minimize warpage on the hinge end was needed. The method I chose was to alternate the heartwood-sapwood sides of the top's laminations. This created a slight washboard effect, but avoided the large distortions that would have occurred without some hold-down method. Other possible solutions to this warpage problem are using two breadboard ends on each leaf, or using oak plywood for the top, thus avoiding the movement problem.

You can experiment with the finish. I used Watco oil, which is easy to care for, but you may prefer a more durable finish for everyday use. □

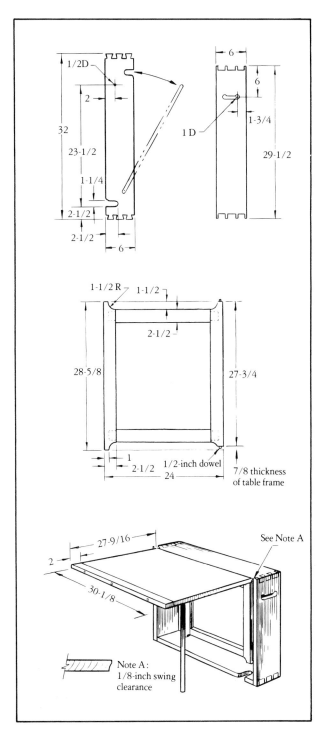

Drop-Leaf and Gate-Leg Tables
Graceful proportions make all the difference

by Simon Watts

Tables with hinged leaves have been made in America for at least 300 years, although no surviving examples date back to before about 1700. The early tables were often used in taverns and, when not in use, could be pushed back against the wall to make more floor space. The first drop-leaf tables had a square edge between the leaf and the top—simple but crude. The barrel of the iron hinge was left exposed and there was a substantial gap when the leaf was down.

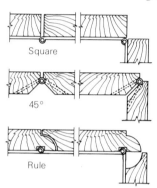

Later tables had a 45° angle cut in the lower edge of each board, with the hinge set in from the underside. At some point an unidentified genius invented the rule joint. This elegant detail allows the hinge to be concealed completely. Special steel table hinges are now made that have one leaf longer than the other. This longer leaf is attached to the table leaf; the shorter leaf is attached to the tabletop. I rout a short recess for the barrel of the hinge but there is no need to set the whole hinge into the wood. It's just extra work, and results in making the hinge more visible when the leaf is down. The mating edge profiles are best cut with a router, although originally molding planes were used. In my experience it is a mistake to make the joint too snug because crumbs and other debris tend to get jammed in it.

The leaves of early tables were supported by slides or swinging brackets, but when larger tables with wider leaves were made, a swinging leg became necessary. These became known as "gate-leg" tables. For convenience I will call the first kind a drop-leaf and the second a gate-leg.

The leaves of a drop-leaf table should not be narrower than about half the width of the top. I usually make the top 18 in. to 22 in. wide and the leaves 10 in. to 12 in. If the table is much narrower the legs get so close together that it might overturn when used with only one leaf up. If the table plus leaves is much wider than about 44 in., it will look bulky unless it is made too long for the average dining room. A table 6½ ft. long seats eight comfortably.

The leaves do not have to be rectangular; they can be curved on the long side, with the slight disadvantage of reducing the space available at the end. I don't like oval-shaped drop-leaf tables because the curve crossing the rule joint makes part of the joint project in an unsightly way. Leaves can also drop from the ends of the table instead of from the side, although it is difficult to gain enough length for a whole place-setting without embracing a leg between one's knees.

The table shown in the photos and drawing was made for a family with three small children. I suggested putting a radius on the corners but the parents decided that would detract from its appearance so the corners were left square. By now all three children have met a corner head-on, and one required stitches. I think a furniture maker is obliged to point out this kind of hazard, but should not insist on doing it *his* way.

The choice of wood and the boards selected for the leaves are important. This is because the drop leaves are not restrained, except along their top edges, and if they cup or twist there is no structure to prevent them from doing so. For this reason I use a very stable wood, such as mahogany, and try to use boards whose annual rings run nearly at right angles to the surface (vertical grain). The leaves have to look good when down and should match the top and each other when up. Ideally, one ought to make leaves and top out of boards cut from the same tree.

Top and bottom surfaces of the leaves must be finished in exactly the same way. Otherwise, the side of the wood with less finish will pick up moisture or dry out more readily than the other, and the leaf will cup.

Simon Watts has been building and designing furniture for more than 20 years. He is author of Building a Houseful of Furniture: 43 plans with comments on design and construction *(The Taunton Press, Box 355, Newtown, Conn. 06470).*

The drop-leaf table shown in the plan drawing on the next page has routed rule joints (see detail in photo at right). Each leaf of the table is supported by four hinges—one pair near the ends, and a second pair inboard of the slide supports.

Photos: Richard Starr

There must be enough knee room for people to sit at the ends of the table. My experience is that a top-to-apron overhang of between one-fifth and one-sixth the length of the table accomplishes this and also looks right. The amount of taper of the legs is also important. Too much taper and the table looks nervous—as if it were about to get up and walk away. Too little taper and the whole piece begins to look clumsy. There are no rules except that what *looks* right generally *is* right. I always put a substantial chamfer around the bottom end of the legs where they meet the floor, especially if the piece is too heavy to lift. Furniture always gets dragged around and the legs eventually wear down. If there is little or no chamfer the legs can splinter.

The most difficult detail on a drop-leaf table is designing the slides so they will support the leaves. Nothing spoils the look of these tables more than drooping leaves. I put a small blocking piece between the slide and the underside of the tabletop. This angles the slide up very slightly, and with a bit of adjustment the leaf can be made to lie dead level. If the leaves do begin to droop due to wear, the blocking piece can easily be replaced with one slightly thicker.

Some people make drop-leaf tables with a hinged bracket to support the leaf. This is not good practice because it strains the hinges and twists the apron. The strength of the table is in the joints between the aprons and the legs, so these must fit well and be properly proportioned. I use a haunched tenon joint and offset the mortises. The tenons should not meet inside the leg. If they do they seriously weaken the joint, which can then be split out by an accidental kick.

The top is attached to the base with steel tabletop fasteners

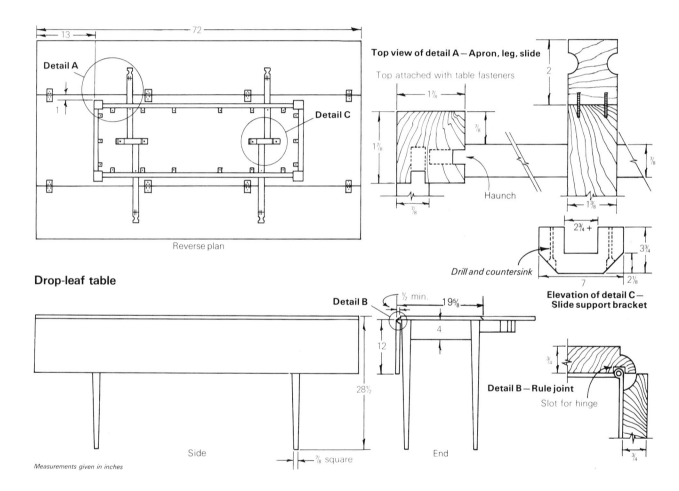

Drop-leaf table

Measurements given in inches

Photograph of a drop-leaf table taken from below, left, shows slides and the support bracket. A brass pin in the slide stops its travel against the bracket when the leaf is down, and against the apron when the leaf is up. Two variations of the drop-leaf table, center and right: leaf with curved edge, and leaves that are hung from the ends of the table.

The top can be attached to the aprons with metal clips or with wooden buttons. Either device is screwed to the tabletop and engages a saw kerf running along the inside of the apron.

that fit in a groove or sawcut around the inside of the apron. They can easily be made in wood but the grain must run at right angles to the lip. The apron should never be screwed or glued directly to the top, as this would prevent movement between the two caused by changes in humidity.

The gate-leg or swinging leg has many similarities. Since the open leaf is supported by a leg and not by a slide, the middle section can be much narrower than the middle of a drop-leaf. This way a table that is rather large when open can be put against the wall when not in use, occupying very little floor space. However, if you make the middle section less than about 12 in. wide, the table is liable to get knocked over when both leaves are down. The maximum depth of leaf for a table of standard height (28½ in.) is about 25 in. Any deeper and the bottom edge gets too close to the floor and will be kicked. The shape of the top can be square, rectangular, round or oval, but if the length is more than about 60 in. a second gate is desirable, which interferes with seating. It also makes for a heavy leaf, awkward for one person to lift.

The rule joint is the same but because the leaf is deeper the choice of wood is more crucial. If a single wide board cannot be found, a number of narrower boards will have to be joined. Opinions vary, but my own feeling is that the heart side and the sap side of adjacent pieces should alternate. I think this reduces the possibility of the leaf's curling if is it exposed to the heat from a stove or radiator. If possible, choose vertical-grain stock.

The boards to be joined should not have any twist or wind as this cannot be taken out by clamping. However, a bowed board can usually be straightened by putting it between two straight pieces or by pairing it with a board bowed in the opposite direction. Mating edges can be planed by hand with a long jointing plane or a power jointer. When using a power jointer, run the boards alternating their faces against the fence. Any errors (due to the fence not being precisely at right angles to the bed) will cancel, not accumulate. It is good policy to plane the boards with a slight hollow (less than ⅛ in. over 72 in.) so that their ends are pressed together and there is less chance of a joint opening under seasonal movement. On no account should there be any camber.

I always glue up stock on edge vertically, holding the bottom board in a vise or standing it on sawhorses. If you try to do it on the flat, the glue always runs down to the lower edge and you get a starved joint. I also dowel with ⅜-in. by 2-in. hardwood pins on 8-in. centers to keep the edges from sliding on each other when clamping pressure is applied. Of course some use a spline for the same reason, but unless its groove is stopped near the ends, it will show.

Before gluing, the boards should be set up dry in final sequence. They should be placed on each other vertically and should sit fair without any rocking. Check one side with a straightedge to be sure the surface is flat, then mark and drill the dowel positions. A quick way to close up the joints before

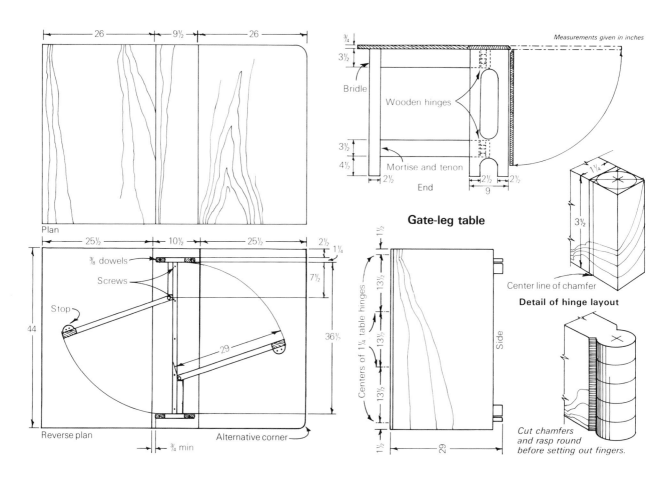

Plan

Reverse plan

Alternative corner

Gate-leg table

End

Bridle

Wooden hinges

Mortise and tenon

Measurements given in inches

Center line of chamfer

Detail of hinge layout

Cut chamfers and rasp round before setting out fingers.

Side

Designed by Simon Watts; Redrawn by Bob Crosby

Gate-leg table in open and closed positions, as shown in the drawing on page 42. The gate-leg principle can also be applied to the more conventional leg-and-apron understructure, by adding a low rail between the legs where the gate can attach.

putting on clamps is to stand the whole assembly on the bench, pick up one end and then drop it—hard. Then pick up the other end and drop it too. It makes an awful racket but is far quicker than winding up the clamps one by one.

The clamps should be alternated from front to back of the assembly, and if the wood is not to be replaned, slip waxed paper or plastic under them to avoid staining the wood. A clamp over every dowel is good practice, and always put one at each end. Bar clamps are rigid but pipe clamps, if threaded at each end, can be made up with couplings to any length required. I like to keep some of each, but bar clamps over 6 ft. long are unwieldy. There should always be plenty of glue squeezing out of the joints, but beware of too much pressure—you can squeeze out too much and starve the joint.

The traditional wooden hinge can be mastered by anyone with a bit of patience who is willing to make one or two practice sets. This example pivots through 180°, but it can be stopped anywhere by varying the chamfer behind the knuckle itself. Square up the stock, then lay out the joint by gauging the stock thickness all around the ends of both pieces. Draw in the diagonals on both edges, to locate the center of pivot, and with dividers scribe the circular shape. The circle crosses the diagonal at the bottom of the chamfer; extend these

points to the sides of the wood and square across. Now add pencil lines where the circle runs out on the faces and ends. The lines mark the point where no wood will be removed.

The layout completed, I saw the chamfers and the bulk of the waste with the table saw set at 45°, then finish the rounds with a rasp and sandpaper. Divide the width of the wood into four or five fingers, saw in on the waste side of the lines, and chisel out the waste from both sides, just as for dovetails. You can get at the inner hollow on the ends with an in-cannel gouge, but between the fingers the waste has to be removed with a chisel, bevel downward. Finally, fit the joint together and drill through both pieces at once for the pin. I usually use a brass pin, peened over at both ends so it can't fall out.

Make the end pieces of the table by cutting a board in half lengthwise; then bandsaw the waste and finally dowel and rejoin the two halves. A saber saw or a small frame saw could make the cutouts without splitting the board, but the finishing tends to be tedious. The frames and gates can be left square, chamfered or radiused. I prefer some rounding.

Any dry, reasonably stable hardwood can be used for these tables. I like walnut, cherry, teak and mahogany. I don't think they look as good when made out of blond woods such as oak or maple, but that's just an opinion. ☐

Cheap clamps

I don't like pipe clamps because the pipes bend under load and mar the work. I can't afford long bar clamps, so I make the 2x4-and-folding-wedge clamps shown in the drawing below.

The materials bill for each clamp is an 8-ft. or 10-ft. utility stud crosscut in half, a foot of 1-in. hardwood dowel, and some scrap for cleats, blocks and wedges. Avoid twisted 2x4s, although a little bow doesn't matter. Make the wedges about 12 in. long, tapering about 1 in. over 9 in., for slow, firm squeeze. Keep the dowel holes about 6 in. apart and span intermediate widths by adding spacer blocks between cleat and wedges. I usually take the clamps apart and use half of each as an assembly bed, then put them together right around the work. Add blocks until the narrow end of both wedges just fits the space, then drive the wedges in together. Keep the joints in line by putting hand-screws across them at the ends, and fine-tune with smaller wedges driven between the clamps and the tabletop.

—*Larry Green*

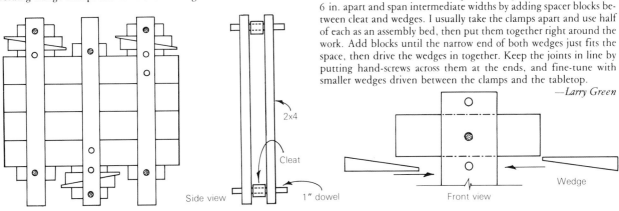

Designing Trestle Tables
Knockdown joinery challenges ingenuity and skill

by Kenneth Rower

Trestle tables are bridges made of two or more standing frames and a top. If the frames are not individually stable they must be connected to one another or to the top. There are different ways to do this, most commonly by fitting a stretcher somewhere between floor level and the top. Most end-frames are T-form, but some are H-form or X-form, and these are sometimes braced on the diagonal to the top instead of being connected to one another. Many trestle tables are designed to knock down quickly. The simplest—indeed, the archetype—consists of a board on two horses, but most have a loose top and a detachable stretcher, which draw-wedged tenons join to the trestle posts.

A trestle table does not always require a knockdown frame; doorways, hallways and stairways are normally wide enough for maneuvering. The top alone can come off quickly, to reduce weight and bulk, and fixed joints can be made at the posts. But if flat storage is a requirement, or if the exercise is to build a rigid table that can be knocked down to elements with only a hammer, then the extra work is justified. Also, sizable draw-wedged tenons showing outside the posts are unsurpassed for strength, and an opportunity for expressive construction. But if flowing lines are planned for the frame, then it will be better to make fixed joints, without projections, at the posts.

Practical dimensions—A trestle table at standard dining height (29 in.) looks and works best when 6 ft. long or longer. At any length, the amount of top between the end-frames compared with the amount outside them is important. Putting about five-ninths between the supports and two-ninths out at each end balances the top against sagging, whatever its thickness (figure 1). But for tables much shorter than 6 ft., the resulting leg room at the ends becomes a problem—much less than 16 in. is uncomfortable. For elbow room, allow 24 in. per person along the sides. As to minimum dining width, around 30 in. is possible, 32 in. is better, and 36 in. provides space for serving dishes in the middle. The ratio between width and length is not critical, but as the

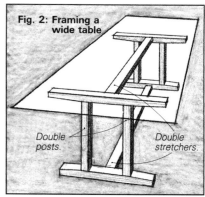

Wide, wedged stretcher bridges the table's posts and stiffens the trestle. It also allows quick assembly and disassembly.

plan approaches square, a leg-and-apron construction is more practical, for stability as well as comfort. A very long table may work better with another support in the middle, in which case the five-ninths/two-ninths rule is of course irrelevant.

The thickness of the top should be judged against the thickness of the posts. Probably the top should be thinner, but how much so will depend on the effect wanted. The width of the posts should be gauged against the width of the top. Two posts might be better than one under a very wide top, but twin stretchers could appear cumbersome. Flat stretchers placed at the floor and just under the top will give an airy effect (figure 2), but cannot do the stiffening work of a deep stretcher placed about halfway up a central post.

The trestle arms should stop about 3 in. short of the edges of the top, for knee room. The feet should be shorter yet, for toe space, but not so short as to allow the table to tip if someone were to sit on its edge. To clear minor irregularities in a floor, the lower edges of the feet can be relieved very slightly—$\frac{3}{32}$ in. is enough—starting 3 in. or 4 in. from each end. Careful beveling of the bearing parts will continue the thin dark line at the floor.

Stretcher depth and height off the floor determine the frame's lengthwise stiffness, as well as the apparent mass of the whole. In the standard knockdown design, the stretcher must

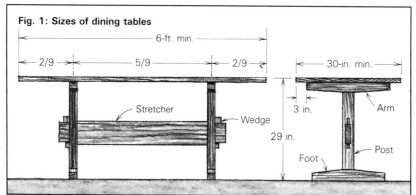

Fig. 1: Sizes of dining tables

6-ft. min.

2/9   5/9   2/9

Stretcher

Wedge

30-in. min.

3 in.

Arm

29 in.

Foot

Post

Fig. 2: Framing a wide table

Double posts.

Double stretchers.

From *Fine Woodworking* magazine (September 1983) 42:42-44

be thick enough to accept wedges that look right, and it is no bad thing to have plenty of weight down low in the frame.

Choices remain in the shaping of the frame parts and the treatment of edges, and different effects can be obtained for essentially the same table. For example, a frame trimmed with stopped chamfers on the posts and stretcher will look quite different from the same frame finished with through chamfers. The posts and the feet can be shaped to flow together at the joint, or they can be of different thicknesses to emphasize the change in direction. For wood of large section or uncertain seasoning, the latter arrangement has advantages.

Joinery—It is more complicated to plan and build a trestle frame than an apron frame. Instead of two sets of similar parts (legs and rails) and eight similar joints, there are four pairs of parts (posts, arms, feet and wedges) plus the stretcher, and three different sets of joints. The posts can be joined to the feet and arms by conventional mortise-and-tenon joints, or they can be bridle-joined by cutting open mortises at each end, with corresponding housings midway along each crosspiece. The latter is perhaps easier to do, and if cut with four shoulders is conceivably a stiffer joint in one direction, but it is particularly sensitive to shrinkage of the post. Certainly the bri-

dle joint is appropriate when the post is thicker than the foot.

Figure 3 shows several ways of joining a trestle to its top. For a fully fixed design, effective joints can be made with stout wood screws through the trestle arms into the top, the top acting somewhat as a stretcher. This, of course, requires careful truing of the mating surfaces (**A**). For a removable top, or if a purely wooden construction is preferred, the simplest approach, if the top is heavy enough, is to cut shallow stopped housings in the underside to fit snugly over the breadth of the arms. Gravity will keep things together well enough, although the housings should be cut hollow in their length to allow for some cup in the top, and long as well to allow for shrinkage (**B**). Alternatively, each arm can be shaped to offer a slightly tapered dovetail cleat along its upper edge, and the top housed to receive it. This device can be found on Italian Renaissance tables (**C**). The joint can be stopped so as not to show and to allow setback of the arm, but the cleat must then be considerably tapered and shortened so the top can drop over it and engage by sliding across the frame (**D**). Another method, which exploits the force of the draw-wedges in the stretcher, requires cutting barefaced dovetail cleats in the upper post tenons where they emerge from the trestle arms. Matching housings in the top are then locat-

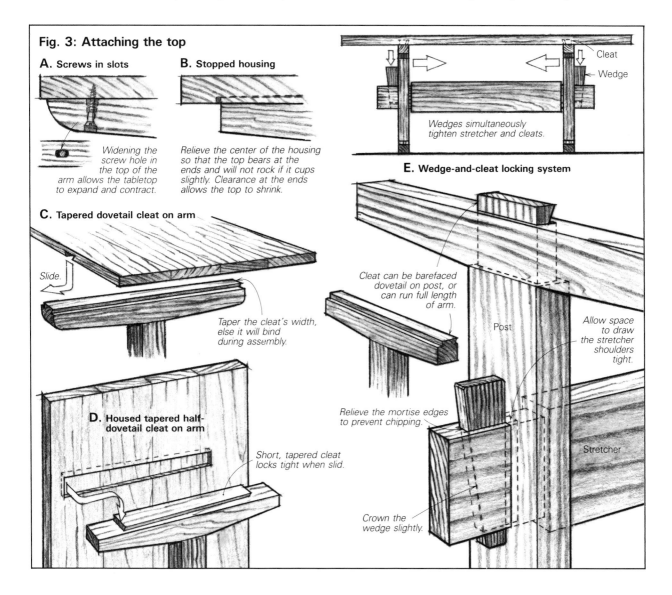

Fig. 3: Attaching the top

A. Screws in slots

Widening the screw hole in the top of the arm allows the tabletop to expand and contract.

B. Stopped housing

Relieve the center of the housing so that the top bears at the ends and will not rock if it cups slightly. Clearance at the ends allows the top to shrink.

C. Tapered dovetail cleat on arm

Slide.

Taper the cleat's width, else it will bind during assembly.

D. Housed tapered half-dovetail cleat on arm

Short, tapered cleat locks tight when slid.

Cleat
Wedge

Wedges simultaneously tighten stretcher and cleats.

E. Wedge-and-cleat locking system

Cleat can be barefaced dovetail on post, or can run full length of arm.

Post

Allow space to draw the stretcher shoulders tight.

Relieve the mortise edges to prevent chipping.

Stretcher

Crown the wedge slightly.

ed slightly farther apart than the cleats as measured when the frame is locked up. This method can instead use the full length of the trestle arm as the cleat. In either case, knocking home the stretcher wedges completes the joint by driving the end-frames toward one another (**E**).

When building end-frames, the post mortises can be chopped right through, ⅛ in. oversize in length, their ends squared, and the tenons later shimmed tightly with 5⁄32-in. slips, taken from the tenons themselves when the narrow shoulders are cut. Dowel pins secure the joints in the other direction.

Mortises through the posts for knockdown stretcher tenons are usually broad and exposed on one side, thus boring and paring is safer than chopping. The stretcher tenons should be a sliding fit in thickness and an easy fit in height, to prevent seizure if the wood swells.

Wedge mortises through the stretcher must be cut over-long to draw the stretcher shoulders tight against the posts. The slopes of the wedges should be slightly relieved toward the ends, and the extremities of the mortises chamfered, to prevent the wedges from catching when driven in or out. Wedge pitch is somewhat a matter of taste, but if it is too steep the wedge will bounce back when struck, and if too gentle the wedge may travel farther than anticipated. The wedges should be made first and used to lay out the mortises. A push fit is about right for the thickness. There is a temptation to make the wedges from harder wood than the rest of the frame, but such wedges may impress shallow grooves in the posts. It is better to use good pieces of the same stock, and to allow the slopes of the wedges to deform and lock against the harder end grain of their mortises.

Pins should also be the same stock as the frame, but selected for straightness in both planes (look at the rays as well as the rings). Square and octagonal pins hold best, but can visibly crush the surrounding wood on the driving side. Where the pins emerge they will be round, and so for consistency drive all pins from the same side. Center the pin holes about 1½ diameters from the shoulders of the joint.

Making the top—In the absence of a single wide piece (not impossible in, say, mahogany), certain strategies remain. A board one-quarter the width required but twice the length and thickness can be crosscut, then resawn. Random stock can be studied for possibilities of unobtrusive joints and some balance in color and grain.

If edge-joining, allow ¼ in. of width for each joint and another ¼ in. for truing the edges of the completed top. Mark the face side at the joints and glue them up one at a time, each time truing the face side of the boards already joined as well as that of the one to be added, to keep the plane of the whole flat. If this work is done well, and all glue cleaned away each time, little final effort will be required to ready the top for finishing.

Any variations in the surface of the underside need to be dealt with only where they count. When the top is fitted to the frame, parallel flats can be planed across the grain where the top bears on the trestle arms. Differences in thickness showing at the edges and ends can be trimmed away on a short bevel, working to a line gauged from the show side. Sometimes this is done anyway, to make the top appear thinner. ☐

Kenneth Rower is a joiner living in Newbury, Vt. Photo by the author.

Altar table's carved lions, below, face the horizons and symbolize the passage of time. Gary Rogowski of Milwaukie, Ore., built the mahogany altar, 62 in. by 30 in. by 40 in. high, for the Lotus Temple of Hermetic Yoga.

Tricky Trestles
Three variations made by readers

These three tables illustrate the vast range of structural and decorative variations that can be developed on the fundamental theme of the trestle. Whether gargantuan or dainty, the trestle keeps the table sturdy. The stretcher's shape, and the way it locks into the upright posts, is part of the woodworker's fun. These are just 3 of the 515 photographs of furniture, tools, accessories and sculpture made by readers of *Fine Woodworking* magazine and published in *Design Book Three*, available from The Taunton Press. ☐

From *Fine Woodworking* magazine (September 1983) 42:44-45

Photos: Douglas Dalton, Harold Wood, Adkins-Burnham Studios Inc.

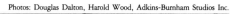

Conference table, 26 ft. long and 7 ft. wide, was designed and built of bubinga solid and veneer by Peter Allen of North Westport, Mass., for the National Fire Protection Association of Quincy, Mass.

The 'Bullet Train Desk' by Robert D. Sorrels of Brazil, Ind., made of spalted mahogany, elm and persimmon, is 60 in. long, 30 in. wide and 31 in. high.

The Torsion Box
How to make strong, light and stable panels

by Ian J. Kirby

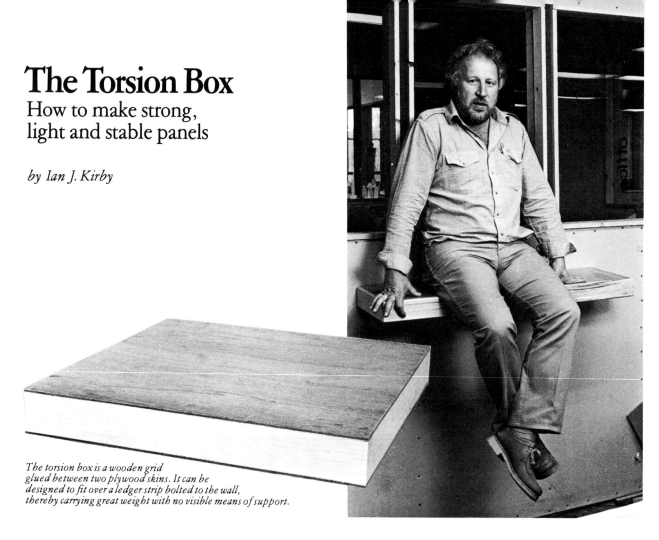

The torsion box is a wooden grid glued between two plywood skins. It can be designed to fit over a ledger strip bolted to the wall, thereby carrying great weight with no visible means of support.

Suppose you wanted to make a low bench about 18 in. wide and 4 ft. long, cantilevered out from a wall with no supporting structure underneath. In solid wood, you'd have to use a plank 2 in. thick or thicker, so this simple bench would consume at least 12 bd. ft. of wood, and it would weigh 40 lb. or more. Then you'd have the devil's own tussle figuring out how to hang it on the wall.

If you used a torsion box, you could make the same bench from less than 3 bd. ft. of wood and 12 sq. ft. of ¼-in. plywood. It could be any thickness you wanted, it would weigh about 10 lb., and it would be child's play to cantilever it from the wall. The torsion box is especially suitable for building high-quality veneered furniture, because it's both lighter and more stable than a conventional lumbercore structure. It's probably the simplest way to make a curved panel, and the ease with which the designer can manipulate the thickness dimension is truly liberating. At the same time, the torsion-box system is well within the technical reach of the amateur craftsman and the small professional shop.

As used in furnituremaking, the torsion box is two thin skins of plywood glued to a core grid of thin wooden strips. The resulting structure has strength not present in either the skin or the core alone—it's strong the same way an airplane wing is strong. In particular, a torsion box has tremendous resistance to twisting and bending forces. This is because the structure's geometry converts any applied force into shearing stress on the glue lines between skin and core grid. And a

sound glue line is strongest in its resistance to shearing stress.

The concept behind the torsion box isn't new. Engineers use it for box beams as well as for airplane wings, and the same concept makes possible the structural steel I-beam. The system described here was developed in Europe during the 1960s for the manufacture of large wardrobes and other case goods for storage. The traditional way of making a wardrobe is to join four pieces of wood at the corners, firmly attach a back, and hang doors on the front. Although the back contributes a great deal to rigidity, the front corner of a 6-ft. wardrobe can still be lifted several inches off the floor with the other three legs remaining on the ground. Any unevenness in the floor will thus twist the case, jamming its doors and drawers. If a torsion box is used to make the back or sides, they will be absolutely rigid, and the rest of the wardrobe, if firmly attached to the torsion box, will also be rigid. The furniture industry hasn't made much use of the system, even though its applications extend far beyond keeping wardrobes free from twist. It can be used in practically every furniture form—storage cases, shelving units, tables, beds and all forms of seating, upholstered or not.

The torsion box is not a shoddy alternative to solid wood. It opens up design possibilities that simply cannot be achieved in solid wood. In the solid, you can usually find a board that's long enough, and the width can be glued up, but the thickness dimension is pretty much limited by weight and commercial availability to 2 in. or less, and you cannot eliminate wood movement. In terms of workmanship, the torsion box is fully as demanding as working in solid, and the result can be furniture of the highest quality. In fact, making a torsion box

Ian J. Kirby is a designer, cabinetmaker and educator in Cumming, Ga.

From *Fine Woodworking* magazine (January 1982) 32:96-102

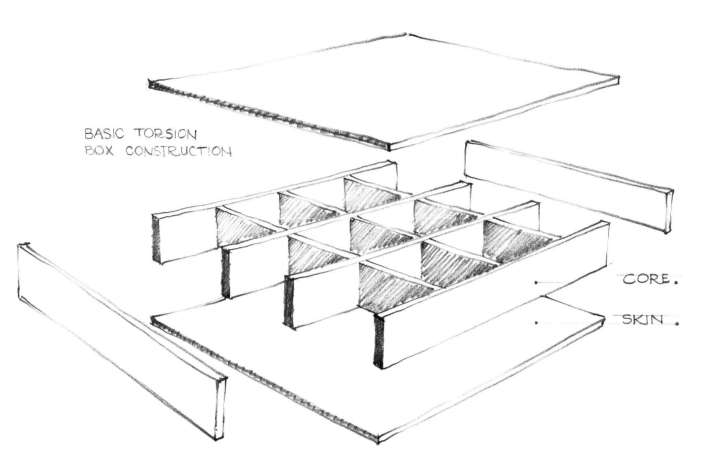

BASIC TORSION
BOX CONSTRUCTION

CORE.

SKIN.

Here is the basic method for making a torsion box. Prepare stock for the skins and core (above), in this example ¼-in. plywood and clear pine sawn ⅜ in. thick by 2½ in. wide. Ordinary staples hold the core together until the skins can be glued on. Start with the outside pieces (right), and the long strips, then fill in the grid (below, left). Run a bead of white or yellow glue on one side of the grid (below, center), roll it out well, and carefully position the skin. Then flip the box over on top of the bench and clamp it down, using curved cauls to distribute the pressure (below, right). Unless you are using a veneer press, it's unwise to glue both skins at once.

requires more thorough planning than working in solid wood, for once you've glued up the box, you cannot change your mind and trim a half-inch off. There's no room here for inadequate design planning or for sloppy workmanship—quite the opposite.

A sample panel—The photo sequence on p. 49 and the following discussion are based on making a sample panel that's 2 ft. square and 3 in. thick, using ¼-in. veneered plywood for the skins and ⅜-in. by 2½-in. softwood for the core. The panel might be for a tabletop or for a shelf—it doesn't matter. The point is to establish the working principles involved. Once you understand the system, you'll see that the core grid and the resulting box can be virtually any shape you want, according to what your design requires. Later on I'll discuss surface and edge treatments, ways of joining two boxes together, and how to attach a torsion-box structure to a wall.

For the core we should use wood of practically any clear species, from poplar to maple, even pine, at 6% to 8% moisture content. But don't mix species in any one core. Differences in shrinkage can make the panel wavy. The thickness of each strip is as much a function of handling as of anything else. We could cut it down to ⅛ in. thick and build the grid on 2-in. centers, but we'd waste a lot of wood in sawdust. We'd also have trouble keeping the 24-in. long strips straight in one direction, and even more trouble handling 121 bits of wood, each 1⅞ in. long and 2½ in. wide, in the other direction. Even so, we could make a 4 sq. ft. core grid from 1½ bd. ft. of stock (not counting kerf losses), the 2-in. spacing would be enough to keep the plywood skin from sagging into the voids in the grid, and there would be about 78 sq. in. of gluing surface on each side—the panel would be plenty strong. If we make the core stock ⅜ in. thick, the strips won't be as numerous or as flexible. Spaced just over 4¼ in. apart, we'll have a 2-ft. square that still consumes less than 2 bd. ft. of material. There'll be 108 sq. in. of glue surface on each side, more than enough. At this point in the analysis we might decide that the grid spacing is too great for ¼-in. plywood, especially if it is to be veneered and used for a table. To keep the skin from dishing into the core voids, we could add a couple of core strips, or use ⅜-in. plywood for the skin instead. There is no hard rule—you decide according to the materials and the ultimate use of the box.

Whatever dimensions you choose, all the core material must be accurately prepared: it must be flat, uniformly thick, and cut off squarely. Both the width and the thickness can be got with a carbide-tipped saw, but it's better done through the thickness planer. Both skins should be made the same size, with their corners truly square, to the finished dimensions of the panel. The core grid, on the other hand, should be made a trifle large, say 1/16 in. over in length and width. Then after assembly it can be planed to meet the skin exactly.

If the finished box is to be veneered, the veneer should be glued onto the skins before they are cut to size. It's bad practice to veneer the assembled box, because the pressure of the press will tend to force the glue away from the core grid, making it puddle up over the voids. The box might end up looking like a lumpy checkerboard.

Joining the core grid—There are no joints in the core grid. The pieces are simply stapled together across the joint lines, top and bottom. Start by stapling together the four outside pieces, then run all the long strips in one direction, using crosspieces as spacers. Hold each piece firmly in place and staple. When all the long strips are stapled on one side, turn the grid over and staple the other side. Then fill in with the crosspieces. It's natural to imagine that staples can't possibly hold this thing together, that some joint must be necessary. Actually, the staples don't hold anything together. They merely stabilize the grid so it can be handled until the core can be glued onto it. The glueline between core grid and skin is what holds the box together. You would have to apply enough force to shear all that gluing surface before any core joinery would come into play.

Having now got the two skins cut to size and the core assembled, the next step is to put the three parts together. Any normal wood glue will do the job; I find it easiest to squeeze white or yellow glue along all the core edges, then to spread it out with a 1-in. paint roller. It is important to wet the entire surface of the core grid, since the skin goes onto it dry. Plant the skin on the core, register one long edge, then align an adjacent edge. If the core seems out of line, pull it into place using the skin as a try-square. Once one corner of the assembly is aligned, the rest of it will be aligned too. You can drive a couple of veneer pins or small brads through the skin into the core to hold it in place. Clamp or press the skin onto the core until the glue cures, then turn the box over and glue the second skin in place, being sure to work from the same edge and corner you aligned on the first side.

A veneer press is the ideal tool for gluing up the box, not because of the pressure it can exert, but because its bed is flat. In whatever shape you hold the torsion box while the glue is drying, that will be its final shape. If it is twisted while it cures, it will stay twisted forever. The veneer press also makes

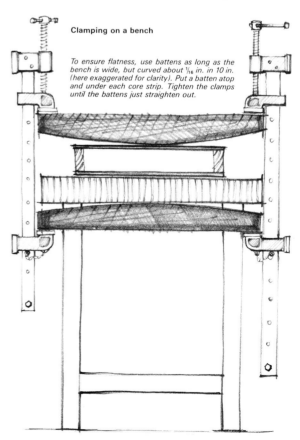

Clamping on a bench

To ensure flatness, use battens as long as the bench is wide, but curved about 1/16 in. in 10 in. (here exaggerated for clarity). Put a batten atop and under each core strip. Tighten the clamps until the battens just straighten out.

it practical to glue both skins onto the core at one pressing.

The best alternative to a veneer press is the top of your bench, but check it for flatness before you spread any glue. You can clamp the core to the panel (panel flat on the bench top) with standard quick-set clamps, as shown on p. 49. Use cambered battens to distribute the pressure. Be sure the clamps themselves don't twist the bench top; don't, for example, anchor clamps to the bench's understructure. The appropriate method is determined by the availability of a press or of clamps and a flat surface, and by the geometry of the workpiece. The important thing is to understand what has to be achieved and to respond accordingly.

Surfaces and edges—The torsion box is well-suited to the application of quality veneers and to the quality cabinet-making techniques that go with veneering. As I mentioned earlier, it's best to veneer plywood skins before you assemble the box. Applying your own veneers gives you easy access to the ebonies and rosewoods and other exotic species that can no longer be had in solid wood. Of course there is nothing wrong with using pre-veneered plywood for these boxes—the only drawback is that your choice of veneers is somewhat restricted.

Whether you apply your own veneer or use pre-veneered plywood, the edge of the torsion box needs to be finished. The most direct solution is to glue a solid wood lipping to the core, of the same species as the veneer or some contrasting species. Mitered corners always look good. If the lipping is to be flush with the surface of the box, it can be registered with a spline or a Lamello, or else it can be milled a little wide and planed flush after assembly. If the lipping must bear a load, a hinged door for example, it should be reinforced with a spline or tongue-and-groove. Grooves can be milled directly into the core of the box, and tongues onto the lipping stock. Of course the lipping can be shaped to virtually any profile. When the surface is an exotic veneer, you can make lipping stock by gluing three or four veneers together.

With the torsion box system, there is no reason to confine your design universe to wood. The stability of the skin allows

When the glue has cured, unclamp the assembly, clean off the glue squeeze and plane the core to the size of the skins. To assess the strength of the box you've just made, clamp one edge in the vise, grab the top corners and try to twist it.

What we've done up to this point is make the basic building brick of the torsion-box system. In order to use the system we must consider how to join two or more boxes together, and how to finish their surfaces and edges. These considerations are part of the design process, not afterthoughts, for most joining methods require some provision in the construction of the core. When you understand the system, the possibilities are limited only by your ingenuity.

you to cover it with virtually any sheet material. Thus you can develop your design with the colors, textures and properties of paint, leather, Naugahyde, cloth, Formica, ceramic tile, slate, metal tile or even sheet metal. There are special adhesives available for most of these materials. Tiles can be laid with adhesive and grouted. A traditional way to attach sheet copper is with decorative nails. Leather and Naugahyde are best stuck down with white glue.   *(continued, next page)*

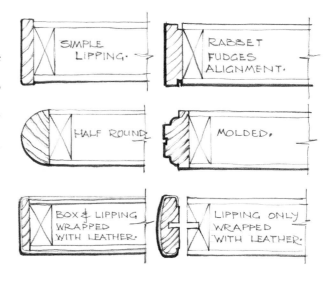

Rich Lippings

When the box is veneered, a leather-covered lipping will be quite rich in look and feel. An upholsterer would make up lipping stock by driving nails through one strip of wood, then gluing a second strip atop the nailheads to capture them. Trim this sandwich to width, profile its edges, glue the leather around it and then hammer it into position.

When the box is covered in leather or Naugahyde, neatly wrapping the corners can be most difficult. You can avoid the grief if you trim the leather exactly flush with the edge of the box, then glue on a solid wood lipping whose width is the thickness of the box plus surface material or even slightly wider, so it stands proud of the surface. The job will be especially rich if you make the lipping as wide as the panel is

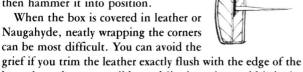

thick without surface material, then plane the panel's top edge down by the thickness of the leather or Naugahyde. This planed margin should be about 1½ in. wide; it can be planed flat or round as shown. Glue on the surface material, trim it back flush, and use a spline to locate the lipping flush with the leather surface.

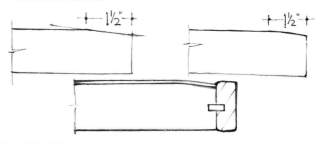

Joinery—The simplest way to join two torsion boxes edge-to-edge is to butt them together with glue. To keep the surfaces in line, use a loose spline or a Lamello spline (figure A). If you're in any doubt at all about the ability of the core to support the joint, double up the core stock in the joint area when you design the box.

A butt joint can also be used to join two boxes with their skins at right angles, as shown in figure B, but usually the core stock must be made doubly thick at the joint. The result will probably be more attractive if the skin of one of the boxes overhangs its core, so it can conceal the joint. Splines can be used to register the parts.

Alternately, the mating edges of the boxes can be mitered and glued (figure C), although once again enough stock must be provided for the miter cut when you are designing the box. The miter is especially strong in this application, since the core strips both present long-grain gluing surfaces, not a near end-grain surface as is usually the case in solid wood. Some form of register is vital, and again a spline will serve.

There's a slightly different strategy for forming a right-angled joint with one box in the middle of another, for example a bookshelf or a wall system. It's best to glue and screw a ledger strip onto the surface of one box (the screws going into a core strip), and to build a pocket into the other box (figure D). The pocket then slips onto the ledger strip. It can be glued in place for permanency, or screwed. The lippings on the boxes will conceal the ledger.

Finally, an intermediate piece of solid wood can always be used at a corner, with the edges of the two boxes glued directly to it, as shown in figure E. *(continued, p. 54)*

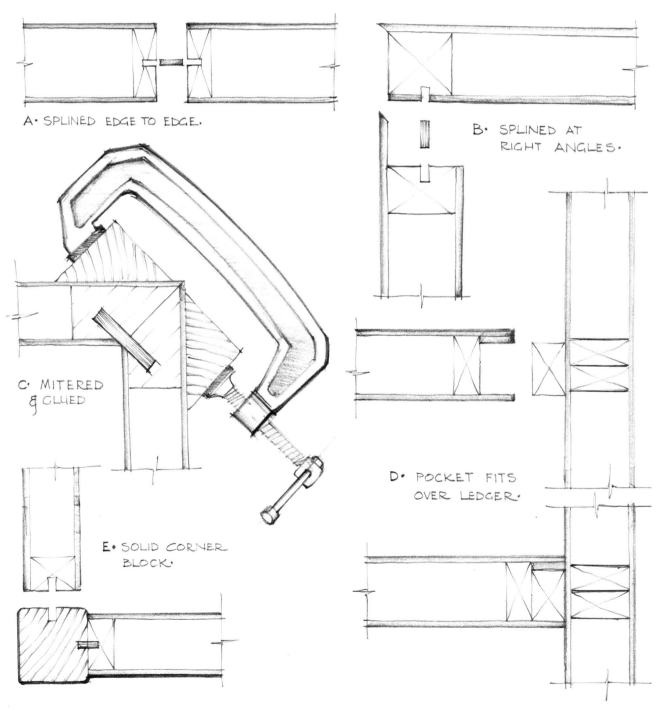

A· SPLINED EDGE TO EDGE.

B· SPLINED AT RIGHT ANGLES.

C· MITERED & GLUED

D· POCKET FITS OVER LEDGER·

E· SOLID CORNER BLOCK·

Some applications of the torsion box, from work done at Kirby Studios.

Top: Three-part core grid made of medium-density fiberboard is 4 in. thick, 6 ft. wide and almost 15 ft. long. Designer-maker Mike Garner skinned each grid with ash-faced plywood, to build a trading desk that had been commissioned by a commodities investment firm.

Center: This four-module coffee table, shown in two of its many arrangements, could hardly have been built in solid wood. As the photo at left shows, each module consists of three torsion boxes. The flat top is veneered with Macassar ebony, the curved verticals are painted. Designed and made by Jim Van Etten (© 1981).

Bottom: David Schwartz joined his table by screwing ledger strips onto the vertical torsion boxes. The strips plug into sockets constructed into the box that is the tabletop.

Wall mounting—One of the attractive characteristics of the torsion box is the way it can be fastened to a wall and made to hold considerable weight with no visible means of support. The usual method is to bolt or screw a ledger strip to the wall, and to construct the box with a pocket at its back edge that exactly fits over the ledger (A). Screws hold the box to the ledger. Thus the whole thing can be removed from the wall. Or the box can be glued to the ledger, in which case the fixture is permanent (B).

The ledger should be a piece of clean, knot-free wood, preferably hardwood. The way it's fastened to the wall depends on the load it's likely to bear—No. 10 screws 1½ in. into the studs will support a phone; seating or shelves for such heavy loads as a television set may require bolts right through the studs. Use 2-in. Rawlbolts into masonry walls. Where the shelf goes into a corner, ledgers should be attached to both walls. Screws through the top skin into the ledger hold the box in place, but if the top skin is ¼-in. plywood it had better be doubled or trebled inside the pocket. Gluing extra thicknesses of plywood inside the flange that fits over the ledger will minimize the risk of the screws tearing out under load (C). This thickness may also permit countersinking and plugging to conceal the screws.

When you wish to eliminate any visible trace of holding screws but still want the box to be removable, you can profile the ledger with a dovetail as shown at D.

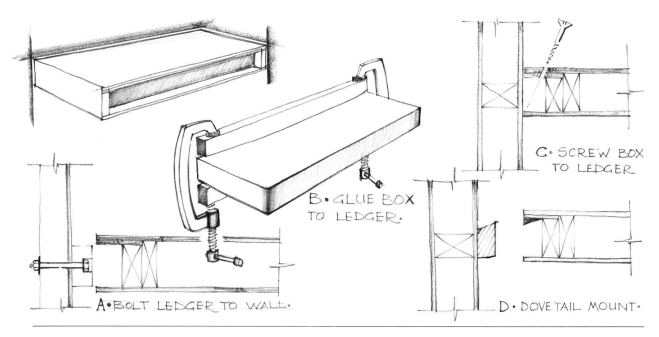

B.GLUE BOX TO LEDGER.

A.BOLT LEDGER TO WALL.

C.SCREW BOX TO LEDGER

D.DOVETAIL MOUNT.

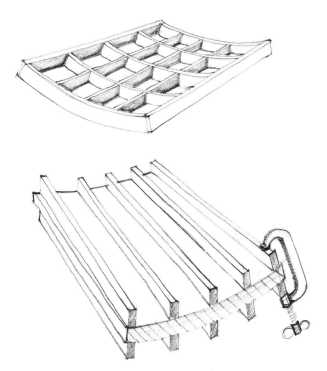

Curved panels—It's relatively simple to make a torsion box that's curved in one plane, such as for a chair seat or back. The method is to draw the curve full-size, then to cut out as continuous strips the core elements that form the curve. Don't try to use short curved pieces between continuous straight pieces, for they would be impossible to align. The outside straight pieces should also be continuous and attached to the end-grain of the curved pieces. This will aid in alignment and will also keep the core from twisting before the first skin is applied. It's best to skin the convex side first—if the finish is to be leather or paint, the skin can be glued and stapled or nailed. If the skins have a show veneer already, they'll have to be glued with the aid of battens and clamps. The battens should be slightly cambered, say ¹⁄₁₆ in. for every 10 in. of length. Place the battens in pairs, one over the other with a core strip between. Hardboard between the veneer and the battens will spread the pressure and keep the skins from scalloping.

In sum—The torsion box should be considered a building block within a system. It is the counterpart, in man-made sheet materials, of the frame-and-panel in solid wood. Both are systems developed in response to the dimensional instability of wood. Either system brings its own limitations and liberations, but these depend mainly on the designer-woodworker's imagination. □

Knockdown Tabletops
Dovetails, not hardware, pin top to base

by Kenneth Rower

For storage or shipment it is often advantageous for a tabletop to be quickly removable, while in daily service the top should be fastened securely enough for one person to be able to shift the table within a room. Here are two construction systems that require no hardware—one for tables with apron frames together with a variation for pedestal frames, and the other for trestle frames.

Apron frame — This method uses dovetail pins cut at the tops of the legs and dovetail housings with escapements chopped across the grain of the underside of the top. To assemble, drop the top over the pins and push it across the frame to lock the pins in their housings. To disassemble, push the top from the opposite side until the pins register in their escapements, and lift the top away. Properly dimensioned, the system is invisible when locked up (figure 1).

When sawing the legs, leave extra length at the top end equal to about half the thickness of the tabletop, and when laying out the rail mortises do not omit the customary allowance above the top of the mortise—about ¾ in. for a 4½-in. rail. Square up the top of each leg and take all measurements from there. Build the frame and assemble dry, leaving the rails strong to be trimmed later. Sketch plans and elevations of the leg tops, bearing in mind that all four pins must be offset in the same direction, and that if the system is to be concealed the pin length must be a bit less than half the leg thickness, an allowance being made for seasonal change in the width of the top. Later in the construction, when the frame has been fitted to housings, the escapements will also be lengthened to accommodate this variation. For ordinary-size frames, about 30 in. across, divide the leg top into two pin lengths, plus ⅛ in. for each length (figure 2), then lay out the pins using a mortise gauge for the side and end lines, and

a small adjustable bevel, set to a beveled guide block (about 78°), for the slopes. Gauge the shoulder lines from the end. Make the four cuts outlining the pins, then saw the shoulders. Trim with a sharp chisel, testing the work with the guide block. Finish all work on the frame except polishing.

Build the top and trim it sufficiently to center the frame. Scribe the outline of the pins on the underside of the top to mark their position when locked up (figure 3), but note that the outline is of the crown of the pin rather than its root, which is actually wanted in this space. Mark near each outline the direction the frame will travel when unlocking. Pencil in a benchmark on one leg and nearby on the underside of the top to register the location, and remove the frame.

Lay out the escapements by extending the scribed sidelines in the proper direction a distance equal to the pin length, and connect the new lines with an end line. Find the centerline along the length of this double box. Measure the width at the root of each dovetail pin and transfer it to the layout of the housing, employing the centerline. If the measurements vary from pin to pin, transfer one at a time. Cut the escapements, first boring out with a Forstner or other short-pointed bit, then chopping square. There is no advantage and some danger in going any more than a trifle deeper than the height of the pin. Test the frame in the escapements to be sure that the shoulders of the legs lie flush with the underside of the top. Level as necessary. Now remove the frame and lay out the slopes of the housings, using the adjustable bevel set to the guide block. Bore out, then with a dovetail saw rough out the slope, keeping a little strong of the line. Chop out the waste, again keeping away from the line. Clamp the guide block at the line and trim with a narrow paring chisel, the final cuts to be taken with the chisel right against the block (figure 3).

Lay the frame in the escapements and see that the pins are

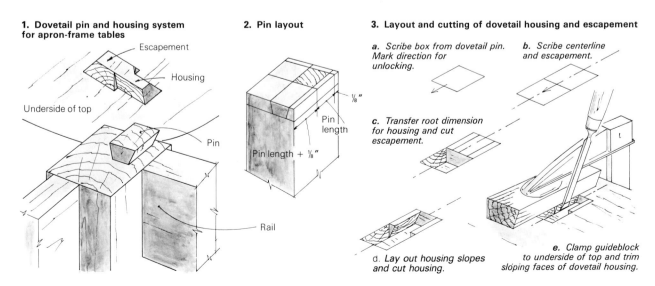

1. Dovetail pin and housing system for apron-frame tables

Escapement
Housing
Underside of top
Pin

2. Pin layout

⅛"
Pin length
Pin length + ⅛"
Rail

3. Layout and cutting of dovetail housing and escapement

a. Scribe box from dovetail pin. Mark direction for unlocking.

b. Scribe centerline and escapement.

c. Transfer root dimension for housing and cut escapement.

d. Lay out housing slopes and cut housing.

e. Clamp guideblock to underside of top and trim sloping faces of dovetail housing.

likely to enter the housings. Then remove the frame and chamfer the leading corners of the pins. Replace and push (or pull). Considerable force may be necessary the first few times—waxing the pins is helpful. However, a driving fit means too much interference. Usually one joint will cause the trouble, or two that are not in parallel across the frame. There will be enough flex in the frame so that tapping at each joint will tell which one is binding. If you trim away too much during adjustments, a piece of veneer or cedar cigar wrapper (.009 in. thick) can be glued into the housing. When all is well, remove the frame and stamp a benchmark into the top of one pin and inside the corresponding escapement. At this point consider the probable shrinkage and expansion of the tabletop, and lengthen the escapements accordingly. Round off all the points and corners of the pins and the entry corners of the housings, as in service the top drops down over the pins, somewhat by feel. Then the near pair of legs can be gripped and the top pushed home with chest or waist.

Pedestal frame — As the arms of a pedestal frame do not offer the appropriate grain for cutting pins, separate pins must be fashioned and joined to the arms. Make up pin blanks of rectangular section, but with one sloping face in the length, then mortise in with a shim to drive the blank against a correspondingly undercut end of the mortise. Saw the slopes once the blank is glued and trimmed.

Dovetail pin for pedestal table

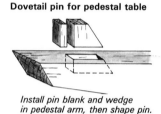

Install pin blank and wedge in pedestal arm, then shape pin.

A blank could be fitted up through the underside of the arm and then wedged below, but shrinkage in the depth of the arm would leave the pin standing proud and the joint loose. The best orientation is for one set of arms to be perpendicular to the grain of the top, the other parallel, with room left in the housings perpendicular to the grain for tabletop expansion and contraction. If you orient the arms at 45° to the grain of the top, the system works but the housings won't be as strong.

Trestle frame — In a knockdown trestle frame consisting of two trestles, a stretcher, and two draw-wedges, the action of the wedges in drawing the trestles tight against the stretcher

shoulders can be exploited to clamp the tabletop to the frame. The system consists of a barefaced dovetail cleat formed by extending the post tenon up through each trestle arm, and corresponding housings cut into the underside of the top where it bears on the arms (figure 4).

When cutting the posts, allow for bringing the tenon through the arm, plus an amount equal to about one-half of the thickness of the tabletop, and square the end of the post. Cut the mortise-and-tenon joint, assemble dry, and mark the tenon where the top edge of the arm crosses the cheeks. Remove the post and using a dovetail plane or a wide paring chisel, cut the slope on the inner face (with respect to the middle of the table) of the tenon. The shoulder should be a little behind the line to allow for shrinkage in the depth of the arm (figure 5). Build the rest of the frame.

Make the top and trim to size. Make up a beveled guide block as before though long enough to be clamped from the tabletop edges, and if the underside of the tabletop is not already flat, plane flats where it will bear on the trestle arms. The flats must be parallel, in plane (check with winding sticks) and wide enough to register the guide block.

Invert the assembled frame and center it on the underside of the top. Scribe the outlines of the cleats and remove the frame, benchmarking one end of the system. The outlines mark the location of the cleat crowns, not their roots. With a steel tape, measure the inside distance from root to root of the cleats, add 1/32 in. (more for a very long table) to provide compression to the system, and transfer to the layout of the housings. Draw another line outside the housings to allow the cleats to enter the housings before locking up (figure 6).

Bore and chop out the housings, keeping clear of the sloped faces. Then clamp the guide block in place and chisel back the sloped faces. Leave a little clearance at the bottom of the housings. Round off the entry corners of the housings and the points and corners of the cleats. To assemble, fit the trestles loosely to the stretcher, spacing them out from the shoulders an amount about equal to the swell in the cleat. The top should now drop easily over the cleats. Drive home the wedges to lock up the trestles and the top. Should the system loosen, tighten it by trimming the shoulders at one end of the stretcher, or by installing a shim in one housing. □

Kenneth Rower makes furniture in Newbury, Vt.

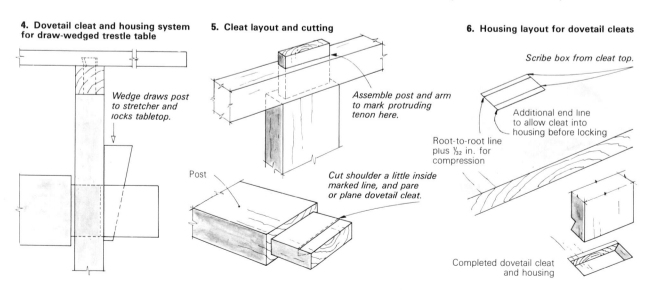

4. Dovetail cleat and housing system for draw-wedged trestle table

Wedge draws post to stretcher and locks tabletop.

5. Cleat layout and cutting

Post

Assemble post and arm to mark protruding tenon here.

Cut shoulder a little inside marked line, and pare or plane dovetail cleat.

6. Housing layout for dovetail cleats

Scribe box from cleat top.

Additional end line to allow cleat into housing before locking

Root-to-root line plus 1/32 in. for compression

Completed dovetail cleat and housing

Orientable
Another knockdown design

by Curtis Erpelding

*Fir, maple and walnut,
60 in. by 36 in. by 30 in.*

The process by which a piece assembles itself intrigues me. Most of my designs incorporate a knockdown feature to emphasize and perpetuate the act of assembly. There is a pleasing gestalt to how a few components, only so many pieces by themselves, transform into a table or chair, and easily disassemble for moving or storage. Stacked and sculptural furniture seems too solid and final in comparison.

Knockdown design assumes easy fastening. The less hardware involved, the purer the design. I cut the compound-angled *V* in the end of the through stretcher tenons with a radial arm saw. A slight tap on the correspondingly tapered wedge that fits through this slot draws the stretcher against the cross member (figure 1). For a more secure fit I routed a *V*-shaped dado into the back of the cross member and chamfered the tenon on both sides to seat into it. But not exactly—the *V* of the stretcher is slightly fatter than the dado in the cross member so it mates ever more tightly.

The top is standard breadboard construction. It is free to contract and expand and easy to remove. Cleats screwed to the underside of the tabletop center it when they're placed to one side of the stretchers. The cleats and stretchers are through-mortised and drawn tightly together by folding wedges whose opposing ends curve. When the top expands, the right cleats are free to move with the tabletop and a gap opens between

cleat and stretcher (at the single arrow in figure 2). With contraction the left cleats are free to move and a gap opens between cleats and stretchers on the left side of the table (double arrow). As the seasons change, the top may position itself up to ½ in. off center, but it will stay flat and intact.

In evolving this table (it had two prototypes, one in fir and one in maple), I added a drawer of walnut and maple, hung under the top by its slide—a bit of whimsy. Instead of the usual square groove, I worked hollows in the drawer and matching rounds with planes. The two slides are connected at the back and the whole unit slips into the stretcher via bridle joints. The slides and the top edges of the drawer are flush with the bottom of the tabletop, which supports the unit.

I chose fir for the table itself because its graphic grain is right for subtle curves and crisp edges. There's a certain delight in working what most people consider a common utility wood. I hand-planed all surfaces, including the top; I had only a 4-in. jointer and no thickness planer. All curves—first bandsawn—I worked with a spokeshave. The realized curve of the legs, though based on the Fibonacci series, comes from tool, hand and eye. I don't use templates or calipers. □

Curtis Erpelding is a professional woodworker and designer in Seattle, Wash.

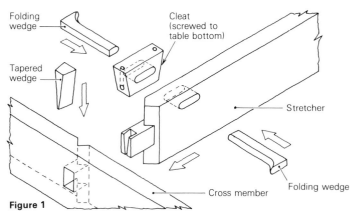

Figure 1

Folding wedge · Cleat (screwed to table bottom) · Tapered wedge · Stretcher · Cross member · Folding wedge

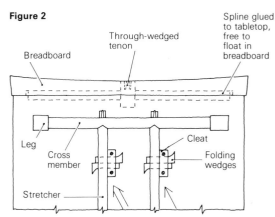

Figure 2

Breadboard · Through-wedged tenon · Spline glued to tabletop, free to float in breadboard · Leg · Cross member · Stretcher · Cleat · Folding wedges

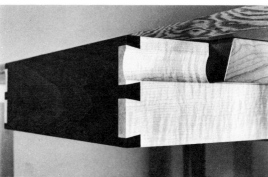

The name 'Orientable' suggests both the orientation of parts into a table and the Oriental influence on the design.

Serving Cart
Sliding top solves design problem

by Alan C. Marks

When first approached to design and build a serving cart, I was excited by the challenge. Most people who come to me have vague ideas of the function and other requirements their piece of furniture can or should fulfill. In this instance my instructions were specific, but rather than restricting the imagination, they liberated me from many critical decisions.

The height was to be 34 inches. The size of the table was to be 24 in. x 15 in., but it had to expand at least half again its length. Because space was limited, it was to take up as little room as possible when not in use. The cart was to roll equally well on linoleum and shag rugs. It had to have a drawer for potholders and carving utensils, which I measured to determine drawer dimensions. A carving board and a serving tray would be stored on a shelf below. Another shelf would carry used dishes and utensils to the dishwasher.

Dark walnut paneling and furniture decorated the room in which the cart would stand. The logical choice of wood was therefore walnut. I am used to designing for light woods, which I prefer, so I decided to make two carts, one of walnut for the client and one of close-grained Douglas fir for myself. I was afraid I would lose enthusiasm for the work if I couldn't look forward to a completed serving cart in a delicate wood like Douglas fir, and losing enthusiasm is the worst thing that can happen to me.

I think dark woods lend themselves best to sculptural pieces where overall shape or form is primary. With light woods small touches, color nuances and molded shapes stand out and enhance large wooden surfaces. This is because shadows produce greater contrast on light woods than on dark woods and describe small shapes well; details are emphasized rather than melting into an amorphous mass. Even details in shadow are light enough to be seen and to contribute to one's appreciation of the whole piece.

My biggest difficulty was how to increase the table surface. Everything else would depend on that decision—shelf placement, type of drawer, legs, everything. Usually some factors take sequential preference in a design problem; it is good to get the sequence right and avoid backtracking. It is best to make unpleasant discoveries on paper, so I do preliminary sketches first. While wildly drawing, I also consider whether it would be possible to build the piece as sketched. I mentally formulate assembly sequences and methods to determine whether or not it can be done.

Available hardware for drop-leaf mechanisms seemed ugly

Alan Marks studied at Carl Malmstens Verkstadsskola in Sweden and apprenticed with Jim Krenov. He makes furniture in Pacific Grove, Calif.

and poorly made. I wanted traditional handles to push the cart around with, and drop leaves on the ends would make this difficult. The leaves would conceal a large portion of the framework, and the hinged joint would not be attractive. So I discarded the idea.

Having two hinged leaves fold out from their resting place on top of the table seemed good. The table leaves would need support, and the handles might be able to perform this function. I would use a set of rails, front and back, and a drawer would slide on a frame on top of these.

Pleased with my preliminary sketch, I proceeded to a full-scale, head-on drawing that included construction details. I was confident I had a good solution. (Sometimes I can skip the working drawing for things easily kept in my head, but the cart was too complex.)

On the drawing, I spread the legs slightly to afford a wider base, because I feared that weight on the unfolded table leaves might tip the cart. This change also increased shelf space, as did tapering the legs, though the latter was mostly for esthetic reasons. Tall, parallel legs on a strict vertical appear to converge when viewed from a normal height, and the piece may look unstable. Tapered, slightly spread legs give a firm impression of stability.

The handle supports had to attach strongly to the legs, to provide enough meat for a cross-member to stabilize the frame and also be convenient to push on, and they had to complement the shape of the legs. There must be other ways of supporting the handles and achieving all this, but I was pleased with this shape and haven't come up with one I feel better about. The upper shelf rail echoes the curve of the handle supports. I didn't want to overdo this, so I left the lower rail straight, and I think it identifies with the floor and makes the cart appear anchored.

I let the tenons of all the bottom rails through the legs for extra strength and wedged them. This seemed unnecessary except where stress might break apart the joints. I didn't intend to join the side aprons atop the legs with this kind of joint, but when building the cart I accidentally mortised the first leg all the way through. Having no extra legs in reserve and being too impatient to start again on a new set, I bowed to fate and let the superfluous tenons protrude. I might pretend things turn out exactly as planned, but often they don't. The appearance didn't suffer too much from this mistake, although the cart in walnut escaped my clumsiness and looks better for it.

While drawing I worked for a general feeling of lightness and so chose spaced-slat shelves. The alternatives to slats would be either veneered and faced lumbercore, or frame-

From *Fine Woodworking* magazine (Spring 1977) 6:58-61

and-panel construction. All would circumvent the problem of wood movement, but slats are airy and light. I ran them across the width of the cart to avoid the sag of longer lengths. I had planned to add rails on the sides of the bottom shelf for stability, and I set the slats below them so dishes couldn't slide off.

When my drawing was complete down to the minutest detail, I stood the drawing board against a wall to get a perspective on the cart.

It was awful. Top-heavy, thick and clumsy. I was annoyed with myself for assuming it would look right; experience teaches to look first and work out details later. The double top had to go. The drawer section looked much too heavy and box-like.

So I taped a fresh sheet on top and traced what could be salvaged—the legs, handles, shelves, and their placement. I mulled over it for some time, but the possibilities seemed to be exhausted. The top had to be made light and graceful, but how? A center leaf with pull-out table halves on extension slides suggested itself, but the slides would have occupied space under the table and made construction clumsy. Then everything popped into focus.

I could rout along the length of the front and back aprons with a dovetail bit and mount runners on the table halves. The halves would pull out and rest on the handles. I would use a veneered tabletop with a stable core to eliminate movement so the runners wouldn't bind. This left a cavity between the rails for storing the carving board/serving tray. The center leaf could store on the shelf. And I could hang the drawer in slots from L-shaped side aprons which also would support the carving board.

I hid the drawer runners behind an overhanging drawer front. Such a big overhang seemed unnecessary except at the top and so I felt free to curve the front at the sides to make

the drawer less boxy; the curve was in tune with the handle style as well. There is a relationship between a serving cart and a carriage, and I emphasized the similarity by shaping the front and back of the drawer to give the impression of containing or carrying something. The simple pull accents the shape of the drawer front.

The tabletop, since it had to be veneered, required banding. I raised the banding to form a lip that would prevent things from sliding off. Usually I cut my own veneer with a band saw, so I can use wood of my choice, cut from the same planks as the rest of the piece. Color and grain structure remain harmonious this way, and I can get veneer of decent thickness, about 1/16 in. As a core, I used 1/2-in. Baltic birch plywood. I have not been able to locate a U.S. source of the 13-mm. lumbercore readily available in Sweden. The veneer grain runs lengthwise and the edge banding is narrow, to emphasize the length. The ends are capped with wider pieces that allow rounded corners and routed finger-grooves for pulling out the leaves.

The table assembly sequence was:
• glue and trim center bandings flush with plywood core;
• veneer (using white polyvinyl glue because it is not affected by moisture as Titebond);
• rout fillets on the inside of the banding;
• glue and trim the lengthwise bandings;
• glue and trim end bandings;
• rout finger grooves;
• shape bandings;
• round the corners.

Fitting the runners to the table halves was tricky. I made them of maple and inset pieces of maple in the aprons to dovetail through. Maple on maple glides beautifully and wears well. I predrilled the runners for screws and positioned them against stops in their dovetailed slots to protrude about

'It was top-heavy, thick and clumsy.'

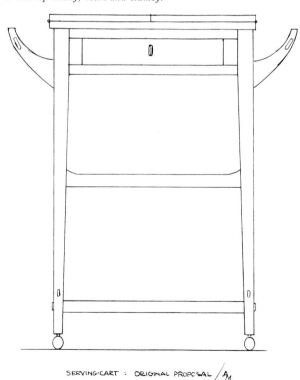

SERVING·CART : ORIGINAL PROPOSAL /A·M

Completed cart, 'made light and graceful,' in Douglas fir.

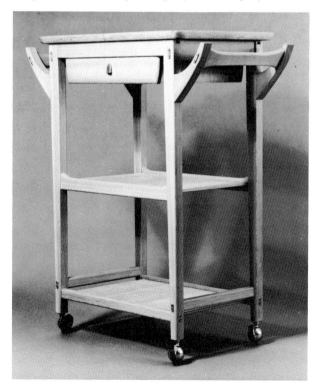

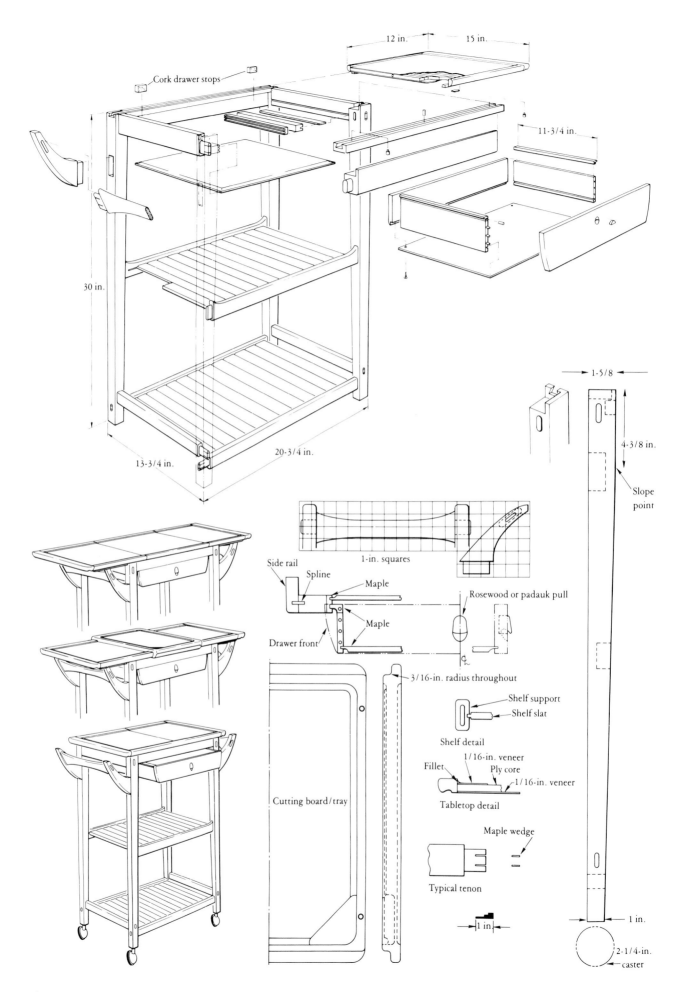

Cork drawer stops

12 in.

15 in.

11-3/4 in.

30 in.

13-3/4 in.

20-3/4 in.

1-5/8

4-3/8 in.

Slope
point

Side rail

Spline

Maple

Maple

Drawer front

Rosewood or padauk pull

1-in. squares

3/16-in. radius throughout

Shelf support

Shelf slat

Shelf detail

1/16-in. veneer

Fillet

Ply core

1/16-in. veneer

Tabletop detail

Cutting board/tray

Maple wedge

Typical tenon

1 in

1 in.

2-1/4-in.
caster

1/32 in. above the apron level. Then I glued and clamped the halves onto them and only then did I screw them in place. In spite of my efforts to be precise, the runners needed a lot of fitting before they would glide smoothly. This was partly because the plywood cores were slightly warped.

With the table halves gliding properly and in position, I glued the handle assemblies in place. I left the table supports a bit higher than needed and carefully filed them down until the runners slid out smoothly. The shape of the handles necessitated special clamping blocks with non-skid, sand-paper-covered surfaces which were themselves clamped to the handle supports.

The steps in glue-up and assembly were:
• shape and mortise legs; assemble legs with front and back aprons and shelf rails; rout dovetails for the runners;
• glue these together with machined and fitted side aprons and side shelf rails with slats and compartment dividing panel in place;
• assemble table halves and center leaf; install runners and fit table halves; install locater for center leaf;
• glue handles into handle supports;
• with table halves in place, glue on handle assemblies;
• assemble and fit drawer, knob and carving board/tray.

Three types of hardware were used, all where they'd hardly be noticed. I used click-stops to mark the table extension required to insert the center leaf. These are ball-bearing catches inset into the dovetail slots that pop into a brass detent plate set in the runners. To prevent the table halves from vibrating apart while the cart is rolling, I used two tiny button magnets oriented so their poles would attract. The center leaf has steel buttons on both sides. I used male and female brass locaters of the type patternmakers use to locate the carving board/tray.

The client's walnut cart was finished with oil. The fir cart has an all but invisible coating of water-white flat lacquer.

I can't say how much time it took to construct my serving cart. I've found that the more attention I pay to passing hours, the less time is available for work. Solutions and decisions become forced, and mistakes occur. Therefore I don't count hours. □

Detail of serving cart shows cutting board/serving tray in place, and drawer pull.

Maple slide runs in dovetail way let through leg and rests atop handle support. Below, drawer hangs from slot in apron piece that also holds divider panel.

Patternmaker's locating pins, left, index cutting board and center leaf. Male pin, below, is set into center of front rail and a notch is cut into sliding leaves to conceal it. Button magnet at center of leaf edge keeps movable parts together. Bullet catches concealed in the ways control the extension of leaves.

Folding Stool With Tray
Knockdown design for a dual-purpose project

by Tage Frid

I was asked to design a folding stool that would be light, take up little space when folded, and serve as the base for a tray. In addition, any parts broken during service would have to be easily replaceable. When the stool was finished it weighed 4½ lb., and measured 1¾ in. folded. Nothing has broken yet, so I haven't had to take it apart, but I could if I wanted to and it would go back together good as new.

I made the stool from ash. If I had used a weaker wood, I would have added to the thicknesses and widths for strength. The seat can be either leather or canvas. The one shown is canvas, with a single row of stitches to make a hem at the edges and a double row to hold the 3-in. overlap.

The stretchers can be held to the legs with either T-nuts or barrel nuts and ³⁄₁₆-in. stove bolts. The stool shown here has T-nuts, which leave the holes in the stretchers open. Barrel nuts would have filled the holes and looked like metal plugs. Where the stretchers butt against the legs there's a hidden dowel (or a steel pin) that keeps the stretchers from turning. A washer between the legs where they cross allows the stool to fold easily, and double nuts are locked together so they don't have to be drawn too tight. If a tight single nut were used, the stool wouldn't fold. Washers under the bolt heads protect the wood.

The legs are identical except for the angle on the foot—the angle makes it a right leg or a left, to keep the dowel holes inside. Mill the leg blanks, square them and cut them to exact length. Set up the drill press with stops to locate the holes, and then drill them all. Notice that the holes for the dowels or steel pins don't go through—make these holes ⅜ in. deep. After you've drilled the holes, taper the legs with a taper jig on the tablesaw or on the bandsaw. Cut a little wide so you can run the edges over the jointer to remove the saw marks, and then cut the foot angle.

The stretchers are all the same length. I made the bottom stretchers ⅛ in. wider than the top because people have a tendency to put their feet on them when they sit on a stool, but the stretchers could be all the same size. Mill them out and cut them to length, then use a stop on the drill press to make the holes for the T-nuts or barrel nuts. For T-nuts, make ⅝-in. holes; for barrel nuts, use ½-in. holes. Of course, regular nuts could be used if the others aren't available, but barrel nuts are easy to make. My students and I use them a lot—they make an attractive and strong joint if a piece has to be disassembled. They can be of ½-in. cold-rolled steel, aluminum, brass, or other rod stock. Cut the nuts to length, so they will be flush with the surface if you want them to show, or shorter if you want to use them in a blind hole. File and sand the ends, then drill and thread holes for the bolts. Use a V-block jig in the drill press to bore the hole. Remember to countersink these holes so the bolt will start easily—when it comes time for assembly, you can wiggle the nut until you feel the bolt start to engage. If you use barrel nuts or regular nuts for the stool, use a ³⁄₁₆-in. stove bolt, 2½ in. long. For T-nuts, use a 2-in. long bolt. Tilt the drill-press table to 90° and clamp a jig to hold the stretchers while you drill the holes

The taper in the legs of this stool cuts down weight, leaves the wood where it's needed, and allows the stool to close up to a snug 1¾ in. T-nuts in the stretchers allow disassembly. You don't have to store this stool in the closet when you're not sitting on it— make a tray that converts it into an occasional table or server, as shown above.

From *Fine Woodworking* magazine (September 1982) 36:68-69

Folding stool with tray

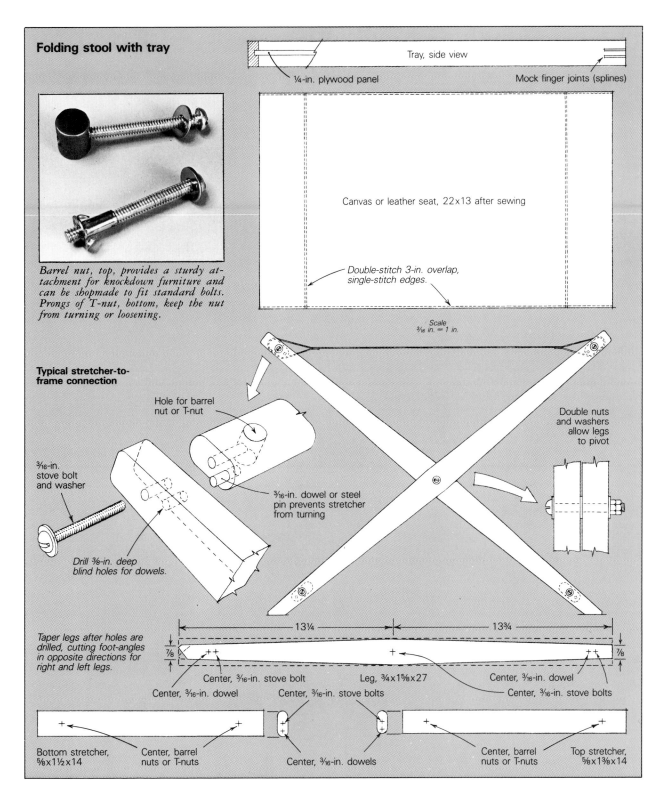

Tray, side view

¼-in. plywood panel

Mock finger joints (splines)

Barrel nut, top, provides a sturdy attachment for knockdown furniture and can be shopmade to fit standard bolts. Prongs of T-nut, bottom, keep the nut from turning or loosening.

Canvas or leather seat, 22x13 after sewing

Double-stitch 3-in. overlap, single-stitch edges.

Scale
³⁄₁₆ in. = 1 in.

Typical stretcher-to-frame connection

Hole for barrel nut or T-nut

Double nuts and washers allow legs to pivot

³⁄₁₆-in. stove bolt and washer

³⁄₁₆-in. dowel or steel pin prevents stretcher from turning

Drill ³⁄₈-in. deep blind holes for dowels.

Taper legs after holes are drilled, cutting foot-angles in opposite directions for right and left legs.

13¼   13¾

⅞   ⅞

Center, ³⁄₁₆-in. stove bolt   Leg, ¾x1⅝x27   Center, ³⁄₁₆-in. dowel

Center, ³⁄₁₆-in. dowel   Center, ³⁄₁₆-in. stove bolts   Center, ³⁄₁₆-in. stove bolts

Bottom stretcher, ⅝x1½x14   Center, barrel nuts or T-nuts   Center, ³⁄₁₆-in. dowels   Center, barrel nuts or T-nuts   Top stretcher, ⅝x1⅜x14

for the bolts and dowels. The stool is now ready to be assembled, but first chamfer all the edges with a router or a plane, then sand and finish the pieces.

Don't make the tray before you have assembled the stool and measured it to be sure that the tray will fit. This one is an ash frame with a panel of ¼-in. walnut plywood in a groove. I didn't use solid wood for the panel because, to remain stable, it would have had to be ⅜ in. thick, and that would have made the tray too heavy to carry around. There's

no trick to making the tray—I cut the corners to 45°, rubbed them together with hot glue, then strengthened them with a mock finger joint, which I learned from that wonderful book on *Joinery* by Tage Frid.   □

Tage Frid, retired professor emeritus of furniture design at R.I. School of Design, is author of three books: Furniture-making; Joinery; *and* Shaping, Veneering, Finishing, *all available from The Taunton Press.*

A Spider-Leg Carriage Table
Turned legs, tray top evoke diminutive elegance

by D. Asher Carmichael

Shortly after I moved to Mobile, Ala., five years ago, Dr. Samuel Eichold asked me to reproduce a table which an antique dealer refused to part with. I met with the dealer, Charles Crane, and coaxed him into letting me make the drawings, measurements and descriptions from which the table shown here eventually developed.

The original table was English, late Georgian (circa 1800), and seemed a tiny cousin to the butlers' tray-on-stand, which was then very popular, primarily for serving wines. The smaller examples—this one is only 21 in. high—were employed in outdoor excursions and were commonly called carriage tables. They are rare today because of their fragility and the rigors of country excursions. The one I copied had probably remained at home most of the time, serving as a chairside table for occasional use.

This table is mahogany with crotch veneer and satinwood veneer border. Like many butlers' tables, it could be made with fancier inlay or even painted and gilded. The top should be veneered rather than made of one piece of solid wood that would likely warp. A butlers' table, of course, has a removable tray, a possible alternative here. Perhaps hinging the top was meant to be insurance against leaving it behind, overlooked at the end of the day beneath some leafy English shrub.

To begin construction, refer to the bill of materials (p. 66) and prepare the rough stock. Dress the stock for the legs, stretchers, cap rails and hinge strip to finished square dimensions, and cut the pieces to length.

Turning the legs—Without a steady rest, legs as thin and long as these tend to whip a good bit on the lathe, but they can, like the original, be turned as one piece. Mount a leg blank in the lathe with just enough pressure to hold it securely—you don't want to introduce any more compression force than necessary, because it will increase the amount of whip. To further reduce whip, start at

the center, work toward the ends and don't remove any more wood than you have to for each step.

Cut the shoulders of the pummels with the long point of a skew chisel, then follow the sequence shown in figure 3, using a small gouge to rough out the legs. Mark the beads. If you are a confident turner, you can round them with the skew. Otherwise, leave them as V-cuts, then shape them with 150-grit sandpaper after you have turned the cylinders to their finished diameters.

An alternative method for making the legs, which decreases whip, is to turn each one as two shorter pieces, then join the pieces with a ½-in. diameter tenon (leg detail, figure 2). Turn the tenon slightly oversize to allow for trimming and fitting. Also, sand the separate leg pieces while they're still on the lathe—it's not likely that the joint will be perfectly centered, and the leg will thus run off-center if you try to sand it on the

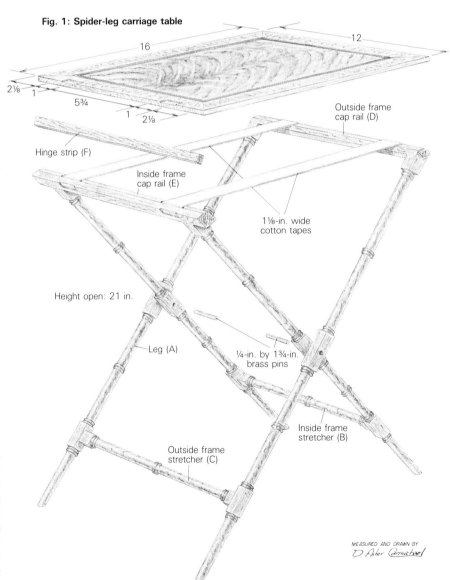

Fig. 1: Spider-leg carriage table

16

12

2⅛ 1

5¾

1 2⅛

Hinge strip (F)

Inside frame cap rail (E)

Outside frame cap rail (D)

1⅛-in. wide cotton tapes

Height open: 21 in.

Leg (A)

¼-in. by 1¾-in. brass pins

Inside frame stretcher (B)

Outside frame stretcher (C)

MEASURED AND DRAWN BY
D. Asher Carmichael

From *Fine Woodworking* magazine (May 1983) 40:70-72

lathe after it's been glued up. Bore the ½-in. diameter mortises in the upper legs with a Forstner or a Power Bore bit chucked in a drill press or in your lathe.

Cap rails and frame assembly—

Before you chamfer the cap rails, lay out and cut the leg and tape mortises. Also, lay out the stretcher mortises in the legs. You can cut the square mortises with a ⅜-in. hollow-chisel mortiser, or you can rough them out with a ⁵⁄₁₆-in. brad-point bit and then chisel them square. Take care cutting the leg mortises in the cap rails. If they are too deep, they will show when you cut the chamfer. To cut the slot mortises for the tape, drill adjacent ⅛-in. holes through the stock, then clean up with a thin file.

Now cut the tenons on the legs and stretchers, using your choice of table-saw, radial-arm saw or hand tools. Also,

bore a ¼-in. diameter hinge-pin hole through the center square of each leg.

I chamfered the cap rails with a hand plane—it's risky to use a tablesaw or a jointer on such small pieces.

When tooling is finished, sand the rails to 120-grit, then glue and clamp the frame assemblies.

Top and final assembly—

You might decide to use ¼-in. plywood for the ground, hiding its edges with a thin band of veneer, but the original table's ground is edge-glued from pieces of quartersawn stock. This choice of grain—along with the maker's care to veneer both sides and apply a good finish—has kept the thin top flat and true.

If you use solid stock, dress the lumber for the ground to ⅜-in. thickness. Watch for tearout as a clue to grain direction, then, to make planing easier,

Fig. 3: Turning the legs

To avoid whip, work from center toward ends, removing only enough wood to allow you to clean up details as you go. As an alternative to turning the beads with a skew, you can leave them V-shaped (as in step 2), then round them with sandpaper after you have turned the legs to finished diameter.

1. Cut shoulders for center square; rough-turn legs to diameter slightly larger than beads.

2. Define beads with V-cuts.

3. Turn short sections to leg finished diameter; shape beads with skew.

4. Turn leg to finished diameter.

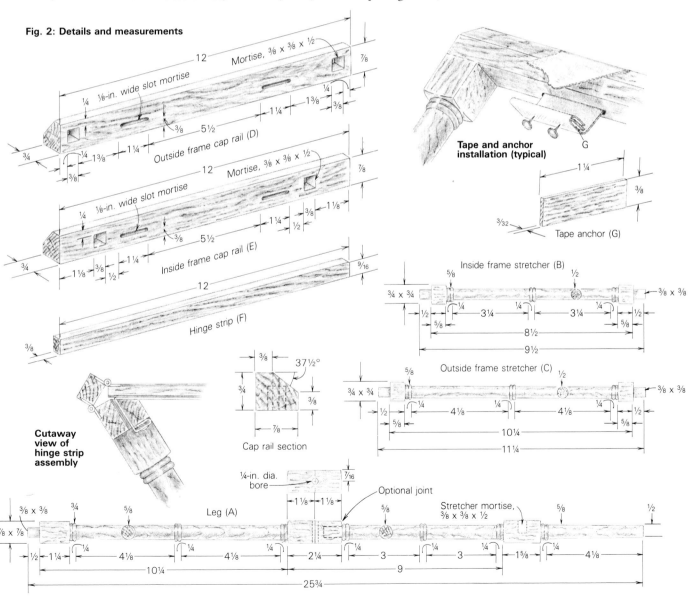

Fig. 2: Details and measurements

Outside frame cap rail (D)

Inside frame cap rail (E)

Hinge strip (F)

Cutaway view of hinge strip assembly

Cap rail section

Tape and anchor installation (typical)

Tape anchor (G)

Inside frame stretcher (B)

Outside frame stretcher (C)

Leg (A)

arrange the boards so that all the grain goes the same way. Edge-glue the pieces to make a panel ½ in. oversize. Plane the panel to about ¼ in. thick, and cut it to final size.

Lay out and cut the veneers, allowing 1/32 in. extra on the counter veneer and the border veneer to ensure complete coverage. Using a straightedge and a razor or a veneer knife, cut the miters from the long point toward the inside, to avoid breaking off the long point. Assemble the veneers as shown in figure 4 with some glue between the joints. The tape will be removed with scrapers and sandpaper once the veneers and ground have been laminated.

When the face veneer lay-up is dry, you can glue up the ground and veneers with yellow, plastic-resin, or hide glue (figure 5). Deep-throated handscrews and C-clamps will supply plenty of pressure if they are arranged evenly over the cauls. (A commercial or shopmade marquetry press would also work.) Get everything ready, then apply glue to one side of the ground (not to the veneer) and center the counter veneer, best face showing. Turn the top over, apply glue to the other side, and center the top veneer, taped side out. Press down to remove any air bubbles, then, to keep it from sliding, secure the sandwich with several small strips of tape. Place either

waxed or plain paper over the veneers as a parting agent, and clamp up.

When the top is dry, remove the veneer tape with a freshly sharpened scraper. Then plane the veneer flush with the edge of the ground. Finish-sand, carefully easing the veneer edges.

Cut and sand the hinge strip and attach it to the top with two 1-in. by ¾-in. brass butt hinges. Let in the hinges so that they are flush. You'll have to pre-drill the screw holes and file the screws shorter to keep them from going through the tabletop. Next, hinge the strip to the inside frame assembly.

Finishing up—Remove all the hinges, clean up any blemishes and give the table a final sanding to 150-grit. If you plan to stain the wood, seal the stringing and border veneer with shellac first. To avoid this step, I used a chemical stain, 2 cups of quicklime (calcium oxide) in 1 quart of warm water, which colored the mahogany black-red without darkening the lighter veneer too much.

Any finish will do, but be sure to apply thin coats rather than heavy ones, which would fill in the grooves at the beads and obscure the detail.

Next, reattach the top. To allow the table to fold, pin the legs with brass rod as shown in figure 1. If the pins do not fit snugly, peen one end oval. Resist any temptation to use epoxy, as this would prevent disassembly of the base frames should the need arise.

Now you can attach the cotton tapes (available from upholstery shops) to the cap rails as shown in figure 2. As with the hinges, pilot-drill the tape anchors to keep them from splitting. It will be easier to attach both tapes to the inside frame cap rail first and then use the top as a gauge to determine their final length.

Set the table up and check for level posture, then mark and trim the bottom of the legs to ensure a stable footing. Seal the trimmed leg ends, then apply a thin coat of wax until the table gleams.

Now that you're finished, the people in your life whom you've neglected so long would probably love to use the table for its original purpose—an outing in the country. If your heart isn't quite that strong, it's up to you to convince them that something a mite more substantial would be more appropriate. □

D. Asher Carmichael works for Emperor Clock Co. In his spare time he draws and makes furniture.

Fig. 4: Laying up the face veneer

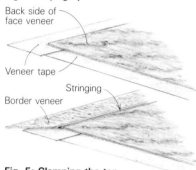

Back side of face veneer
Veneer tape
Stringing
Border veneer

Fig. 5: Clamping the top

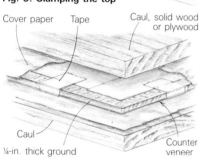

Cover paper
Tape
Caul, solid wood or plywood
Caul
¼-in. thick ground
Counter veneer

Marilyn Tario

The carriage table, even in semi-repose, tells tales of elegant Georgian picnics. It folds up for easy carrying, and the tray is attached with hinges so you won't accidentally leave it behind.

No. of pieces		Description	Dimensions (net) L x W x T
BILL OF MATERIALS			
Mahogany:	4	Legs (A)	25¾ x ⅞ x ⅞
	1	Inside frame stretcher (B)	9½ x ¾ x ¾
	1	Outside frame stretcher (C)	11¼ x ¾ x ¾
	1	Outside frame cap rail (D)	12 x ⅞ x ¾
	1	Inside frame cap rail (E)	12 x ⅞ x ¾
	1	Hinge strip (F)	12 x 9/16 x ⅜
	4	Tape anchors (G)	1¼ x ⅜ x 3/32
	1	Top (ground), can be plywood	16 x 12 x ¼
Veneer and stringing:	1	Counter veneer	16 x 12 x 1/28
	1	Figured face veneer	14 x 10 x 1/28
	50 in.	Holly-ebony-holly stringing	⅛ in. wide
	60 in.	Satinwood border veneer	⅞ in. wide
Hardware:	2	Cotton tapes	18 x 1⅛
	4	Brass butt hinges	1 x ¾ (open)
	2	Brass pins	1¾ x ¼ dia.
	8	Brass tacks or light upholstery nails	

Versatile Plant Table
Redwood slats support your fine-foliaged friends

by Frederick Wilbur

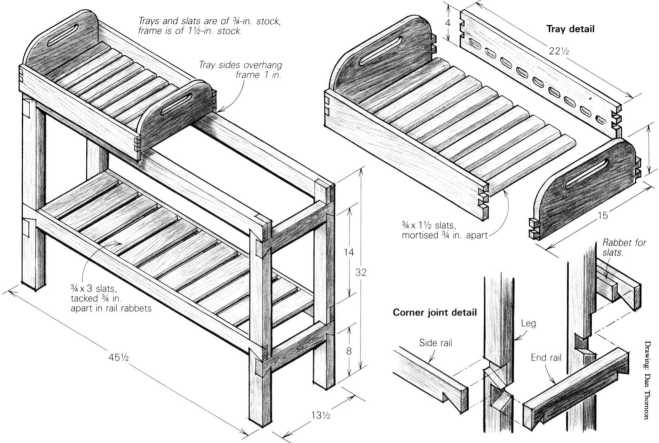

Trays and slats are of ¾-in. stock, frame is of 1½-in. stock.

Tray sides overhang frame 1 in.

¾ x 3 slats, tacked ¾ in. apart in rail rabbets

45½

14

32

8

13½

Tray detail

4

22½

¾ x 1½ slats, mortised ¾ in. apart

15

Rabbet for slats.

Corner joint detail

Side rail

Leg

End rail

Drawing: Dan Thornton

For those of us who have a house full of herbaceous friends crowding every windowsill and end table, this redwood plant stand will make them more enjoyable. The stand supports two removable trays at a height that makes admiring and caring for their occupants convenient. And the trays also allow you to carry the plants outside for sun, or for a bath—the tray bottoms are slatted for drainage. The stand includes a bottom shelf for more plants, ones that require less direct sun, or for the paraphernalia that accompanies enthusiastic plant care.

I recommend using redwood, though cedar or cypress would last as well. If you have an absolute jungle and plan to produce these stands by the score, consider the economy of pressure-treated lumber. One could, I suppose, adapt the design, fabricating copper tray inserts and making the trays and frame of any fine cabinet wood.

The plant stand requires a modest amount of both ¾-in. and 1½-in. stock. I make the two trays first from the ¾-in. stock, using through dovetails for strength, although finger joints would also work well. Cutting dovetails in redwood takes a little patience because the wood is brittle and easily splits. When laying out the joint, note that the sides project below the ends so that they straddle the frame. The end curves are bandsawn, and the handles cut out with a coping saw. To mortise the sides for the slats, I used a simple router template made from ¼-in. plywood, and positioned the mortises so that the slat bottoms would be in line with the bottom edge of the ends. I rounded the slats on a stationary sander to fit the round-cornered mortises. The length of the slats must ensure that they don't fall out after assembly.

The supporting frame is made from

the 1½-in. stock. The top rails of the frame must be spaced close enough that the sides of the trays fit outside them. Other than this, the configuration of the frame can vary to suit. I lay wide slats into rabbets in the long rails at the bottom for a balanced appearance. Though this stand is lap-dovetailed and glued into one unit, through mortise-and-tenons or bolted lap joints (for a knockdown version) would work well too.

I sanded the trays for this stand and rounded their corners, but I didn't apply any finish to the redwood, not knowing what effect some chemicals might have on delicate houseplants. Water stains are inevitable, so I didn't worry about preventing them. Redwood turns a mellow gray in time, contrasting nicely with the lush greenery of happy plants. □

Frederick Wilbur operates Braintree Woodworks in Lovingston, Va.

Two Game Tables

Morris Sheppard's opulent game table, right, unfolds along the chessboard center line to reveal a backgammon well. The table is solid rosewood; inlay and playing surfaces are ivory and ebony; price tag is $30,000. Sheppard, of Big Sur, Calif., spent 1,500 painstaking hours making it.

The chessboard squares contain the pattern shown in the diagram, in ivory and rosewood for the white squares, ebony and rosewood for the black. Sheppard assembled a log for each color, and sliced each into 32 squares, like bologna. The white log began with a square block of ivory, to which he epoxied four triangular prisms of rosewood, then four more of ivory, four more of rosewood, and a final course of ivory. The log was carefully scraped and sanded after each glue-up to maintain symmetry and squareness, and checked with a micrometer and dial indicator. Sheppard says he quickly learned the precise thickness of a single scraper shaving. He used a fine tooth, plastic-cutting band-saw blade to cut the logs into thin squares. The epoxy didn't always hold the ivory, Sheppard found, and squares that fell apart were reassembled with cyanoacrylate "super glue." His careful work paid off: The 64 squares fit together so tightly there wasn't a single gap to fill. The playing surfaces were sanded to 600 grit, polished with jeweler's rouge, sealed and French-polished.

Joe Tracy, of Mt. Desert, Maine, used a thickness planer and a scarfing jig to produce the playing surfaces for 12 backgammon tables, below. The efficient solution, he says, came from realizing that a backgammon board could be divided into 12 parallel strips, each containing half of the spear pattern at each end. Such modules could be made by scarfing a wide board at each end, gluing in place an identically tapered wedge of wood of a contrasting color, and slicing the assembly into strips. Furthermore, 12 modules could be stacked up to make a "backgammon sandwich," which then could be bandsawn into 24 slices for 12 complete tabletops.

After roughly bandsawing the tapers, Tracy devised a simple jig that would hold each board at a constant angle as it was fed through the thickness planer. The jig was made of 1-in. hardwood lumber, with a combination of small clamping wedges and wooden stops to hold each piece in place. All 12 boards were run through with the thicknesser setting unchanged, then the boards were flipped end-for-end in the jig and run through again. Additional stops allowed him to use the same jig for making the contrasting wedges. He writes, "The trick throughout was to control the feather edges and to work with enough accuracy to make the spear halves meet in uniform points."

He glued and clamped the modules in another jig that held the ends tightly in place, inserting a layer of contrasting veneer to outline the spears. Then he ran all 12 modules through the thickness planer again, continuous side on the bed, and glued the sandwich together. A sharp band saw and a steady hand sliced the stack into 24 identical boards, ready to smooth in the thicknesser and glue to a plywood ground.

Tracy made the table itself and the main part of the board of cherry; the spears are kiln-dried pear (dark orange) and air-dried pear (white), outlined with walnut veneer. The tables were selling for $400 each.

The same jig could be used to prepare two modules for one backgammon board. It could also be used with a hand plane, the sole bridging the jig's parallel sides.

—*John Kelsey*

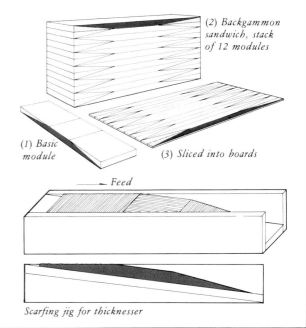

(1) *Basic module*

(2) *Backgammon sandwich, stack of 12 modules*

(3) *Sliced into boards*

— *Feed*

Scarfing jig for thicknesser

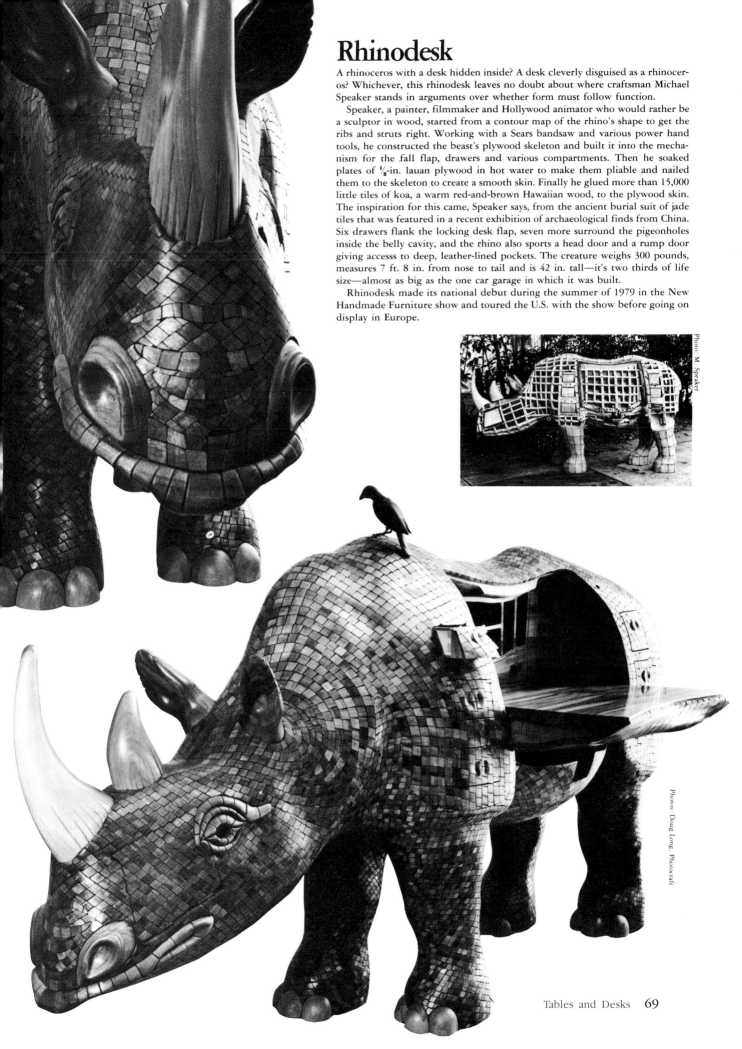

Rhinodesk

A rhinoceros with a desk hidden inside? A desk cleverly disguised as a rhinoceros? Whichever, this rhinodesk leaves no doubt about where craftsman Michael Speaker stands in arguments over whether form must follow function.

Speaker, a painter, filmmaker and Hollywood animator who would rather be a sculptor in wood, started from a contour map of the rhino's shape to get the ribs and struts right. Working with a Sears bandsaw and various power hand tools, he constructed the beast's plywood skeleton and built it into the mechanism for the fall flap, drawers and various compartments. Then he soaked plates of $\frac{1}{8}$-in. lauan plywood in hot water to make them pliable and nailed them to the skeleton to create a smooth skin. Finally he glued more than 15,000 little tiles of koa, a warm red-and-brown Hawaiian wood, to the plywood skin. The inspiration for this came, Speaker says, from the ancient burial suit of jade tiles that was featured in a recent exhibition of archaeological finds from China. Six drawers flank the locking desk flap, seven more surround the pigeonholes inside the belly cavity, and the rhino also sports a head door and a rump door giving accesss to deep, leather-lined pockets. The creature weighs 300 pounds, measures 7 ft. 8 in. from nose to tail and is 42 in. tall—it's two thirds of life size—almost as big as the one car garage in which it was built.

Rhinodesk made its national debut during the summer of 1979 in the New Handmade Furniture show and toured the U.S. with the show before going on display in Europe.

Photo: M Speaker

Photos: Doug Long, Photocraft

Shaker Lap Desk
A challenging exercise in hand dovetailing

by Brian Considine

The Shaker lap desk may be considered the predecessor of today's briefcase. Like modern briefcases, lap desks were convenient for carrying papers. In addition, one can write on either the slanted top or on a special surface inside the desk.

These desks are fine examples of the thought, care and skill the Shaker woodcrafters put into even the smallest piece. The variety and detail of the joints in this piece make it a challenging project for the modern craftsman.

The general procedure for making these is to make and assemble the four sides and shelf, then the bottom and top, and finally the drawer.

First make patterns of the large and small ends on pieces of manila cardboard and lay out and cut the dovetails' outline on these patterns. (In making dovetail joints, I like to make the tails first.) Next, size and plane the stock from the cutting list. Cut the pieces for the front, back and ends 1/8-inch over in width so that you can plane down the top edges when it's together. Cut the angle on the top of both the ends and leave a little over.

With a marking gauge, scribe the depth lines of the dovetails on the end pieces. Now align the patterns along the bottom of the end pieces and transfer the dovetails with a scribe or awl. Then cut and clean them. Now position the four sides as they are to be and code the corners that are to be dovetailed together. Then one by one mark the lines for the

pins from the tails and proceed to cut them out. To help in the chiseling process, I like to make relief cuts with a bandsaw into the waste sections of the pins. But take care to place the piece on the saw table with the wide part of the pins up so that you don't cut into them by accident. Then fit the dovetails together, carefully paring down the pins where necessary.

Size the shelf and lay out the grooves to hold it on the inside of the four sides. The bottom of the shelf should line up with the bottom edge of the small end. Cut the groove for the shelf with a router or with knife and chisels, but be careful not to go to the outside edge and cut through the dovetails. Then glue the sides together, placing glue blocks just beyond the dovetails so that they can close all the way. Clean any dried glue off with a chisel and smooth the corners with a block plane. Plane the bottom edges so that box sits flat. Plane the top edges so that they all lie on a plane.

Size the bottom piece, round the edges and glue it on. Size the top. Glue on bread board ends (tongue should be 3/16-inch wide). Cut 1/8-inch molding to go around the mouth of the drawer. It should be rounded on the edge and protrude slightly. (The drawer will slide straight if you put extra molding behind the two sides of the opening. This should be done before gluing on the bottom of the desk.)

Now size and fit the drawer front and proceed to dovetail

This lap desk was made of 200-year-old pine (on commission), although the author prefers to use cherry for the desks. Shakers often made dovetails as shown here, but to be more correct, dovetails should have been laid out to begin and end with half-pins, not half-tails.

From *Fine Woodworking* magazine (Spring 1976) 2:48-49

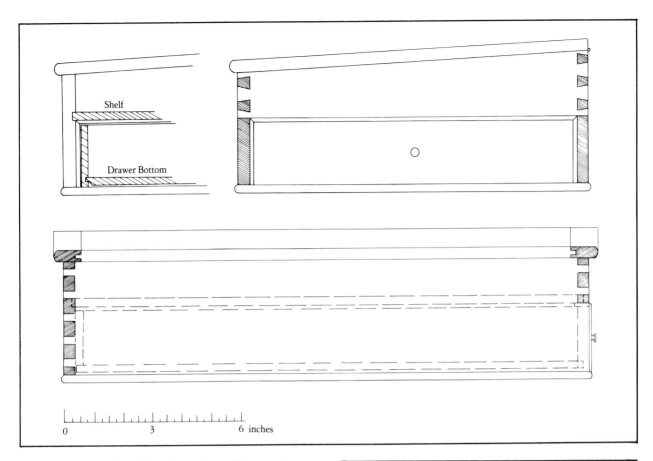

Shelf

Drawer Bottom

0   3   6 inches

the drawer together. The front dovetails are of course half-blind.

Dovetail the sides to the front first, put them together and slide them in the drawer opening. Cut the sides a little long so the drawer front will protrude at first. Then measure and cut off enough from the back end of the sides so the drawer front sits flush with the side of the case.

You still have to size the drawer back and bottom and dovetail the back to the sides. First cut a groove on the inside of the sides and front to hold the drawer bottom. Note that it is essential that the bottom edge of the groove be above the bottom half-pin. Otherwise when you pass the pieces through the table saw you will cut the dovetail. After you make these grooves, size the drawer bottom to go in the grooves and bevel the edges. Then measure for the back piece. It will be as wide as the drawer front but its height will be the distance from the top edge of the groove to the top of the sides. Dovetail this back to the sides by repeating the procedure for dovetailing the case. Finally, the drawer bottom should be slid in and nailed to the back piece from its underside.

Once the drawer is completed, bevel the back edge of the lid so it is flush with the back edge of the box and hinge it.

Desk Parts	
Large End	3/8 x 4-3/8 x 12
Small End	3/8 x 2-1/8 x 12
Back	3/8 x 4-3/8 x 18
Front	3/8 x 3-3/4 x 18
Bottom	1/4 x 12-1/2 x 18-1/2
Shelf	1/4 x 11-1/2 x 17-1/2
Top	3/8 x 12-3/8 x 18-3/4
Drawer Parts	
Front	3/8 x 2-1/8 x 11
Molding	1/8 x 1/2
Sides	1/4 x 2-1/8 x 17-1/2
Back	1/4 x 1-3/4 x 10-5/8
Bottom	1/4 x 10-5/8 x 17-1/2

Q & A

Source for typewriter lift mechanism

The Pfaff Sewing Machine Co. makes an elevator mechanism that features positive lock stops at the top, and at 3⅜ in. and 15 in. down from the top. A spring winding device counterbalances the weight of a sewing machine or typewriter, allowing fingertip control while the elevator platform moves vertically along the two tracks. Using this mechanism would provide a normal desk-height work surface, a lower typing platform and a complete typewriter disappearing act. Check with your local sewing-machine dealer, or write the manufacturer: Pfaff Handelsgesellschaft, fur Haushaltnahmaschinen mbH, Subsidiary of G.M. Pfaff AG, D 7500 Karlsruhe 41, West Germany.
—Wayne Hope, St. Albert, Alta.

Tambours

Precise measuring and machining make slats run smoothly

by Alphonse Mattia

Tambours are flexible doors, made up of a series of thin wooden slats. They are either glued to a fabric backing or threaded together with wires. The slats have tongues at each end, which run in tracking grooves cut into the carcase. Tambour doors can open vertically, as in a roll-top desk, or horizontally, as in a buffet.

Most people refer to tambours as "roll-tops" because of the familiarity of the American oak roll-top desk. Tambours, however, originated in France during the 17th century. Tambours were very popular in Louis XV (1715-1774) and Louis XVI (1774-1792) work, and again in England during the Sheraton period in the early 19th century. They did not reach the general public in America until the oak roll-top desk came into fashion early in the 20th century. Tambours are also used in Scandinavian contemporary furniture.

Tambours are efficient and offer several advantages over other door systems. Space is saved because doors do not swing out from the carcase. They give greater access to the carcase opening than sliding systems where the doors must overlap. Tambours can also follow or accentuate graceful curves in the piece. Wired tambours offer the advantage of allowing the back of the tambour to be exposed, since it is not covered with fabric. The fabric-backed method stabilizes the tambour and controls warpage better. I prefer the fabric method and will concentrate on it in this article.

Design

Tambours are a sophisticated door system, which must be an integrated element of a total design, not attempted as an afterthought. Every aspect of the piece should be planned out, from shape or form right through to details, because tolerances and clearances are very important considerations.

The initial concept should be developed through sketches and made final in accurate full-scale drawings. Mock-ups should be made where full-scale drawings do not supply enough information.

Precision is essential. The tongues must be of a shape and size that will slide smoothly in the grooves. The carcase must be glued up square with duplicate tracking grooves directly opposite each other. Design a form that you will be able to control accurately through the building stages. This is not to say that your piece must be a rectangle, but keep your first attempt fairly simple and small.

With vertical tambours, weight becomes important. A large tambour that opens from the bottom may be too heavy, and one that opens from the top may fall open under its own weight. If you plan to have a reverse curve in the track, you will have to cut a clearance angle on the sides of each slat.

One common problem with tamboured pieces is that warpage in the carcase will affect dimensions between the tracking grooves, usually at unsupported corners or over long expanses. Be sure your carcase is structurally sound. Internal parts can be designed to add rigidity to the carcase. Tamboured pieces often have a false back and sides, which conceal the fabric side of the tambour when it is opened and also prevent the contents of the cases from interfering with the travel of the doors. They may also support compartments, partitions, shelves or drawers. These parts have to be located to allow enough clearance for movement of the doors. I try to

Designer/craftsman Alphonse Mattia teaches woodworking at the Program in Artisanry in Massachusetts.

Left, author's writing cabinet, bubinga and figured maple. Above, detail of Richard Tannen's tall maple cabinet; fixed slats are filler strip.

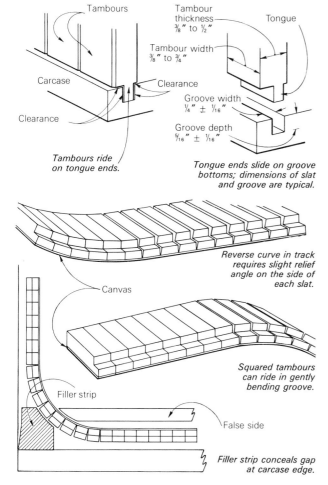

Tambours

Tambour thickness
⅜″ to ½″

Tongue

Tambour width
⅜″ to ¾″

Carcase

Clearance

Clearance

Groove width
¼″ ± ¹⁄₁₆″

Groove depth
⁵⁄₁₆″ ± ¹⁄₁₆″

Tambours ride on tongue ends.

Tongue ends slide on groove bottoms; dimensions of slat and groove are typical.

Reverse curve in track requires slight relief angle on the side of each slat.

Canvas

Squared tambours can ride in gently bending groove.

Filler strip

False side

Filler strip conceals gap at carcase edge.

provide as much clearance as possible to prevent later problems, such as rub marks on the tambour surface. The space where the tambour enters the carcase can be made to appear narrower by use of a filler strip or a thickened carcase edge.

Tambours are usually shouldered on the exposed side to conceal the carcase groove. The tambour can then be fitted to the groove at the tongue without distorting the shape of the tambour. Tracking grooves vary in width, depth and radius of curve. Generally speaking, tracking grooves range in width from ³⁄₁₆ in. to ⁵⁄₁₆ in. They may be smaller in delicate, silk-backed work, or larger in heavy applications. Grooves should be a little deeper than they are wide. A ³⁄₁₆-in. groove should be about ¼ in. deep; a ¼-in. groove should be ⁵⁄₁₆ in. deep.

Tambours for a ¼-in. groove might range from ⅜ in. to ¾ in. wide, and from ⅜ in. to ½ in. thick. The tambour width is the dimension parallel to the direction of the groove; the tambour thickness corresponds to the width of the groove. A rectangular tongue (wider than it is thick) will ensure steadier travel in the groove. For a narrow tambour, say ⁵⁄₁₆ in., I would probably switch to a ³⁄₁₆-in. groove for this reason.

The radius of the tracking grooves should be checked carefully to make sure that the tambour can travel the bend comfortably. This can be checked on paper. Draw the groove by using a compass to construct two parallel lines at the proper radius. Be sure that a paper rectangle the size of the tambour tongue will fit in the groove. This will tell you a lot, but is no substitute for routing a sample groove to the desired radius in a piece of scrap plywood and testing a glued-up sample of

your tambour. A 6-in. square of tambours can easily be made by cutting the appropriate tongues on one end of several short strips and gluing them to the fabric with Titebond. This should not take long and will be well worth the effort.

One last word about design—you should decide how you will attach the handle to your tambour, because the attaching strip may interfere with internal parts of the cabinet.

Making templates and routing grooves

A template, or pattern, for routing the tracking groove is needed to transfer the groove accurately from the drawing to both sides of the carcase. The easiest way to make grooves is to run a router against the template. It is best if a single template can be reversed for alternate sides of the carcase, so that slight inaccuracies in the curve will be duplicated.

Before you make the template, decide how it will guide the router. I usually use rub collars, which are available for most routers in a variety of sizes. Choose a size that has a convenient distance from rub surface to cutting edge. You will have to account for this distance when you construct your template. A ¼-in. bit with a ½-in. O.D. rub collar will give you a difference

Router and rub collars.

of ⅛ in. This means the template has to be ⅛ in. smaller than the inside line of the groove.

You could run the router directly off the edge of the router base, but this can be inconvenient. The router will be more difficult to handle and discrepancies in the template will be magnified because of the large distance from the base-plate edge to the groove.

Get the bit and collar before making the template. It is very annoying to construct a template for a ½-in. rub collar and then find out that the local hardware dealer has every size except ½ in. A new carbide bit will help make a clean, clear track.

Once you know the size of the rub collar, you can construct accurate template lines on the full-scale drawing. To parallel a curved line, set a compass to the distance that you want between the two lines. With the point on the original line, lay out a series of arcs from the line. Then construct a new line through the top points of the arcs by using a French curve, flexible drawing spline or bending sticks. Circular arcs can be drawn with a compass.

When you draw the template, consider reference points that you can use to orient the template on both sides of the carcase. The template can be laid out to conform to some fixed line or shape on the carcase, such as a bottom edge or corner where the groove does not pass. Templates can be clamped in place, or better yet, screwed down in two or more inconspicuous spots that can be filled later. Screwing the template down will save you the aggravation of having to move clamps during routing. These screw positions can also provide an ideal reference for locating the template on the sides. A template attached in this manner can be removed, cut down and relocated to pattern other grooves in the cabinet (unless you plan to make a duplicate cabinet, in which case you'll want to keep all the templates intact). For example, the same template could be used to flush-trim the outside shape of the

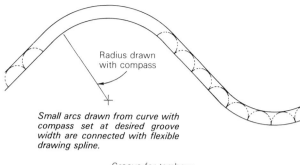

Radius drawn
with compass

Small arcs drawn from curve with
compass set at desired groove
width are connected with flexible
drawing spline.

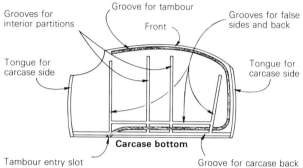

Grooves for
interior partitions

Groove for tambour

Front

Grooves for false
sides and back

Tongue for
carcase side

Tongue for
carcase side

Carcase bottom

Tambour entry slot

Groove for carcase back

*Template (above) guides grooves
for tambour. Internal cabinet
parts (left) add rigidity.*

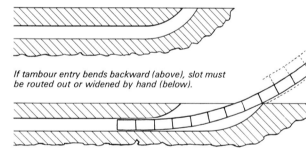

*If tambour entry bends backward (above), slot must
be routed out or widened by hand (below).*

carcase, then be removed, cut down and relocated to rout the tambour grooves, removed, recut and relocated to cut grooves for the false sides, back, shelves and other internal parts.

Template lines should be transferred from the full-scale drawing to the template with tracing paper. I glue the tracing to a piece of Masonite or Baltic birch plywood using spray adhesive or rubber cement. Fir plywood has too many voids that will cause problems when routing. Cut the template as accurately as you can, cutting on the waste side of the line. Lumps can be filed, but be sure you check the accuracy of the template against the full-scale drawing. If inaccurate, it's best to get a new piece of Masonite and start over.

Note that tambour entry slots can be part of the template, or hand-cut later if that is easier in your particular design. Remember that if the entry slot bends backwards, you have to cut a clearance angle on the tambour, or else widen the slot.

To familiarize yourself with the feel of running the router against the template, fasten the template to a piece of scrap

plywood and make a trial cut. The router cuts best when run against the direction of rotation. This may mean that on one side you will have to lower the router down into the wood to start the cut. This is awkward, but is better than trying to run with the rotation. I usually rout at full depth with a carbide bit. Most routers are slightly inaccurate, and two settings may make a tiny ledge in the groove that will cause later problems. Make sure the bit is fastened securely in the router. Some ½-in. routers do not hold ¼-in. shank bits snugly. It is common for a ¼-in. bit to slip in the collet. If this happens you will have to fill the grooves, reset the bit and rerout. Other routing mistakes can sometimes be repaired the same way. It may be necessary to widen the groove slightly at a tight radius, to aid tambour travel. This can be done by removing the template, filing the radius a tad, relocating and rerouting. Or the radius can be eased during sanding.

After the first groove is routed, orient the template on the other side. Double-check positioning and rout again. I sand grooves with little fitted sanding blocks. They should be sanded as smooth as possible without deforming them. Finish with a coat of thin shellac and polish with paste wax.

With the grooves complete, continue building the rest of the carcase. Prefinish the inside before assembly. Take precautions to ensure that no glue will run into the grooves or into areas with limited access, such as between a false side and the carcase side. Make sure that your cabinet is glued up square.

Machining the tambours

Tambour slats will be ripped longer than their finished size. Then they will be shaped, presanded and glued to a fabric backing. After gluing up, the tambour will be cut to its final length, and shoulders and tongues will be cut on the ends. Plan on making about one-third more tambours than you need. If you need 60, make 80 or 90. This will not require that much more time or material, and it is convenient to be able to discard chipped or warped tambours. Tambour stock should be sawn down to 3-in. to 5-in. widths, 1 in. or so longer than the finished length. Anything much wider will be difficult to resaw. Then resaw the sections about ³⁄₁₆ in. thicker than the finished thickness. (This depends on the length of the tambour—shorter tambours require less excess than longer ones.) These slats should be allowed to warp, at least overnight and preferably for several days. Then the slats should be dressed down to the finished thickness.

Now slats should be ripped to width. Rip a few to see if they are coming off the saw fairly straight. A little bit of warp can be tolerated in this dimension. A light jointer pass between each sawcut will help keep the tambours straight. If they are warping too much you will have to rip them oversized, allow them to warp again, dress them on the jointer and either thickness-plane or rip them to exact width. It is best to avoid running them over the jointer—this is dangerous with such small strips. If you must, make sure the jointer knives are sharp and use a push-stick. Now cut the strips to length, leaving ¼-in. to ½-in. excess at each end. Remember to account for the tongues.

When the tambours are cut to size, they should be stacked with stickers between them so they are exposed to air on all sides. Stickers should be of equal thickness and should be placed directly over each other just as when stacking lumber. I find it is better not to restrict movement and warpage. Later, before assembly, you can discard the worst tambours.

Tambours can be machine-shaped in many ways, but if you plan to do this there are a few things to remember. If they are completely rounded over on the top surfaces, you may have to cut the tongues ahead of time, because a rolled-over tambour might not sit flat on the glue-up board. Rounded tambours and most other shapes require presanding. Tambours that have a relief angle to travel in a back curve can also require presanding. On a first attempt keep shaping fairly simple, such as a simple chamfer or cove cut on the edges of the tambours to accentuate the individual strips.

To shape the tambours you will need a shaper or a router mounted in a table. Set the chamfer or cove bit to the proper height. Clamp a fence at the right distance. Clamp finger boards in place to hold the tambours tightly against the fence and table. Push each tambour through with the next one. Try not to pause when picking up the next one, as this can cause burn marks. Repeat on the second edge of each tambour.

If you have to cut a relief angle, make a jig that will hold the tambour securely as it is slid past the angled blade of the table saw. You need hardly any angle at all. Slide the tambours through once for the first side and again for the second.

If you are going to presand, make another jig to hold the tambour. A few minutes of work here will save a lot of time later. Rabbet a piece of wood to receive the tambour and hold the tambour in place with two small stop blocks. Tambours should be stacked again with stickers while you prepare a glue-up board.

Gluing up

You will need to make a board that will hold your tambours tightly together and flat and square while you glue the fabric onto the back. I use a piece of ¾-in. chipboard. It should be about 2 in. wider on each side and about 8 in. longer (2 in. at the back, and 6 in. at the front of the board) than the size of the tambour you are gluing up. Make sure you figure on enough tambours to recede into the carcase, so that you will not see the last slat when the door is closed.

Dress two pieces of wood about 1¼ in. to 1½ in. wide and as long as your glue-up board. Cut a rabbet in each piece that will receive the thickness of the tambour. The rabbet should be tight, so that when the strips are screwed down they will clamp the tambours firmly to the board. For the ends of the jig, make three thinner strips to fit under the rabbet. These should be the same length and thickness as the tambours, and about 1¼ in. to 1½ in. wide. Also make two or three pairs of opposing wedges the same thickness as the thinner strips. These will be used to clamp the tambours tightly together.

Screw the first rabbeted strip down to the particle board. Then screw down one of the thinner strips, checking with a framing square to be sure that it is 90° to the rabbeted strip. Put the tambours in place, face down, and screw down the other rabbeted strip. Once the strips are aligned, loosen the screws and remove the tambours.

Lay out the tambours on a flat surface, face up. Sort out the worst and arrange the remaining ones for color and grain pattern. You can tolerate a reasonable warpage between tambours, because it will be forced out by the clamping action of the glue-up board. Discard any tambours that arch severely away from the flat surface.

Slide tambours face down into the jig in the order you want. Keep in mind where the handle will be attached. Slide

Stickered tambours dry unrestrained; warped ones will be discarded.

Finger board holds tambour against fence, for shaping.

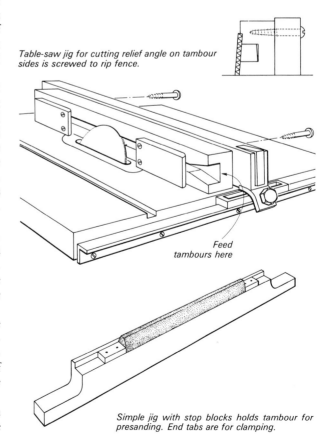

Table-saw jig for cutting relief angle on tambour sides is screwed to rip fence.

Feed
tambours here

Simple jig with stop blocks holds tambour for presanding. End tabs are for clamping.

Glue-up board

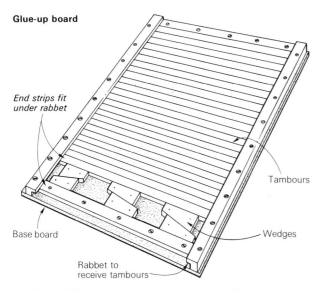

End strips fit under rabbet

Tambours

Base board

Wedges

Rabbet to receive tambours

Glue is brushed on a tambour section. Then a veneer hammer, working from center to edges, smoothes out the canvas.

After tambour is glued up, tongue shoulders are sawn (left), then waste is routed from front and back (above). Canvas flap is for attaching handles.

in one of the remaining thinner strips. Screw down the last strip about 2 in. behind the second strip, depending on the size of the wedges. Then tap the wedges into place to squeeze the tambours together tightly. You don't need any more pressure than is necessary to take out warps and close gaps, to prevent the glue from oozing down between the tambours. Screws in the rabbeted strips should be snug but not all the way home. While tightening the wedges to close gaps, you may need to tap the tambours down flat to the board with a scrap piece. Continue to tighten the screws in the rabbeted pieces and the wedges until the tambour is tight and flat. Then lock the wedges with a few brads.

An alternative method eliminates the third thinner strip and the wedges. Draw the whole tambour up tight with two or three bar clamps. Then screw down the second thin strip and remove the clamps. This works, but you must be careful not to deform the glue-up board with clamp pressure.

While silk, linen and leather can be used as a tambour backing, I prefer unprimed canvas. A good art-supply store will have a selection of canvas types and weights. Generally, 10-oz. canvas is best.

Now calculate the distance between the shoulders of the tambours. The tambours are still longer than final dimension and you want to be sure the canvas will clear the tongues. Remember, canvas stretches. Subtract about an additional ⅜ in. on each side. The canvas should be about 2 in. or 3 in. longer at one end than the tambour, for attaching the handle.

Now you are ready to start gluing. You can use Titebond or liquid hide glue, but I recommend hot animal glue for two reasons. Hot glue can be reheated with an iron, allowing you to correct minor problems. And, if used at the right consistency, it will not penetrate between the tambours. It should just begin to bead up as it runs off the mixing stick—like a thick syrup. You will need a veneer hammer or a suitable wooden alternative.

It is important to get a good bond on the first tambour. Be careful not to get glue on the adjacent thin strip of the glue-up board—wax or masking tape can be used as a glue resist. Spread the glue with a 1-in. or 2-in. brush over about a 4-in. section of the tambour. Start at the handle end. Move quickly—you do not want the glue to cool. Lay the canvas over the tambour, and remember to allow for the overhang for the handle. Be sure the canvas is straight and centered. Now, using the veneer hammer, work from the center toward the ends to even out the glue and smooth the canvas. You don't need a lot of pressure. Draw the hammer parallel to the tambours. If you draw the hammer perpendicular to the tambours you will stretch the canvas, causing the tambour to roll backwards when taken out of the glue board. Then the tambour will not lie flat. You are trying only to even out the glue, smooth the canvas and ensure a good spread of glue. Try not to overwork, or you will saturate the canvas with glue, causing it to become brittle when dry.

Working quickly, flip the canvas back over the area you have just done and pull the canvas back from the glue about ½ in. in a straight line. This will ensure a good overlap of glue. Spread another 4-in. section, lay the canvas back over the tambour and smooth out with the hammer. Repeat over the entire tambour. Don't wait for the glue to dry each time. You may be surprised at how easily the canvas pulls back from the glue. Don't worry—the bond will not be strong until the glue has completely dried and matured. Don't tug on

Making tongues

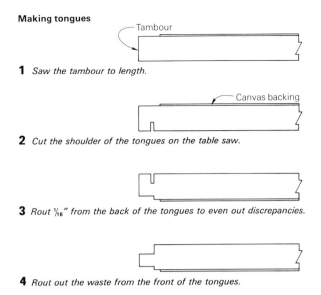

1 *Saw the tambour to length.*

Tambour

Canvas backing

2 *Cut the shoulder of the tongues on the table saw.*

3 *Rout* 1/16" *from the back of the tongues to even out discrepancies.*

4 *Rout out the waste from the front of the tongues.*

Making handles

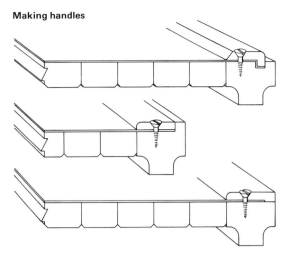

Handles, whatever the design, are usually attached with a backing strip that is screwed to the back, sandwiching the canvas. A lip conceals the canvas from view.

the canvas. Let the tambour dry overnight before you remove it from the glue-up board. Leave the tambour straight after you remove it—don't flex the joints yet.

Fitting tambours

All tambour measurements should be tested with an extra tambour strip and checked at intervals along the grooves in the carcase. It is common to have some variation in the distance between the grooves, so measure for a tight fit at the narrowest point. The tambours should run on the ends of the tongues, not on the shoulders, to avoid causing rub marks on the carcase. It is better to start with a tight tambour and to plane or sand it to a perfect fit.

First cut the tambour to exact length. Trim excess canvas from the back end and tape the handle flap out of the way before running the tambour through the table saw. To figure the length, measure the distance from the bottom of one groove to the bottom of the other groove at the narrowest part of the carcase. The tambour should be just shy of this dimension (about 1/32 in. shorter). Since you will want to center the canvas over the tambour, you will need to make two settings on the table saw, running the best edge against the fence in the first pass.

The tongues are formed by first sawing the shoulders, then routing out the excess wood above the tongues. This way, the router will not chip the exposed edges of the tambours. To make the shoulder cut, set the saw fence to the length of the tongue—much safer than running the whole tambour between the blade and the fence. Make sure the shoulder cut allows clearance between the tambour and the carcase. Finally, you'll need to remove 1/16 in. from the back of the tongue after the shoulder is cut, to even out discrepancies. Therefore set the height of the blade 1/16 in. lower than the thickness of the finished tongue.

After cutting the shoulders, I remove the excess wood with a shaper or router table setup. Set the fence a little short of the length of the tongue (the saw kerf from the shoulder cut is a safety zone) and use a straight cutter bigger than the length of the tongue. Set it just high enough to kiss off the back of the tambour—1/16 in. is plenty—and run both edges. Then raise the bit, flip the tambour over, and rout the front

side. Whole chips will fly off, so safety glasses are essential.

Now try the tambour. It probably won't fit. Try to figure out which dimension is off before going wild with the rabbet plane. Problems can be caused by too long a tambour, too thick a tongue, too little clearance at the radii, or shoulders that rub. A sharp rabbet plane, a crisp 90° sanding block and patience are necessary to fit the tambour. As you get close to the final fit, use finer sandpaper. When the tambour is running smoothly, polish with paste wax. You can also lubricate sparingly with paraffin, but too much will gum up the track.

Handles, finishing and stops

The tambour handle should be an integrated part of the total design, relating to other details on the piece. You want a handle you can grasp easily. One that is too narrow or extends out too far will be prone to binding. If you wish to install a lock or latch, you will have to design the handle with enough material to accommodate it.

Cut stock for the handle with tongues on the ends. This can be done by hand, with a dovetail saw. Try the handle in the groove to check the tongues. Then do all necessary shaping and sanding. The canvas should be trimmed slightly smaller than the width of the handle. I like to size the canvas end with a little Titebond to prevent unraveling.

Handles are usually attached with a strip of wood that is screwed to the back, sandwiching the canvas. I like to cut a slight lip on the edge of the attaching strip to conceal the canvas when the door is open. This lip is easier to cut before the strip is ripped off a larger piece of wood. Attach the handle to the tambour on a flat surface and make sure it is tight against the first tambour before you try to install it in the carcase. Once the holes are drilled you can remove the handle, install the tambour in the carcase and screw on the handle.

Apply finish before you install the tambour. Spread the tambours open, and use a dry brush or rag between them. Don't get finish on the fabric or you will shorten its life.

Plan on making a stop. The handle won't do because repeated use will weaken the canvas where the handle meets the tambour. A ripped canvas will mean a big repair job. Stops can be strips screwed or glued to the inside of the back of the carcase or small pieces screwed into the grooves. ☐

Automatic fall-flap supports

Where can I find slide supports that extend automatically for a slant-front desk or secretary?
—*Steve Zanki, Long Beach, Calif.*

I've seen this method (below) used on a number of pieces that I have repaired in my shop. I don't know of a supply source for these, but they can easily be made of sheet brass or steel, fastened with rivets. —*W.J. Given, Foley, Ala.*

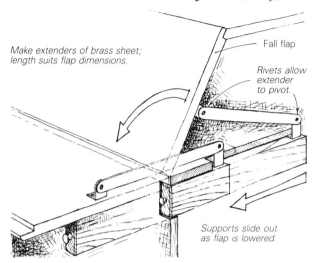

Make extenders of brass sheet; length suits flap dimensions.

Fall flap

Rivets allow extender to pivot.

Supports slide out as flap is lowered.

Durable table finish

I have constructed a dining-room table of walnut and walnut veneer over Novaply. It is good looking but won't stay that way if we keep using it. The linseed-oil finish cannot take hot and cold dishes or moisture. Is there a finish I can apply over the oil that will take everyday use? Or could I strip the oil and apply epoxy resin or some other clear matte plastic finish?
—*Roland H. Norton, Shalimar, Fla.*

The linseed should be removed completely before refinishing with a modern polyurethane varnish. To remove linseed oil, soak the wood with lacquer thinner and wipe off with a clean rag. Repeat several times, until the thinner has nothing more to dissolve, using a small, stiff brush to reach into corners.

The success of your refinishing depends on how clean the wood is. Scrub it down thoroughly with water and brown soap or laundry detergent. This may leave the grain slightly raised, so use 220-grit sandpaper or finer to make it smooth again, and brush off the dust.

The pores of the wood are still sheltering minute particles of the old finish. I wouldn't attempt any further cleaning; I would, rather, seal them in there. For sealer, use a well-diluted solution of your new finish, or use commercial shellac, orange for dark wood and white for light, diluted one part to four of alcohol. Let dry for 24 hours or more, sand through 120 and 150, and you are ready to apply new stain and finish—the wash coat of shellac won't interfere with either. —*George Frank*

[EDITOR'S NOTE: Labels on polyurethane varnish usually warn against applying over shellac, but manufacturers advise that this is because a thick coat of shellac under varnish is liable to chip readily, taking the varnish away with it. There will be no problem with most varnishes if the shellac coat is thin and sanded well.

However, some professional finishers report varnish peeling off in sheets when applied over shellac. This probably is most common with the "moisture curing" variety of polyurethane, which sets by chemical reaction with water vapor in the air and is very sensitive to impurities. The answer is to use a dilute solution of the varnish itself as a wash coat.]

Designing Tambours
Some considerations

by Mark Sfirri

I wanted to design a cabinet with a tamboured front. Since I often feel that traditional tambours read visually as a bundle of sticks, my goal was to design something more imaginative than a simple rounding or beveling over the length of the tambour.

There are two limitations: The backs of the tambours must be flat, and the width across their face must be uniform. These considerations ensure a smooth, clean travel as the tamboured door "disappears" into the cabinet.

I designed a tambour that gracefully bellies out two-thirds of the way down the length. When determining the curve of the tambour, it is important to draw a plan view of the cabinet showing the track of the tambour, false sides, actual sides and the cap piece. This drawing is needed so that allowances can be made in the carcase for the curve of the tambour. The cap piece will have to be shaped on the inside to accommodate the curve. Because of the curve, more space is needed between the track and the actual side. It is also a good idea to make several tambours and mock them up in the curve of the tracks, paying particular attention to any tight radii. It may be necessary to ease off the radius so that the tambours will not splay open as much.

To reproduce the desired shape precisely on each tambour, I made a flush trimming jig for the shaper out of three pieces of plywood. The bottom piece (3/4 inch) has the exact shape of the tambour bandsawed out. The middle piece (1/4 inch) is notched out so that a tambour will fit in snugly. The top piece (3/4 inch) serves as a clamping surface for two eye bolts. The eye bolts also act as handles for the jig. The bottom part of the jig rides against a ball-bearing guide and the cutter shapes the tambour.

Each tambour was individually shaped in the jig. I then laid them out and realized that they still looked like flat sticks. The only place where the shaping could be seen was where the tambours disappeared behind the cap piece.

At this point I decided to bevel the tambours to bring out the three-dimensional quality of the shaping, for esthetic reasons and also out of necessity. The track that the tambours run in has a reverse curve. If the tambours were not beveled, they would bind at the points where they belly out. The beveling can be done on the table saw but a more effective method is to set up the router with a straight bit on a router table and tilt the router to the desired angle. Using the router leaves a smoother surface which requires less sanding. After beveling, the already shaped tambours are narrowest where they belly out the most and wider at the ends, where they are thinner.

Next I glued the tambours to #10 canvas with animal hide

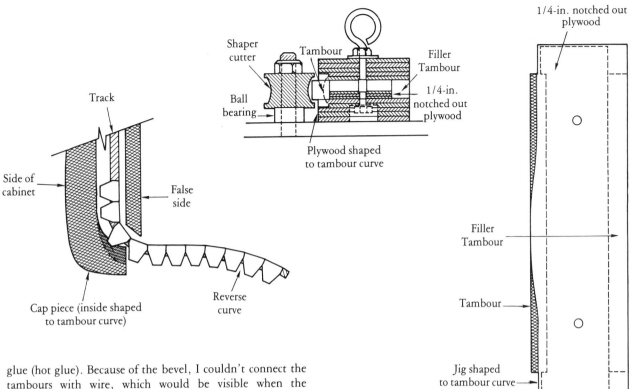

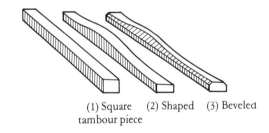

glue (hot glue). Because of the bevel, I couldn't connect the tambours with wire, which would be visible when the tambours went around the curve of the track. After I got the tambours assembled and working in the cabinet, I realized that canvas was visible between the tambours where they turned a tight radius. I stained the canvas black to make it less noticeable behind the dark walnut. Fortunately the animal hide glue also took the stain. Had I used some other type of adhesive, this might not have happened. If you plan to stain the canvas, be sure that the glue you are using will take the stain.

When the shaped tambours are together, the subtle contrast of form and shadow creates an intriguing visual effect. This effect is illustrated in the liquor cabinet I have designed and constructed.

(1) Square tambour piece   (2) Shaped   (3) Beveled

[AUTHOR'S NOTE: For readers interested in pursuing the subject of tambours further, I recommend *The Encyclopedia of Furniture Making* by Ernest Joyce (Sterling, 1979) as the best source of general information.]

Walnut liquor cabinet by the author is 58 inches wide, 34 high. Plan drawing (upper left) is necessary to determine carcase clearances needed for shaped tambours (above). Flush trimming jig for shaping tambours is at top center and right.

Original 'bureau du roi Louis XV,' 1760-69, was made by Oeben and Riesener. It is now on display at the Louvre in Paris.

Roll-Top Desks
How King Louis hid his clutter

by Alastair A. Stair

Writing desks, whether for business or household, need a larger work surface than one might otherwise desire in the room. They also need some means of rapid closure, whereby clutter and important papers may be concealed from snoops, protected from thieves, or merely swept out of sight when guests arrive. The usual solution, found on all manner of furniture since the 17th century, is a hinged flap that becomes a writing surface when open and a locked door concealing drawers and pigeonholes when closed.

The falling flap (often called "slant top") is direct and straightforward in construction, although a variety of ingenious means of supporting the opened flap have been devised. Its two disadvantages, if such they may be called, are that the working clutter must be cleared off the writing surface before the desk may be closed up, and that the flap is of necessity flat. Many designers would not consider this flatness a handi-

cap, but it apparently troubled the master cabinetmakers at the court of Louis XV of France (1715-1774).

Their answer, probably the creation of Jean-Francois Oeben (1720-1763), was the "secretaire a cylindre," the cylinder bureau or roll-top desk. Oeben's masterpiece was made for his patron, Louis XV, and quickly became known as "le bureau du roi," the king's desk. The French court at that time was the center of high fashion, and the desk with its broadly curved top receding into a slot above the pigeonholes was widely imitated.

The king's cabinetmaker and the king himself shared a passion for mechanical devices. Typical of Oeben's work are complicated locking devices and mechanisms that release or raise drawers by hidden processes. Louis XV devoted a considerable amount of time to his own workshop and hobby, the then-fashionable practice of ornamental lathe turning. He

From *Fine Woodworking* magazine (November 1978) 13:60-63

had one of the world's first elevators installed at Versailles in 1743, for the convenience of Mme. de Chateauroux. A little later, he commissioned "tables volantes" which, by rising and sinking through the floor, enabled him to entertain without the intrusion of servants.

Whether the cylinder desk was an original idea on the part of Oeben is difficult to answer. The earliest description of such a mechanism dates from about 1760, although something like it can be seen in an engraved design for wall decoration from about 1750. The source may have been Oeben's early experiments, or Oeben may have picked up the idea from elsewhere. In any case, Oeben's work is the first documented example of furniture of this type.

Begun in 1760, the desk took a full nine years to complete. Upon Oeben's death in 1763, Jean-Henri Riesener (1734-1806), his first journeyman or foreman, married Oeben's widow, carried on the workshop and completed the important work left by the master. (It was common in the 18th century for a cabinetmaker's widow to remarry in this way.) Oeben had left the desk in a fairly advanced stage of construction, with the working mechanisms completed. Riesener can be credited with the lavish pictorial marquetry of holly, boxwood, purpleheart and other exotics. He hired specialty craftsmen to complete the clock, Sevres porcelain plaques, gilt bronze sculptural figures and ormolu mounts that unite to make the desk a tour-de-force of French decoration. Its completion in turn established Riesener as a worthy successor to Oeben. His monogram has been found on several other spectacular cylinder desks now in prominent collections. One is at Buckingham palace, another is in the collection of the Duke of Bedford, and two are in the Rothschild collection at Waddesdon Manor.

Desks with fall flaps often had cupboards or drawers above the writing surface and were of architectural scale in a room. The early cylinder desks were often of a similar scale, matching the large writing tables inherited from the first half of the

century. But the fashion soon turned to smaller, less formal furniture, made for wealthy patrons who preferred the intimate life of the boudoir to the formal salons of an earlier generation. Cylinder desks were more suited to the smaller scale, and as they became smaller they also became daintier, more delicate in character.

There were exceptions to this trend, notable among them a large roll-top attributed to David Roentgen (1743-1807), master cabinetmaker to Louis XVI, which was made around 1785 for Catherine II of Russia. Roentgen, like Oeben, was famous for mechanical ingenuity, and his works are full of springs that release panels and uncover secret drawers.

By about 1780, the French fashion had taken hold elsewhere, aided no doubt by warfare throughout central Europe that deposited German artisans at all the royal courts. Many of the prominent cabinetmakers of Paris were German emigrants known for their skill at marquetry, who returned to the small German courts of the electoral princes when hostilities subsided, taking the latest fashions with them. The cylinder-fall writing table became popular in London about the same time, with a number of designs featured in such books as Thomas Shearer's *Cabinet Maker's London Book of Prices* (1788) and Thomas Sheraton's *Drawing Book* (1791-94) and *Cabinet Dictionary* (1803). Sheraton explains that the place of the familiar slant-top desk had been "amongst fashionable people" taken by a secretary or bureau with a roll-top or cylinder front. He uses the term "cylinder desk and bookcase" to describe an elegant, light piece mounted on tapering legs, with the drawers and pigeonholes enclosed by a tambour front and supporting a low case of shelves with square doors. A similar piece is illustrated by George Hepplewhite in the *Cabinet Maker and Upholsterer's Guide* (1788), where it is called a "tambour writing table and bookcase."

By the time the design reached Sheraton, the cylinder top had been connected via an iron trammel to the writing surface, which automatically slid out as the top was raised. Sher-

Three roll-top desks of diverse styles: Early tambour desk, above, c. 1760, is attributed to Jean-Francois Oeben. Note elaborate floral marquetry and gilt bronze decoration.

Small Sheraton roll-top desk, about 1790, is veneered in harewood and has china cabinet on top.

Roll-top, made by David Roentgen c.1780, has several hidden mechanisms and secret compartments. Woods include sycamore, burl walnut, tulipwood, satinwood, white mahogany, ebony and greenheart.

Extremely rare English cylinder bureau with bombé base in the French style, c. 1790, measures 46½ in. high, 34 in. wide, 22 in. deep closed and 32 in. deep open. A concealed mechanism links the writing surface to the cylinder, which opens when the writing surface is pulled out to reveal various compartments and pigeonholes.

aton s *Cabinet Maker and Upholsterer's Drawing Book* was the first to describe the mechanism. The plates in his drawing book show great fertility of imagination. Some show a low arched top containing small unenclosed drawers, while others retain open shelves with brass galleries and several are surmounted by china or book cupboards with glazed doors. Still others have extra writing slides that pull out from either side of the frame. These desks, lighter and simpler than their predecessors, often had tamboured roll-tops.

The original cylinder was a rigid quarter-round pivoting on a concealed bracket, usually guided by a tongue on the edge, which ran in a semicircular groove. It opened into a slot above the pigeonholes and disappeared behind them. Cylinders were usually made of two or more full-width staves of wood, edge-glued and planed to a circular arc, then veneered. Some were guided by a solid rail tongued across the ends of the boards, a more stable construction, while others had tongues worked directly on the boards themselves. Because it was rigid, the shape could only be an arc of a circle, sometimes a full quarter-circle, more often a sixth-circle, and as much space had to be left behind the cylinder as in front of it. This necessitated a bulky design, and also forced the pigeonholes or drawers to be foreshortened to fit the cramped space. Making a quarter-cylinder is basically the same as making barrels, and the cooper is the likely source of the technique.

It wasn't long before some cabinetmaker, probably in France, observed that the boards of the cylinder didn't have to be glued together into a rigid shape. They would still follow the curve, and other curves as well, if they were glued to a flexible backing. (See "Tambours," pages 72-77.) The usual tambour backing is stout canvas, although sometimes a strong wire is threaded through a hole in each tambour instead. The slats could be made very small (and would then follow a very tight curve), they could be molded into an interesting variety of profiles, or they could be left flat and veneered just as if they were solid, and the veneer subsequently slit. Tambours enjoyed great popularity in England (where they were often called reed tops) and gave rise to a welter of new designs.

When used to replace the cylinder fall, the tambour has the advantage of requiring little space at the back, for when opened it will drop behind the pigeonholes in a straight line. Tambours also can be fitted horizontally to cover an opening like shutters, replacing the usual doors. Tambours that slid

Bedside table, c. 1790.

sideways were found to be satisfactory on all manner of small pieces other than desks, where no great strength or security was required, including sewing cabinets, the lower cupboard of sideboards and bedside tables. When used on large pieces, however, tambours do have disadvantages: They are insecure, and they are liable to injury, often requiring repair. Both cylinder tops and reed tops in general have suffered the ravages of too-constant use over the centuries. Many French flat desks, according to one antique dealer, started life as cylinder

Lady's roll-top writing desk with cabinet on top was made in Baltimore c. 1800 and closely follows patterns given by Sheraton.

Sideboard, made in Baltimore c.1795, of mahogany with inlay and silver and glass panels. Tambour hides containers for tableware.

desks. They appear in today's shops with their tops removed.

One of the loveliest tambours in existence occurs on an American Federal mahogany sideboard, made in Baltimore c. 1795-1800. This elaborate Sheraton-style sideboard was ordered by David van Ness for his country house on the Hudson and is one of the most elaborate pieces of furniture executed in the United States. Its huge tambour structure conceals elaborately fitted containers for knives and forks.

Baltimore produced furniture that closely followed English precedents because it was settled almost entirely by the English and Irish. Its furniture was based primarily on pieces featured in Hepplewhite's *Guide* (1788) and Shearer's *Book of Prices*. Unknown in other areas of the United States was the highly individual style of lady's writing desk, derived from plates 44 and 47 of Sheraton's *Drawing Book* (1793). Such Baltimore desks were elaborately decorated and always had a folding top or a roll-top.

The cylinder form was also popular in the cabinetmaking centers of Massachusetts. In the Boston Museum of Fine Arts, there is a group of cylinder and tambour desks by John Seymour (c. 1738-1818), an English emigrant whose work owes much to the elegant styles of Sheraton and Hepplewhite. The Winterthur (Del.) Museum houses a group of cylinder desks from Baltimore, Salem, Pennsylvania and New York.

Because the revolving top was a great convenience for hurriedly hiding papers from indiscreet eyes, the appeal of the cylinder desk increased during America's Empire period (1815-1840). In the 1890s, manufacturing firms in Grand Rapids and elsewhere turned out roll-tops by the dozens, some of mammoth proportions constructed for the American businessman. During this "Golden Oak" period, Sears Roebuck catalogs contained ads for "curtain-top desks." These roll-tops had spring locks, with "all drawers locking automatically when the curtain top is pulled down." Such a desk, 5 feet wide, sold in 1897 for $20. And in the first two decades of this century, even Gustav Stickley, the father of the Arts and Crafts movement in America and a strict individualist in design who despised reliance on traditional forms, made concessions to public taste—he occasionally made roll-top desks for offices. □

Transplanted Englishman Alastair A. Stair deals in antique furniture in New York City.

Roll-top desk by Gustav Stickley, shown open and closed, was made in 1904 of quartersawn white oak and is typical of business furniture of the time. It is 46 in. high, 60 in. wide and 31 in. deep.

Shaped Tambours

by Bob March

Traditional tambours run on horizontal or vertical tracks and they can follow various curves. But they always have a flat back, which make it difficult to do a lot of shaping on the front. While it would be possible to make the tambour thicker, it could become so heavy that it couldn't be opened easily. This can be overcome with a system of concealed counterweights, which I considered for the desk shown here.

A counterweight didn't seem in keeping with the open nature of the desk I was making, so I decided to eliminate the flat backing. The tambour top is 48 in. wide, so I reduced the canvas to two 10-in. strips down the edges. Then, with conventional shaper jigs, I shaped the tambour slats in the center so they would curve back behind the plane of the canvas.

The first problem that arises when you shape a tambour this way is that it will not be able to go around a corner unless you also taper the portion that is behind the plane of the canvas. The amount of taper can be figured by drawing an end view. In this desk I decided to exaggerate the taper, so there would be open slits in the center portion of the tambour. I felt this would go well with the rest of the desk, which has many open slits in the end and across the back. The slats were tapered with the thicknesser. Then the tambour was hot-glued to the canvas with a veneer hammer.

The handle was attached with hot glue after the tambour was installed in the desk. It was designed with two gripping points, one at each end, which transmit the stress of opening and closing directly to the canvas strips. Its form also seemed to go well with the concave shape of the front.

The additional work this approach requires is well worth the increased shaping possibilities. On this desk the shaping was quite subtle, but the soft curve of the tambour, the top and the back slats made a significant difference. One could also exaggerate the shaping, possibly even making the individual slats from laminations. ☐

Bob March, a graduate of the R.I.T.'s School for American Craftsmen in Rochester, N.Y., teaches at the Worcester (Mass.) Craft Center.

Desk, of vermilion, is 58 in. by 26 in. by 46 in.

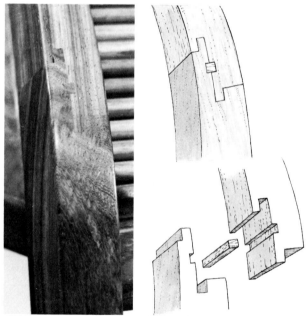

Chinese keyed splice shown in photo and drawings joins leg to desk.

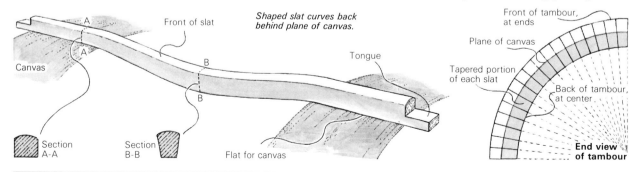

Plans for a Pigeonhole Desk
Design suggests the best woods

by Simon Watts

This folding desk is one of the more complicated pieces, in terms of joinery, made in my shop. The folding front flap is only to make the piece more compact and to give easy access to the drawers. It does not conceal the pigeonholes, as does a conventional roll-top or slant-top desk. I've made nine over the past 14 years, each one a little different from the last. The drawings and photos show the final version, and there are no more changes I want to make to this particular design. It has been made in teak, mahogany, cherry, walnut and padauk but not in any blond woods such as oak or ash.

The matter of choosing an appropriate wood for a particular design is difficult, but not as subjective as it appears to be. Leaving aside questions of cost and availability, there are certain criteria that always apply. Most obviously, the wood chosen has to have the right mechanical properties for its particular function—which may mean using more than one species in the same piece of furniture. Years ago chairs were commonly made out of three different woods: pine for the seat, since it could be easily carved; maple for the legs and rungs, which was ideal for turning; and oak for the back, because of its bending properties. One also needs to think of the suitability of the wood to the tools and construction techniques and the climate to which the finished piece will be exposed. For example, if there is to be a lot of hand-dovetailing, oak is a miserable material because its coarse grain makes it difficult to cut cleanly; if there is a lot of machining and you don't have carbide cutters, you should avoid teak; climates where there are great fluctuations in humidity demand a stable wood such as mahogany.

Stability, ease of working, durability, strength, hardness and resistance to decay—all these have to be considered, but often this still leaves considerable possibilities. Why is it that certain designs look better in one wood than another? Part of the answer lies in the color and texture of the wood. All woods have grain patterns, which range from the almost invisible, as in holly and ebony, to the inescapable, as in red oak. If you use an aggressively grained wood to make a piece like this desk, which is characterized by simplicity and careful proportions, the result is visually confusing. It may be striking and dramatic, but it is not anything a sensible person would want to live with. My general rule is, the smaller the surfaces and the finer the detailing, the more restrained the color and figure should be, but, like any rule, mine can be disregarded by the true genius with triumphant results.

Another point to consider is the hardware that will be used and how it will look. Certain combinations are more pleasing than others: polished brass with walnut or mahogany, wrought iron and oak, stainless steel and rosewood. Similarly, if more than one wood is used, it is important that they enhance each other and that both be subordinated to the overall design. A colleague of mine once made a small oval vanity table, the surface of which was veneered with alternating strips of ash and ebony. Superbly executed, the result was a visual nightmare; but a large table in ash, with a thin edging or inlay of ebony or rosewood, could be both striking and tasteful. If the contrast between the two materials is too subtle, there will be an irritating doubt as to whether, in fact, there is more than one wood and you will get what a teacher of mine called "the monotony of faint variation."

There is also the matter of tradition and historical precedent. A furniture-maker is not bound by these considerations but should be aware of them. This desk has some close relatives in the past at a time when walnut and mahogany were much in vogue, and this may explain why these two woods are my favorites for this particular design.

Some of my customers would want to select a wood not because it was appropriate for the design but because their living room was mostly cherry or oak and they thought that any additional furniture should be in the same wood. My argument is that it is not matching the wood and finish that makes two pieces of furniture good neighbors, but the less easily defined qualities of scale, simplicity and proportion.

Construction — This is a difficult piece of furniture to make, and I urge anyone who is not familiar with a specific technique to try it out first on scrap wood and avoid the frustration of spoiling good material. For example, if you have not made a haunched tenon before, make one, and if necessary, go on making it until you can do it with confidence. It is also prudent, when making a number of identical parts, to make up one or two extras—five legs instead of four, for example. Then, if you make a mistake on one piece, you won't have to repeat each step in its production. The extra piece, if not needed, can be kept as a pattern for future projects.

The time required to construct this piece will vary according to your experience and whether a planer or other machines are available. I would expect to spend about 120 hours in a well-equipped shop. At the end of this article I will discuss how to make up a materials list so that you can estimate the cost and order the right amount of lumber.

Assuming you have a pile of rough lumber, and the plans for this desk, a general cutting procedure would go as follows: Select the best boards for their width, figure, straightness and color. These will be used for the carcase and writing surface. Cut an inch off one end and examine it for checks. If it is clean mark off the length you want and add at least an inch, before cutting. Run the board, concave side down, over a jointer (or hand-plane it) until you have one flat surface.

Putting this flat surface *down*, run it through a thickness planer. Examine it after the first pass and, if it is chipping up, turn it end for end, still keeping the flat surface down. If you're going to glue up, plane to ⅛ in. oversize and, if your planer is wide enough, plane the whole assembly to the final thickness. Otherwise, plane to finished thickness, turning it

Desk of mahogany with rosewood pulls and oak understructure (42½ in. by 28⅞ in. by 42 in.) is a subtle blend of good design, careful choice of woods and hardware and fine joinery. Construction drawings are on pages 88 and 89.

end over end after each pass to avoid moisture imbalance that can cause cupping and to maintain grain direction through the knives.

Next, joint (or plane) the best edge and saw the board to width, allowing ⅛ in. to ¼ in. for cleaning up. With a knife, mark the ends to the exact length and cut off the waste.

The 10½-in. top should be one piece, but unless 18-in. boards are available the side pieces will have to be joined up, then dovetailed into the top, using a half pin at the corners as shown in the scale drawings on pages 88 and 89. The front and back rails can be either one piece or laminated. They should be lap-dovetailed into the sides as shown. This whole assembly is called the carcase. Now rout the ¼-in. groove for the back panel around the inside of the back of the carcase, taking care to stop the groove in the side pieces so that it does not show from the top. The back panel can then be joined up and planed to its finished thickness of ⅜ in.

The grain of a rectangular panel should parallel the rectangles's long axis, to minimize seasonal change. If your wood is *recently* kiln-dried, you should allow between $\frac{1}{32}$ in. and ⅜ in. per foot for expansion, or from ¼ in. to ½ in. for a 16-in. panel. The exact amount depends on the species. Teak and mahogany are at the lower end of the scale, beech and oak at the upper. There is practically no movement along the length of the panel, so it can be fitted quite snugly. With a plane, feather the panel to fit the groove after rough-cutting it to the approximate bevel on the table saw.

To make the understructure, tenon the five drawer supports into the front and back rails, but glue into only the

front rail to accommodate seasonal changes in the carcase. Rout or saw a ¾-in. groove ⅜ in. deep in each side to hold the stationary piece of the desk top. Stop these grooves when they meet the back-panel groove, or they will show from the back. After sanding the inside surfaces, glue up the carcase and flush the dovetails off with a sharp plane.

I use Titebond (aliphatic resin) glue and plastic-resin glue such as Weldwood. Titebond sets up quickly (one to two hours) thus freeing up clamps and speeding the work. However, it has a short assembly time (five minutes or less), cannot be easily sanded off and deteriorates in ultraviolet light. It is subject to creep under stress and should not be used for heavy, bent laminations. Plastic resin permits longer assembly time (10 to 20 minutes), but takes at least six hours to set up at 70°F. Unlike Titebond, it is practically waterproof.

In general, I use resin glue for dovetails and any complicated joint requiring long assembly time and for joints exposed to sun and water. I use Titebond for small laminations and for simple joints that will not be heavily stressed.

It is convenient to make up the base now, to have something on which to set the carcase. The legs should be of the straightest stock you can find, for strength and for appearance. Rough-cut the taper on the band saw or table saw (don't use the jointer) and then clean it up with a plane. I like to plane the legs slightly convex, otherwise perspective makes them appear hollow. A haunched tenon attaches the legs to the aprons. The aprons are rounded on the underside and also have a slight curve—an important detail because it helps to keep the desk from looking too severe. After cutting the groove for the tabletop fasteners or buttons (see pages 41-42 for description and photo), you can glue up the base. Do this in two stages: two pairs of legs first, and then the whole assembly. Check with a tape to make sure the legs are parallel, as shown in the drawing. (They should actually toe out very slightly because perspective makes two verticals, when seen from above, appear to converge.)

Next select the stock for the writing surface, join it up and plane it to fit the ¾-in. groove. The stationary piece can be joined up out of ordinary stock but the front flap, like a table leaf, is not restrained by any structure or frame and should therefore be of vertical-grain stock and preferably one piece. Cut the stationary piece to size and slide it into the carcase until it stops against the sides. It should overhang the front by ½ in. and is kept in place by a single, long wood screw counterbored on each side. But don't fasten it yet; the top must be off to fit the slides and drawers—the next steps.

The slides that support the flap can be of maple or oak, faced with the same wood as the carcase. These facings are offset to act as stops when the slides are pushed all the way in, ½ in. short of the back panel; too close and carcase shrinkage would cause them to project. Attach the facing to the slides with plywood splines as shown in the drawing. Stop the slides in their extended position by putting a peg in the stationary part and a slot in the underside of the slide; the length of this slot determines how far out the slide will travel.

Now set the slides in place and measure the horizontal dis-tance between them, subtracting 2½ in. for the five ½-in. dividers. Divide the remainder by four to get the exact width of each drawer. To avoid the difficulty of making drawers to fit precisely an existing opening, make the drawers first in the usual way (through dovetails at all four corners) and then fit them as follows: Cut some pieces of 3x5 index card. Place the slides, all the drawers and as many of the dividers as will fit. Then slip a piece of card into each gap, at the front and back. Remove, plane and test-fit the dividers until the assembly fits without forcing. Then clamp the dividers and screw them from the underside. (The drawer fronts, which will overhang the drawers, will be stopped against the front edge of the dividers, so not only must they be spaced accurately, but their front edges must be aligned.) When you remove the cards, the drawers will have the right clearance. Now cut out the false fronts and screw them to the drawers from the inside—don't use glue. Make these fronts slightly oversize so they can be trimmed to fit the openings and each other. I like to make the drawer fronts and the slide facings out of the same piece of wood, to give a consistent grain pattern.

The drawer fronts look better set back between 1/16 in. and 1/8 in. from the carcase front. To do this, block them out with one or two pieces of index card, plane or scrape them all off flush with the carcase and remove the card.

Turn the knobs or pulls out of a wood that contrasts with the carcase without being too extreme. For example, a walnut or cherry desk with rosewood pulls looks good, but ebony pulls on a maple desk draw one's attention, detracting from the overall appearance. If no lathe is available, you can carve pulls or substitute small brass knobs.

Cut the front flap as shown in the drawing and attach it to the stationary part using brass hinges, which have to be scribed and set into the writing surface. Rectangular hinges are easier to fit than the ones with semicircular ends. I strongly advise a trial fitting on a piece of scrap before cutting into the desk top.

The final step is to make the pigeonhole unit and fit it into the carcase. Dovetail the outside box together out of ½-in. stock and rout slots for the dividers. Cut a shoulder in the front edges of the dividers to cover the rounded end of the slot left by the router bit. Then slide them in from the back, gluing only the long, vertical ones. The small drawers are best lap-dovetailed but a simple rabbet joint, glued and nailed with panel pins, could be substituted.

Plane the sides of the pigeonhole unit to a slight taper so they fit snugly in the carcase. Then secure the whole assembly with four brass or wood pins as shown. You could make knobs for the small drawers from the same brass rod. All finishing should be done before the unit is fastened in place.

I usually finish with Watco, a synthetic oil that polymerizes on exposure to the air. I apply it at 24-hour intervals until the wood will absorb no more, wet-sanding with the grain, using 600-grit waterproof sandpaper for the final application. If this process is repeated every six months or so, an attractive patina develops. There is no need to oil the understructure because movement within and around it has been allowed in the construction. Wherever wood is sliding on wood I use a good-quality paste wax. This makes for a smooth action and reduces wear. The insides of the drawers are best waxed, too. It makes them easier to keep clean. ☐

Figuring your materials

When buying lumber wholesale, in quantity, you cannot specify the exact widths and lengths of the boards you want, nor, generally speaking, can you pick them out. Consequently you have to order more than you need—but at a lower price. Buying retail by the board is considerably more expensive, but you have less left over.

If you choose to make this desk in *Afzelia*, or some other exotic wood you don't plan to use again, then buying retail makes sense. If you decide to use a more common wood, such as walnut or cherry, which will be used for other projects, then you should buy wholesale at a better price and have the additional advantage of being able to select boards for their figure and color.

You figure the amount of lumber required by making a complete bill of materials. I follow the format given in the example below:

	Size (in.)	Area (sq. in.)	Area (sq. ft.)	No.	Total (sq. ft.)	Total (bd. ft.)
4/4 stock, walnut						
Aprons	2½ x 40	100	0.69	2	1.39	1.53
Drawer fronts	3¼ x 42	137	0.95	1	0.95	1.05
8/4 stock, walnut						
Legs	26 x 2 x 2	104	0.72	4	2.88	3.17

The last column is arrived at by multiplying the total in square feet by 1.1. You do this because when you buy a board foot, its actual size is 12 in. long by 11¼ in. wide; it shrinks that much across the grain from its cut-green width of 12 in. If you need 141 sq. ft., say, you will have to buy 141 x 12/11 (or approximately 1.1) = 155 bd. ft. A materials table like this one should be made for each different kind of wood and for each thickness. You must also allow for waste. If you buy FAS (first and seconds select), 20% is a commonly accepted figure. A lower grade will mean more waste. In addition to hardwood, you will need ⅛-in. plywood for drawer bottoms. You will also need tabletop fasteners (unless you make your own buttons), three brass hinges and some small pieces of hardwood for the knobs. *S.W.*

Simon Watts makes furniture in Putney, Vt.

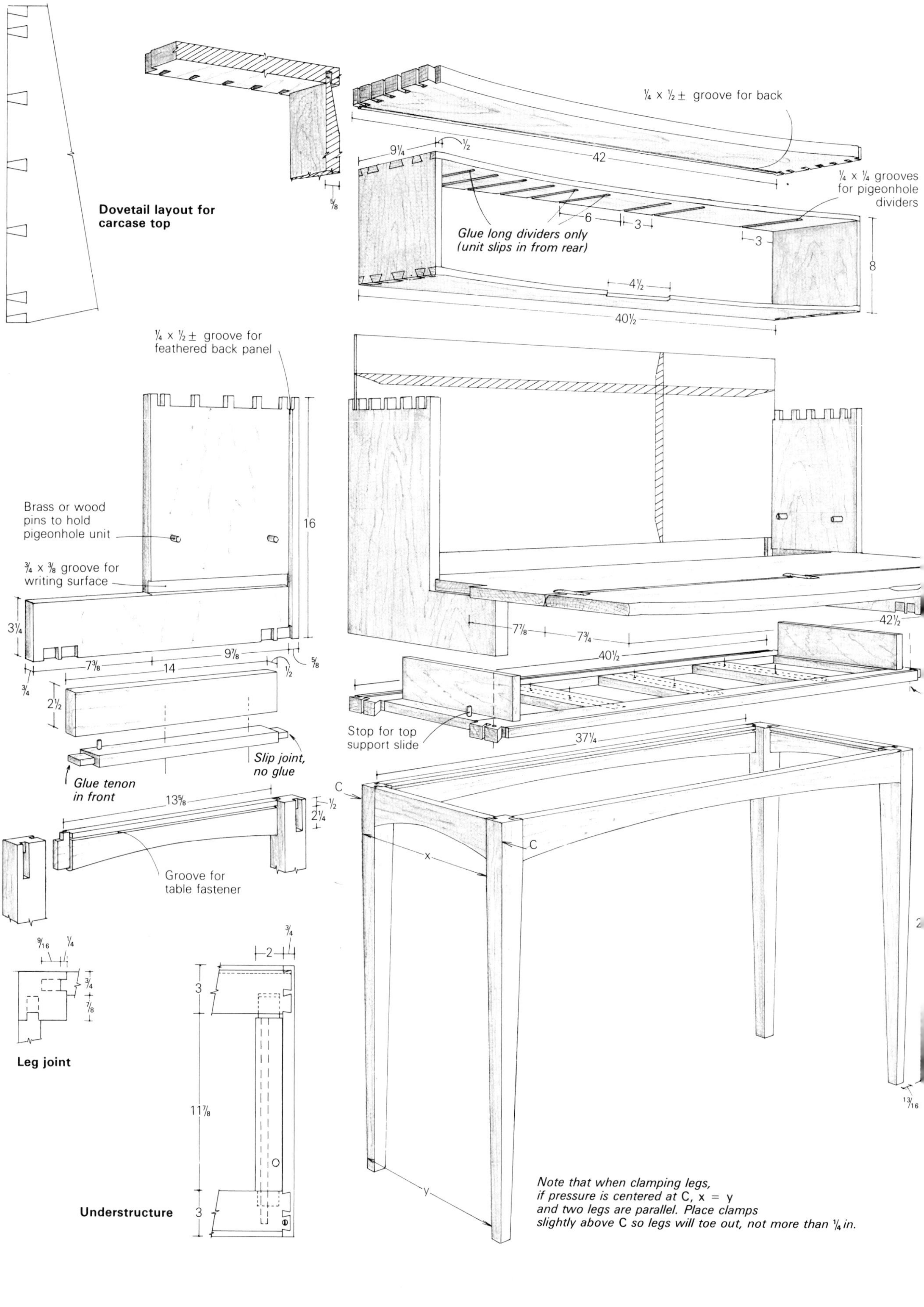

Dovetail layout for carcase top
5/8
1/4 x 1/2 ± groove for back
9 1/4
1/2
42
1/4 x 1/4 grooves for pigeonhole dividers
6
3
3
Glue long dividers only (unit slips in from rear)
8
4 1/2
40 1/2
1/4 x 1/2 ± groove for feathered back panel
Brass or wood pins to hold pigeonhole unit
16
3/4 x 3/8 groove for writing surface
3 1/4
7 3/8
14
9 7/8
1/2
5/8
3/4
2 1/2
Glue tenon in front
Slip joint, no glue
13 5/8
1/2
2 1/4
Groove for table fastener
7 7/8
7 3/4
42 1/2
40 1/2
Stop for top support slide
37 1/4
C
C
x
y
13/16
9/16
1/4
3/4
7/8
Leg joint
3/4
2
3
11 7/8
3
Understructure

Note that when clamping legs, if pressure is centered at C, x = y and two legs are parallel. Place clamps slightly above C so legs will toe out, not more than 1/4 in.

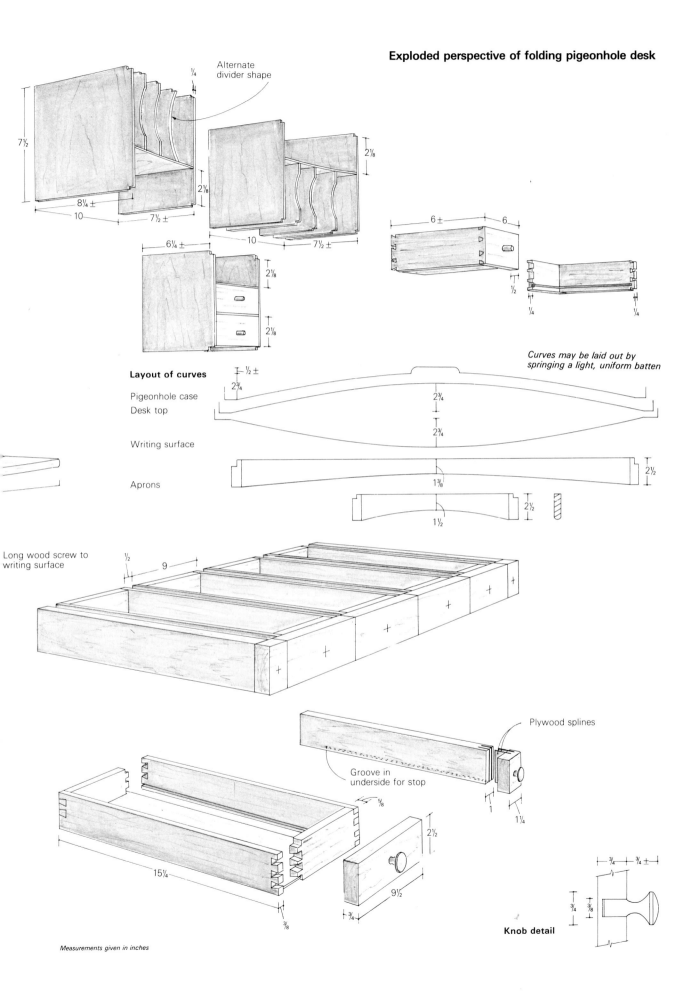

Exploded perspective of folding pigeonhole desk

1/4

Alternate
divider shape

7½

8¼ ±

10

7½ ±

2⅛

2⅛

2⅛

10

7½ ±

6¼ ±

2⅛

2⅛

6 ±

6

½

¼

¼

Curves may be laid out by
springing a light, uniform batten

Layout of curves

Pigeonhole case
Desk top

½ ±

2¾

2¾

Writing surface

2¾

Aprons

1⅜

2½

1½

2½

Long wood screw to
writing surface

½

9

Plywood splines

Groove in
underside for stop

5⅛

1

1¼

15¼

3/8

2½

9½

3/4

3/4

3/4 ±

3/4

3/8

3/4

Knob detail

Measurements given in inches

Tambour tips

The magic of tambours—"doors" that can follow curves horizontally or vertically, that can disappear partly or completely—has long challenged woodworkers. Alphonse Mattia (see pages 72-77), Mark Sfirri (pages 78-79), and Bob March (page 84) provide a variety of styles and applications; their articles prompted readers to respond with their own variations and helpful tips.

Beveling jig for tambours

The use of a jig provides a simple means of cutting the bevels on slats for tambour doors. Make a jig of ³⁄₄-in. plywood or particleboard wide enough to handle a number of slats and a few inches longer than the longest slats. The jig consists of grooves on both sides as shown in the drawing. Cut the grooves with a dado head on the tablesaw. The grooves on one side should match the desired bevel angle on the slat. The grooves on the other side should be twice the bevel angle. The jig illustrated makes a slat with a 10° bevel on each side.

To use the jig, first place the slats in the grooves that have the shallower angle. Then run the setup through a thickness planer. Make sure to run all your slats through before adjusting the planer for additional cuts.

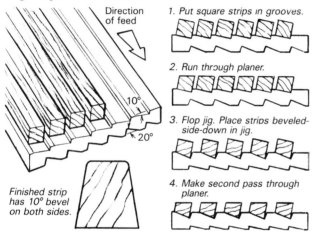

Direction of feed

1. Put square strips in grooves.

2. Run through planer.

3. Flop jig. Place strips beveled-side-down in jig.

4. Make second pass through planer.

10°
20°

Finished strip has 10° bevel on both sides.

After finishing the first bevel, turn the jig over and place the slats in the deeper angled grooves, with the uncut edge up. Again run the jig, slats up, through the planer.

This process provides a smooth bevel cut with the same degree of angle on each side of the slat. The main advantage of this process over using a tablesaw is the smoothness of the cut. Upon completing the bevel cuts, add small rounds to the two exposed edges of the slat with a shaper or a router table.   —David M. Lynch, Janesville, Wisc.

Doweled tambour slats

In 1967 I made a hi-fi cabinet out of walnut wood. Due to space limitations I could not use sliding or swinging doors, so I decided on tambour doors. Each slat was ½-in. walnut, 9¾ in. by 1½ in., with each outer side slightly beveled. I used a ¼-in. dowel at each end of each slat; thus the curve was made with a much shorter radius than using the tongue in the groove would have allowed.
—Leonard K. Pfiffner, Riverside, Conn.

Dyeing tambour canvas

In many articles on roll-top or tambour-top desks, white (un-primed) canvas is suggested for fastening the tambour slats together. This white canvas shows through even the slightest opening between the slats, especially if the wooden slats are

stained a dark color. To eliminate this problem, I first dye the canvas black, iron it and then apply it with glue to the unfinished backs of the stained and varnished tambours. Staining and varnishing must be finished before gluing because the slats stick together if they are finished after gluing up.
—Charles L. Robers, Waukesha, Wisc.

Pre-shrinking canvas

In making tambours, make sure you wash and dry the canvas before gluing to pre-shrink it. If you don't, the water in certain glues will shrink it for you.
—A. Smith, Sudbury, Mass.

Ball-joint tambours

In his discourse on tambours (pages 72-77) Alphonse Mattia comments that the thin wooden slats are either glued to a fabric backing or threaded together with wires. However, I can remember a huge oak roll-top desk in my grandparents' attic that had jointed tambours that were a variation of a hinged joint. To the best of my recollection, the tambours were jointed as illustrated in the accompanying sketch. I don't recall how the tambours tracked in the groove, but tongues and dowels are both possibilities, using the dimensions and clearances recommended by Mattia.

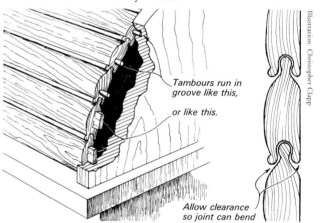

Tambours run in groove like this,

or like this.

Allow clearance so joint can bend

Illustration: Christopher Clapp

The female part of a joint such as this is cut in two operations. First, a groove is cut either on a tablesaw or with a straight router bit. Next, a ballnose router bit is run through the groove. The groove must be wide enough to allow the shank to pass through without binding. The ballnose cannot be withdrawn vertically once the cut is started—it must be run through from one end of the groove to the other. The bit can be backed out of the groove in order to clean out chips if they accumulate.   —John R. Beck, DeKalb, Ill.

Tambour clamp

Considering the small degree of difficulty involved in making tambours, they can add immensely to the attractiveness of a piece. A friend showed me a method of clamping that certainly saves headaches. When the slats are ready for gluing to a canvas back, place them face down and close together. Spread just enough glue on the canvas (yellow glue works fine) to cover the first four or five slats. Lay the canvas over the slats, and with a hot iron, iron the back of the canvas; this sets the glue and you're ready to continue. Spreading the glue on the canvas helps prevent seepage between the slats.
—Michael Turi, Eureka, Calif.

Source for oak tambours

Constantine's, 2050 Eastchester Road, Bronx, N.Y. 10461.

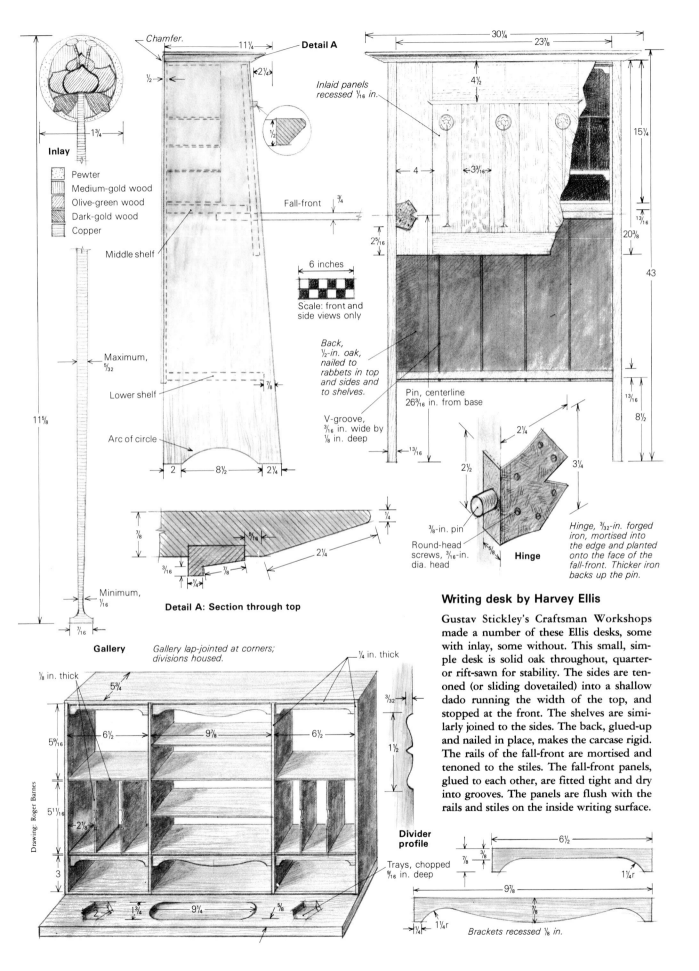

Inlay

Pewter
Medium-gold wood
Olive-green wood
Dark-gold wood
Copper

Middle shelf

Maximum, 5/32

Lower shelf

Arc of circle

Minimum, 1/16

Gallery

Detail A

Chamfer.

Fall-front

Detail A: Section through top

6 inches

Scale: front and side views only

Inlaid panels recessed 1/16 in.

Back, 1/2-in. oak, nailed to rabbets in top and sides and to shelves.

V-groove, 3/16 in. wide by 1/8 in. deep

Pin, centerline 26 3/16 in. from base

3/8-in. pin

Round-head screws, 3/16-in. dia. head

Hinge

Hinge, 3/32-in. forged iron, mortised into the edge and planted onto the face of the fall-front. Thicker iron backs up the pin.

Writing desk by Harvey Ellis

Gustav Stickley's Craftsman Workshops made a number of these Ellis desks, some with inlay, some without. This small, simple desk is solid oak throughout, quarter- or rift-sawn for stability. The sides are tenoned (or sliding dovetailed) into a shallow dado running the width of the top, and stopped at the front. The shelves are similarly joined to the sides. The back, glued-up and nailed in place, makes the carcase rigid. The rails of the fall-front are mortised and tenoned to the stiles. The fall-front panels, glued to each other, are fitted tight and dry into grooves. The panels are flush with the rails and stiles on the inside writing surface.

Gallery lap-jointed at corners; divisions housed.

1/8 in. thick

1/4 in. thick

Trays, chopped 9/16 in. deep

Divider profile

Brackets recessed 1/8 in.

Drawing: Roger Barnes

Mechanical Desks
There's more than meets the eye

by Alastair A. Stair

The eighteenth century was the most vigorous period of letter writing in human history, not only as literary invention for use by published authors, but as a fine art and general pastime for personal pleasure. As such, it took on the aspect of an elaborate ritual, inspiring its own accessories and methods of dispatch. It provided a theme of interest for painters, and most importantly, it stimulated the contemporary cabinetmaker to create all manner of intricately designed writing chairs, desks and writing tables. The English cabinetmaker, in particular, proved himself worthy of the challenge posed by a large clientele of literary ladies and gentlemen throughout the century by supplying bureaux, "scritoires," and different sorts of chests, bookcases, cabinets, wardrobes and tables of all descriptions fitted with writing slides and secretaire drawers. It is toward the middle of the eighteenth century, however, when the demand arose for specialized forms to meet the needs of artists, architects and draftsmen, that the ingenuity of the English cabinetmaker becomes truly admirable. Fully developed desks and tables were introduced that relied upon inventive me-

Estate desk top and till can be raised by crank inserted in holes in upper drawer fronts. Closed desk is shown above.

From *Fine Woodworking* magazine (Spring 1976) 2:33-36

chanisms to delight the contemporary client, and which continue to astonish today.

There is ample evidence in the pieces themselves and in the copious notes in such design books as Chippendale's *Director* and Sheraton's *Drawing Book* that considerable attention and care were given to the equipment and refinements of library writing tables and desks. Designed for prominent locations, these pieces were rectangular or kidney-shaped, usually of open pedestal form, or were designed with recessed central cupboards; they were also made with drawers or cupboards at both front and back, and these are termed "partners" desks. Ingenuity was shown in the disposition of numerous drawers, partitioned cupboards for folio volumes and rising tops which, when adjusted by a ratchet and removable bar, were able to receive large prints, estate maps and folios.

Sheraton also offered a design for an oval library table with rising reading stands fitted in the end drawers, explaining it was "intended for a gentleman to write on, or to stand or sit to read at." In 1766 John Bradburn supplied the Queen with "an extraordinary neat mahogany Library Table." It had 12 drawers, four cupboards, four rising desks for reading and writing, with invisible spring locks in the top.

One of the most remarkable of the pedestal desks is the great estate desk in which the complete top rises to any height by means of a mechanical crank, along with a hidden till with a series of drawers and compartments that when let down is level with the rest of the top. In this way the desk can be used in a seated or a standing position and can meet any demand the user makes of it, with much space for storage of papers and other materials.

Another form with a mechanically rising top is the "Harlequin Pembroke Table" that appears in Sheraton's

Drawing Book. Many variations on this theme were made in the London workshops of the eighteenth and early nineteenth centuries, as seen for example in one compact piece, probably by Shearer, in which the flaps fold out on hinges, containing various compartments hidden by lids. The back draws up when a spring is released to reveal a series of drawers and pigeonholes. The bottom holds a cupboard enclosed by a tambour. The entire piece is an exercise in space-saving technique and provides the maximum convenience for the writer in a small space.

Another mechanical form, lighter and more readily portable and convenient than the ponderous mechanical pedestal

Architect's tables were made in various shapes and styles. Some had a double ratchet arrangement to give greater height and permit work standing up (below), while others had only a single

ratchet. Slide-out front revealed another writing surface (sometimes also ratcheted) plus storage. Book rest sometimes retracted or reversed to give a flush appearance.

Ratchets

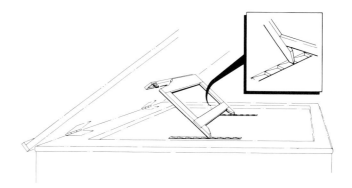

Single ratchet arrangement used in architect's tables folds out of the way when table top is down. Double ratchet below gives greater height. Raising the top also reveals a series of compartments in the table illustrated.

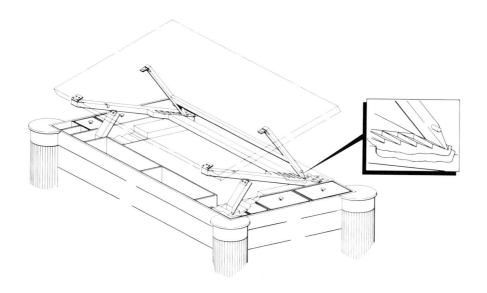

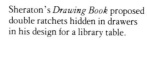

Sheraton's *Drawing Book* proposed double ratchets hidden in drawers in his design for a library table.

Double ratchet "gout stool" uses a reverse arrangement with the hinges and ratchets which means that if applied to architect's table, top would tend to come forward as it's raised.

desks is the so-called ''architect's table,'' well represented in contemporary trade catalogues and ideally suited to the needs of architects, painters and draftsmen. The painter Nathaniel Dance considered the table so desirable that he persuaded John Cobb, the cabinetmaker who purportedly brought such tables into fashion, to allow him to paint his portrait in exchange for one.

In this specialized form the area of the top is considerably increased by a pull-out front supported on the front sections of two straight legs. The front contains a well with numerous small compartments and a writing slide that lifts or pushes back. Often small drawers swing out from the sides for drawing materials. Some were solid with drawers to the floor.

These tables had rising tops which could be fixed at different heights by means of racks, stays, ratchets and struts, ''so healthy for those who stand to write, read or draw,'' and were often fitted with candle brackets and a lock. A number of these tables were mounted on a pillar with tripod feet. William France supplied one of this type for Lord Mansfield's library in 1770 (now in the Victoria and Albert Museum) and described it as ''a large Mahogany Reading Stand on a Stout Pillar and Claw, with a screw nutt, work'd very true capable of screwing to rise 10 ins if required.''

It is desks and writing tables such as these that reflect the mechanical genius of the eighteenth-century English cabinet-maker. ☐

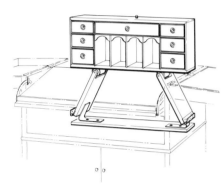

Harlequin Pembroke table pulls out all stops with tambour doors, drawers, drop front with ratcheted writing surface, fold-out top also used for storage, and a disappearing till made in the form of a box that rises when latch is released. Spring and roller arrangement raises the till.

Q & A

Felt writing surface

I need to replace the felt writing surface on an antique desk. What materials should I use and how should I prepare the surface? —Robert J. Atwell, Columbus, Ohio

Felt, sold in fabric or department stores, is made in a variety of weights and thicknesses. The felt I'd recommend for recovering the writing surface on your desk is the heaviest generally available—about 70% wool and 30% rayon. In the old days, felt was applied with hot animal glue, but unless its consistency is just right, hot glue can bleed through and discolor the felt. Instead, I recommend one of the tacky fabric glues sold by fabric stores. I've had good results with Aleene's Original Tacky All-Purpose Glue (made by Artis, Inc., Box 407, Solvang, Calif. 93463).

Remove all the old felt and scrape off the old glue with a properly sharpened and burnished hand scraper. Sandpaper the surface thoroughly, then apply masking tape to any adjacent wood to protect it from the glue. If the new felt is wrinkled, smooth it out with a steam iron before cutting it to size.

Brush the glue over the wooden surface, but don't apply any to the felt. Lay down the felt and apply pressure with a veneer roller. Where feasible, clamp a flat board over the felt to press it firmly against the glued surface until the glue has dried. —*Franklin H. Gottschall*

Small-Scale Cabinetmaking
With measured drawings for a roll-top desk

by James H. Dorsett

Four years ago I built a scale model of the Stanley-Whitman house in Farmington, Conn. It's a post-and-beam structure with a framed overhang, built in 1660. While I could have built a believable model using the plywood shell that is standard in miniature house construction, I chose instead to research and to replicate the framing of the original—stick by stick, joint by joint, from the sills up to the ridge pole.

Miniatures such as this have universal human appeal. As children, we don't have to be taught to enjoy dollhouses or model trains, and as adults only the most prosaic of us have outgrown a fascination with toys. We just develop more sophisticated tastes, appreciating greater realism in the objects we fancy. The more faithfully a model follows its full-scale original, the greater our wonder in beholding it. It is, after all, the contrast with the real world, pronounced in a miniature's detail, that captures the eye and stirs the imagination. And it is the execution of these minute details that most challenges the craftsman and rewards his efforts.

Scale cabinetmaking has become more than an increasingly popular hobby. The greater demand from collectors, and with it the higher prices they are willing to pay for commissioned pieces, have made modelmaking more attractive to serious woodworkers. Encountering the craft of making miniatures for the first time, the full-scale cabinetmaker will recognize similarities as well as differences between working full size and working to scale. To illustrate the shared and unique elements of miniature cabinetmaking, I will describe the construction of the 1/12-scale roll-top desk shown below, including

plans that could serve to help reproduce the original, down to the carving on the drawer pulls. This example will show how the scale modeler selects materials, buys, adapts and improvises tools, and devises special techniques to produce precisely detailed replicas in miniature. But first some discussion of the scale modeler's ethos is necessary.

In the past a dollhouse or a piece of doll furniture was judged for its visual impact, not for its structural integrity or its replicative accuracy. During the past ten years, as interest and sophistication in the craft have grown, there has been more attention to the fidelity of the replication to the original. Yet there are all kinds of miniatures being built, and a useful distinction can be made between *simulations*, essentially furniture for dollhouses, and *replications*, miniatures that conform to a particular scale and to the standards of construction and design of particular periods and prototypes. While various scales are currently used, ranging upward from 1/2 in.:1 ft., the de facto standard has become 1 in.:1 ft. This 1/12 scale, like HO scale in model railroading, combines the advantages of a reasonable level of achievable detail with an economy of space and material costs.

Though the movement has been toward more accurate replication, the other pole—simulation for affective impact—continues to help define the range of approaches the craftsman may take in designing and constructing a miniature piece. Simulation creates in the viewer the belief that the miniature is real, for if it is successful, he will perceive all of the form and detail that exist in the original, whether or not they are actually built in the miniature. The viewer will believe that joinery systems undergird the surface of the piece, that doors swing and that drawers may be opened. On the other hand, replication's primary appeal is for the craftsman himself. Alone in his shop, he feels challenged to incorporate in the miniature details of cabinetry that may never be seen. He takes pride in the quiet integrity of his piece, and can, with an audience, show that his piece works.

Every miniature combines simulation and replication. In the best pieces there is a sensitive balance between the two. It is not only that materials reach a point of intractability, but also that the degree of perceived detail reaches a point of diminishing returns. Even if techniques, tools and materials allow the craftsman to model the detail of a shell or

This desk may look like the real thing, but it is only 4 in. high and 5 in. long. Built to 1/12 scale, it exactly replicates the full-size original, incorporating all its structural and decorative details. The measured drawings beginning on p. 98 show how to construct the miniature, or they can help in reproducing the original desk at full scale.

foliated carving, the viewer's eye need see only the primary and some secondary motifs to be convinced of the carving's quality and authenticity. To do more would look cluttered. Also, the scale cabinetmaker may deviate from exact replication in order to maintain the sense of proportion in the original piece. The heavy cabriole leg of a Chippendale chair, for instance, may be carved undersize on the miniature because the bulk of the precisely proportioned leg might overwhelm the visual balance of the miniature. Thus the aesthetic sense of the craftsman is the final arbiter between simulation and replication.

The tension between simulation and replication is not essentially a difference between greater or lesser levels of craftsmanship. Considerable skill, though often of different sorts, is required to do each well. Compare the dioramist—an architectural scale modeler who uses multiple vanishing points and other modes of artifice—with the tool-and-die maker, who must work to close tolerances. Both sets of skills mingle in the work of the experienced miniaturist.

The selection of materials for a miniature is critical to the success of the project, and points to the necessity of balancing replication with simulation. No matter how painstakingly accurate the planning and the execution of the construction of a piece may be, improperly chosen materials can ruin its effect. And the reason is plain. While dimensions lend themselves to scale reduction, texture often does not. Two materials that can quickly destroy the illusion created by the miniature are wood and fabric. Wood grain in particular is inherently resistant to scale reduction. Exactly replicating the materials of the original piece does not yield a successful miniature.

A successful miniature begins with a complete understanding of the original to be copied. In this respect the scale cabinetmaker is like his full-scale counterpart. The poorly designed and poorly made miniature typically reveals the builder's inadequate knowledge of full-sized furniture. Only beyond this common starting point do the differences between the scale modeler and full-scale cabinetmaker become apparent. The differences include design decisions, material selection, tool choice and use, and special techniques for achieving effects comparable to those in the full-scale craft.

I constructed the $\frac{1}{12}$-scale roll-top desk illustrated here as the design model for an article that appeared in *The Scale Cabinetmaker* 3:4 (Summer 1979, pp. 23-28). The structure and detail of the original were no mystery to me; it is my own office desk at which I have worked for years. I rescued it from the attic of a Kansas lumberyard and rebuilt it entirely. The design of the miniature began with a set of sketches and measurements of the original—useful in building either a full-size duplicate or a scale model. For several reasons, I chose to replicate the original as closely as tools and skills would allow. First, I wanted to see if a tambour curtain could be designed and built in scale that would articulate over the S-curves of the desk sides in the same way and with the same look as in the original. Second, I wanted to illustrate the use of machinist's slotting saws for cutting the mortise-and-tenon joints in the desk's rail-and-stile base and top panels.

Having decided to reproduce the frame joinery of the original, I decided to match the other joints as well—the dovetails in the drawers and the tongues and grooves in the pull-out writing boards. Actually, I excluded from the model only one feature of the original—the spring-loaded latching bars that lock the drawers shut when the tambour curtain is low-

ered. Originally I intended to make this hardware item as well, but in the end I let the challenge pass.

The original roll-top desk has quartersawn oak in its framing members and drawer fronts and plainsawn oak in the panels. But for use in the miniature, oak with its open pores and flaring grain is inappropriate. Miniatures require a medium-hard, close-grained, finely textured wood. For that reason, many miniaturists use satinwood, pearwood, holly, boxwood and cherry. Walnut, while widely used, varies considerably as a satisfactory material, according to its growth rate. Walnut from semi-arid regions is more likely to yield usable material for models than are faster-growing eastern varieties. Basswood is probably the most widely used material for miniatures because of its availability and low price. It is easily worked and offers the appearance of a wide range of full-scale grains from bird's-eye maple to quartersawn oak. However, while it serves as a ground for simulating a variety of wood grains, its short fiber and surface fuzz make tight joint lines and surface preparation a serious problem.

The scale cabinetmaker has the same jealous regard of his materials as does the full-scale woodworker, squirreling away select stuff against future need: pieces of crotch and burl, or boards with special grain. From such a pile I chose some quartersawn cherry for the desk. It was cut from a heavy branch rather than from a trunk section, where annual rings produce too broad a grain. The ray fleck in the cherry provides a believable substitute for the distinctive look of quartered oak. Lighter-colored boards I set aside for the pigeonhole unit; darker wood I used in framing the main carcase, and boards with a more pronounced figure I ticketed for panels.

I might have used commercially produced hardwood boards. However, such material is typically flatsawn, and therefore yields too few boards with useful figure. And it is commonly supplied in fractional rather than in scale thicknesses. If in a $\frac{1}{12}$-scale project the modeler wishes a board that is a scale 1 in. thick, commercial material offers him either $\frac{5}{64}$ in. or $\frac{3}{32}$ in. thick. Since in $\frac{1}{12}$th scale, one inch is 0.0833 in., the commercial stock is either 0.011 in. too thick or 0.005 in. too thin. So the scale cabinetmaker is better off ripping and sizing his own stock. The materials in the desk are precisely scaled to the materials in the prototype with one exception: the entire cubby unit was built of scale $\frac{1}{4}$-in. thick material even though some of the vertical and horizontal dividers in the prototype are $\frac{1}{8}$ in. thick. With scale lumber, a piece that is 0.0104 in. thick simply has no structural stability, and could not be used.

Tools and workbench techniques also change as scale reduction takes place. Some full-size shop tools are useful in preparing materials—table saw, bandsaw, jigsaw, jointer and thickness planer. However, beyond the useful limits of these tools, the maker of miniatures is forced by the inadequacies of the marketplace to become inventive in his search for functional precision tools. While it is possible to build an excellent miniature with a jackknife, as one outstanding craftsman indeed does, precision tools of high quality do increase the chances of achieving good results. The hobby industry produces some good-quality hand and power tools—knives, handsaws, clamps, power hand grinders, belt and disc sanders, and jigsaws. However, many hobby tools are either overengineered toys or underengineered tools. For example, small (4-in.) table saws with tilting arbors appear to incorporate all the features of a full-sized shop machine, but their

(text continued on page 102)

Roll-top desk: front elevation

Plans are 1½ times the size of the miniature.

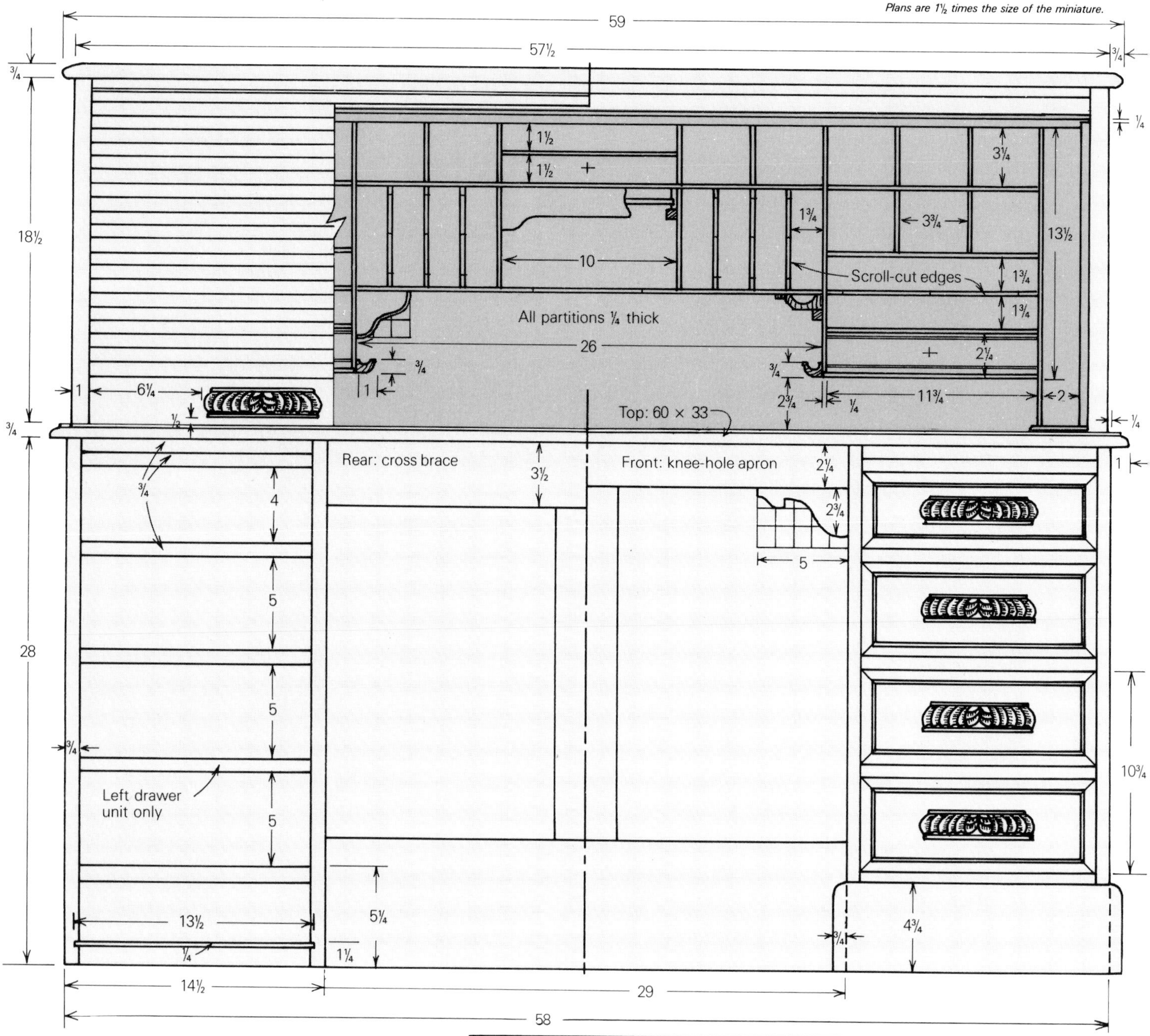
59
57½
¾
18½
28
1½
1½
3¼
1¾
3¾
13½
10
Scroll-cut edges
1¾
1¾
All partitions ¼ thick
26
2¼
¾
1
6¼
1
2¾
¼
11¾
2
Top: 60 × 33
½
Rear: cross brace
3½
Front: knee-hole apron
2¼
2¾
5
4
5
5
5
Left drawer
unit only
10¾
13½
5¼
4¾
1¼
14½
29
58

Scroll profiles

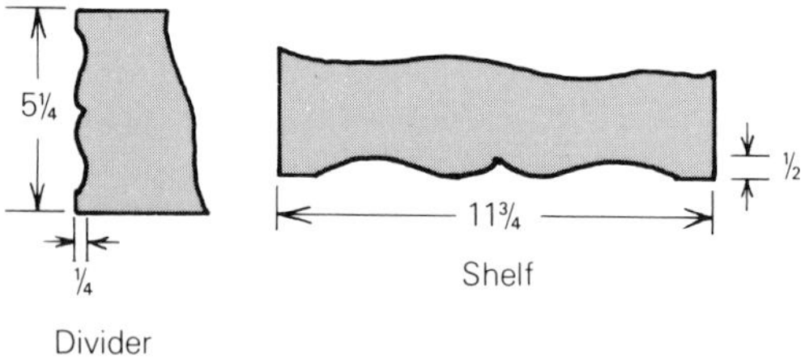
5¼
¼
Divider
11¾
½
Shelf

Plan of central shelf

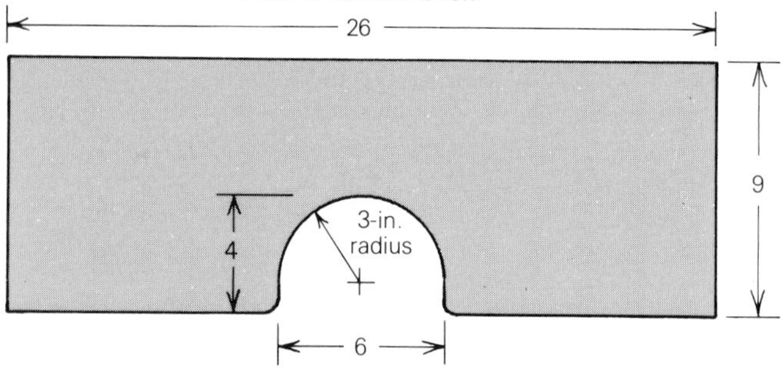
26
9
4
3-in.
radius
6

Typical of early 20th-century factory-made office furniture, the original desk was designed for machine production. If you use these drawings to make the piece full size in your own shop, you might want to improve upon the existing joinery. The main vertical dividers in the pigeonhole unit could be dadoed or routed for dovetail housings to receive the shelves. Likewise, the main shelves could be routed to receive the minor dividers. To secure the writing surface (desk top) to the drawer units, cut square, wedged tenons on the stiles at the four corners, and mortise the desk top to receive them.

Drawer-pull detail

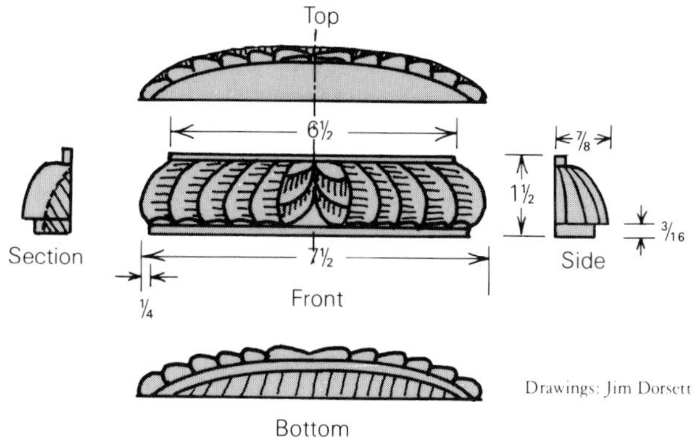
Top
6½
Section
7½
Front
¼
⅞
1½
³⁄₁₆
Side
Bottom

Drawings: Jim Dorsett

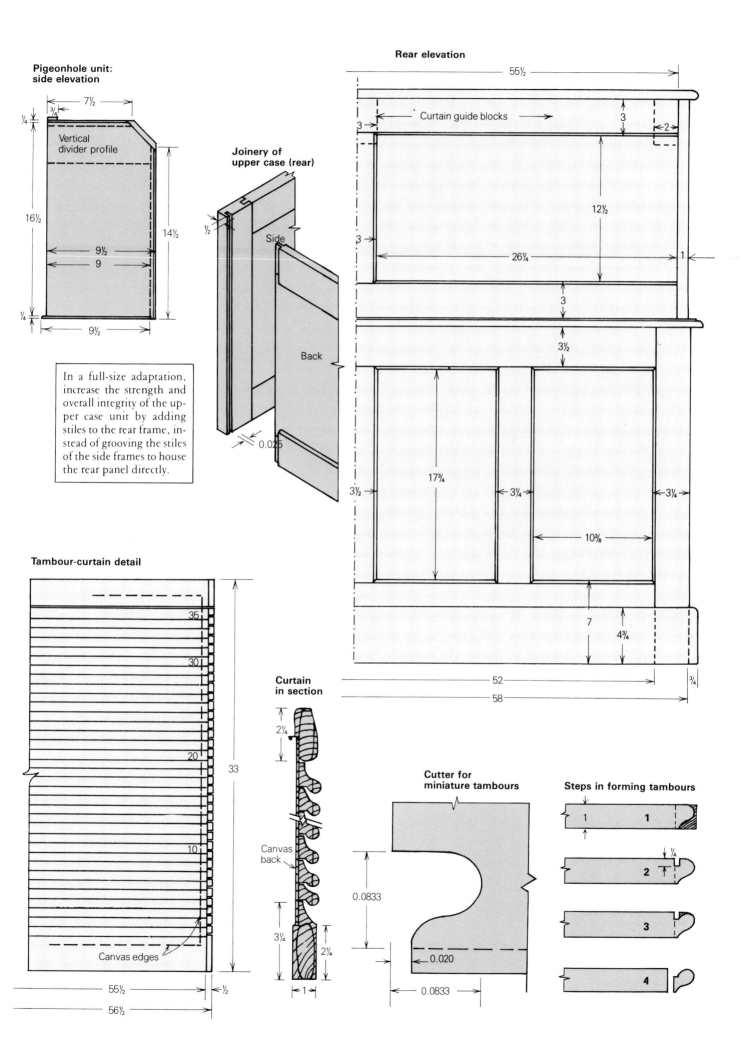

Pigeonhole unit: side elevation

7½
¾
¼
Vertical divider profile
16½
14½
9½
9
¼
9½

In a full-size adaptation, increase the strength and overall integrity of the upper case unit by adding stiles to the rear frame, instead of grooving the stiles of the side frames to house the rear panel directly.

Joinery of upper case (rear)

½
Side
Back
0.025

Rear elevation

55½
Curtain guide blocks
3
3
2
3
12½
3
26¼
1
3
3½
3½
17¾
3¼
3¼
10⅜
7
4¾
52
¾
58

Tambour-curtain detail

35
30
20
10
33
Canvas edges
55½
½
56½

Curtain in section

2¼
Canvas back
3¼
2¼
1

Cutter for miniature tambours

0.0833
0.020
0.0833

Steps in forming tambours

1   1
¼   2
3
4

Case assembly for left-hand drawer unit

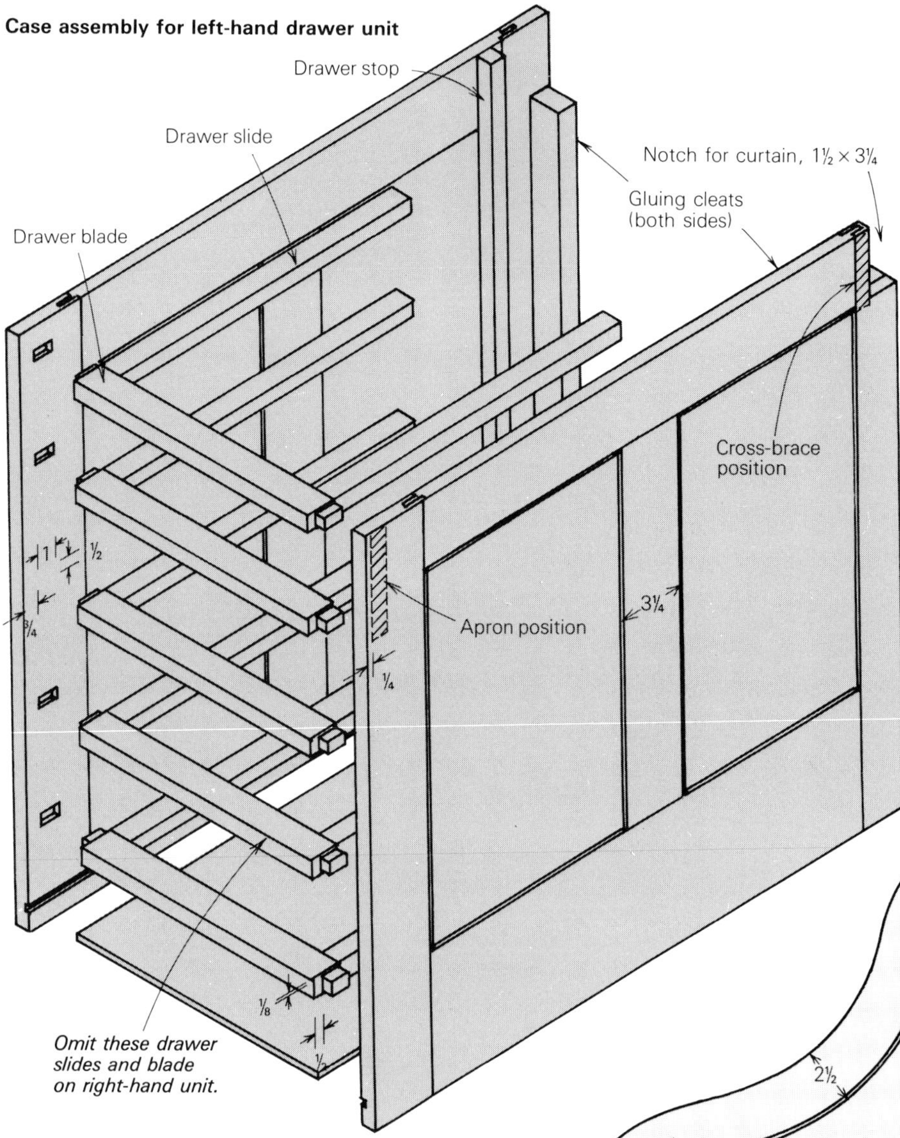
Drawer stop
Drawer slide
Notch for curtain, 1½ × 3¼
Gluing cleats
(both sides)
Drawer blade
Cross-brace
position
Apron position
3¼
1
½
¾
¼
⅛
½
Omit these drawer
slides and blade
on right-hand unit.

You can improve the case joinery of the original by increasing the length of the tenons on the frame rails and muntins. Double tenons on the drawer blades will make the drawer units stronger. In finding means for attaching the drawer guides to the inside of the case, be sure to take wood movement into account.

Side elevation

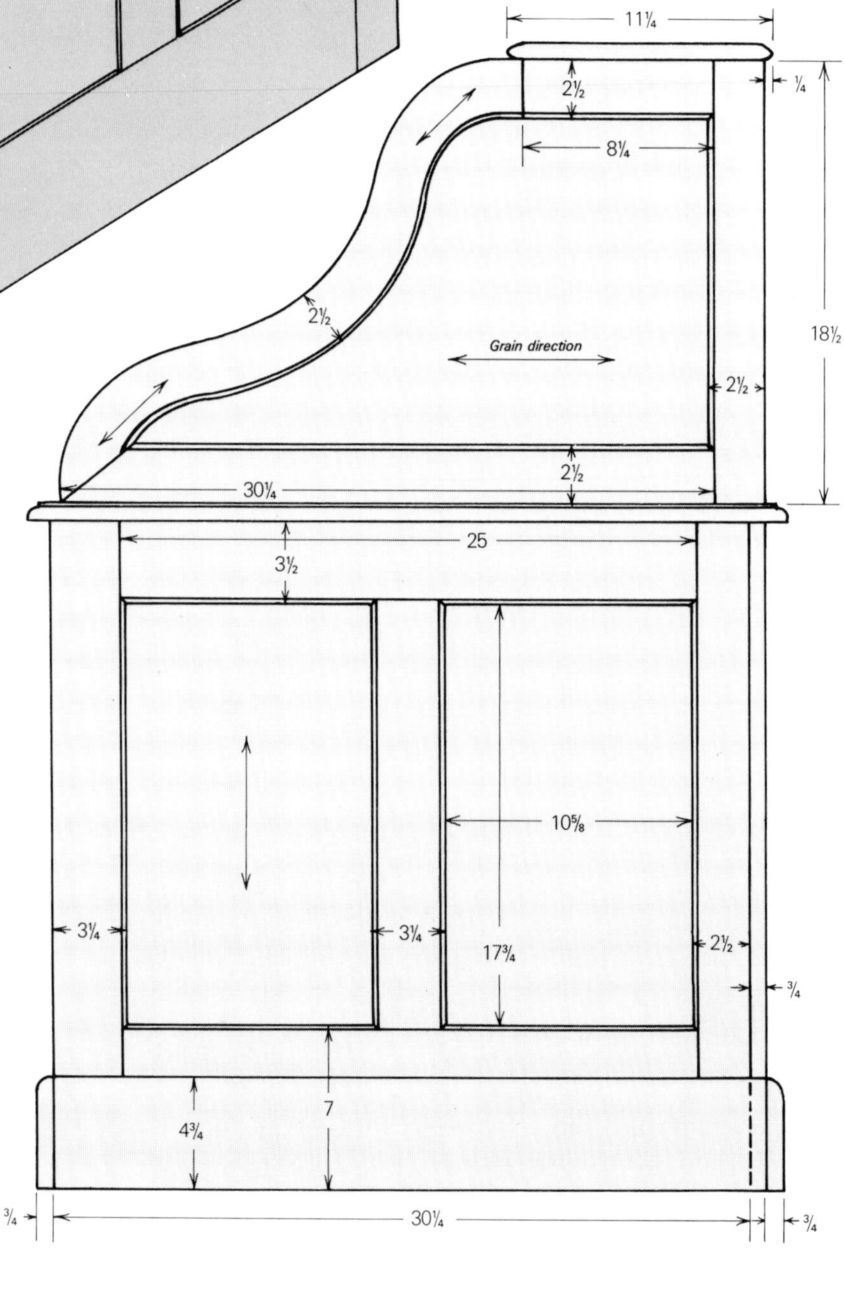
11¼
¼
2½
8¼
18½
2½
Grain direction
2½
2½
30¼
25
3½
10⅝
3¼
3¼
17¾
2½
¾
7
4¾
¾
30¼
¾

Frame assembly for drawer unit

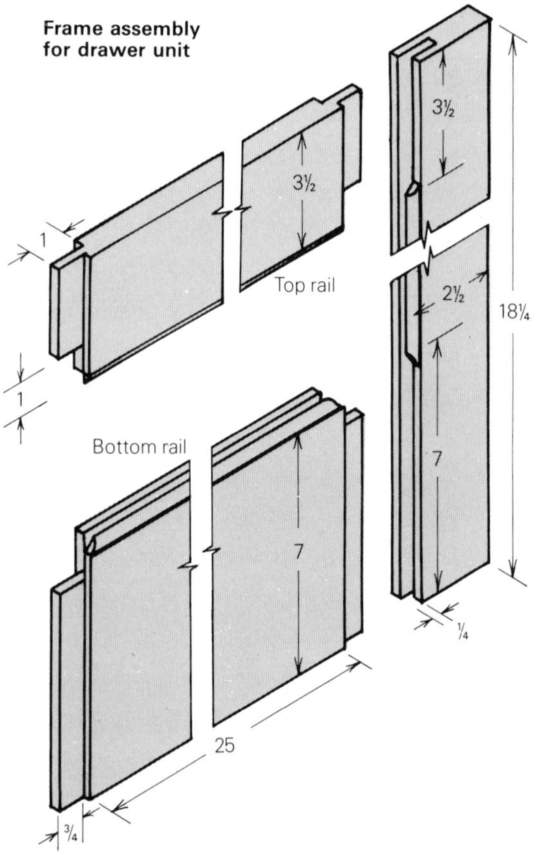
3½
3½
1
Top rail
2½
18¼
1
Bottom rail
7
7
¼
25
¾

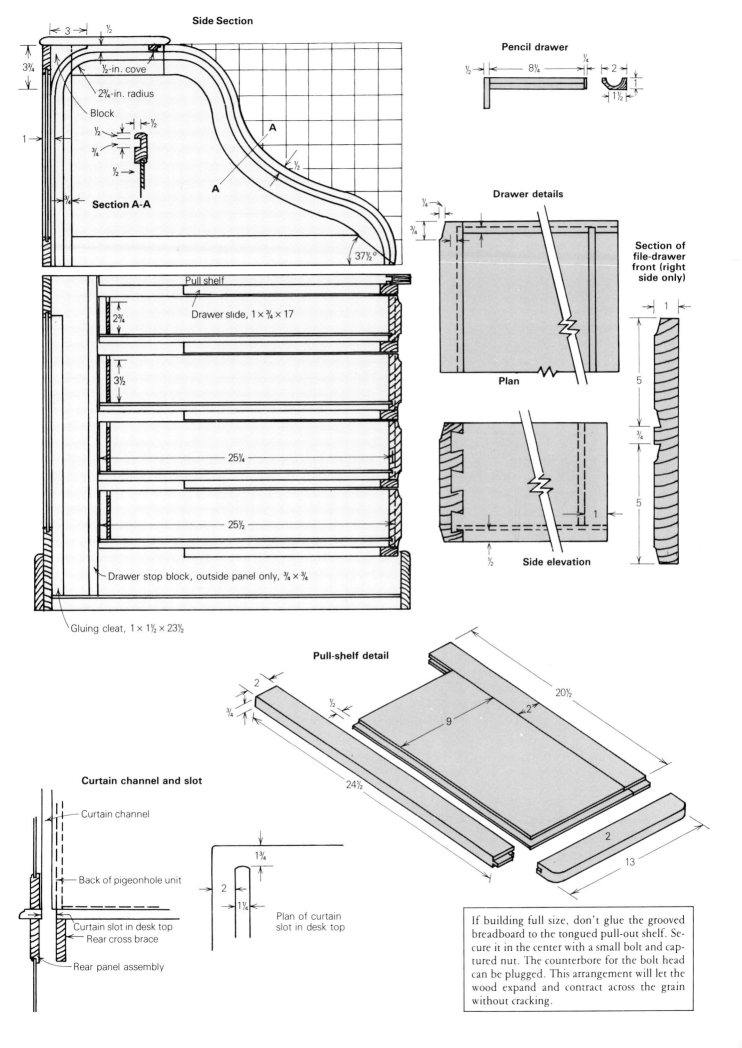

Side Section

3

½

½-in. cove

2¾-in. radius

Block

3¾

1

½

½

¾

½

¾

Section A-A

A

A

½

37½°

Pencil drawer

½   8¼   ¼   2

1½   1

Drawer details

¼

¾

Plan

½

Side elevation

Section of file-drawer front (right side only)

1

5

¾

5

1

Pull shelf

Drawer slide, 1 × ¾ × 17

2¾

3½

25¼

25½

Drawer stop block, outside panel only, ¾ × ¾

Gluing cleat, 1 × 1½ × 23½

Pull-shelf detail

2

¾

½

9

2

20½

24½

2

13

Curtain channel and slot

Curtain channel

Back of pigeonhole unit

Curtain slot in desk top

Rear cross brace

Rear panel assembly

1¾

2

1¼

Plan of curtain slot in desk top

If building full size, don't glue the grooved breadboard to the tongued pull-out shelf. Secure it in the center with a small bolt and captured nut. The counterbore for the bolt head can be plugged. This arrangement will let the wood expand and contract across the grain without cracking.

To thickness his stock to precise dimensions, the author first sands to rough thickness using a drum sander mounted in his radial-arm saw and feeding the boards between the rotating drum and the fence.

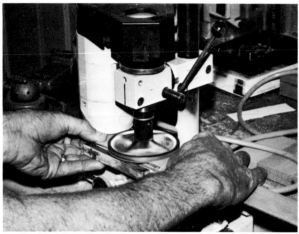

For final finishing, he chucks a sanding disc in his Unimat drill press and draws the stock between the disc and the milling table beneath.

A better method for thicknessing stock employs a tapered sanding disc mounted on a direct-drive mandrel opposite an adjustable fence. This device will give accurate results, thicknessing 1½-in. wide planks to tolerances of 0.003 in. edge to edge.

blades, bearings, fences, work surfaces and power lack the degree of precision and durability that is desirable.

Probably the most adequate and widely used power tools produced for the scale modeler are small machine lathes (Unimat, Sherline, Taig, Machinex). Yet even here the tools were not designed for the woodworking miniaturist. They are essentially down-sized versions of full-sized machine lathes, useful in metalturning. Still, offering such auxiliary capabilities as drill press, table saw, milling machine and disc sander, the small machine lathe is affordable, and essential.

Beyond the limits of available, useful hand tools, improvisation must be practiced at the miniaturist's workbench. Dental burrs and chisels become molding cutters and wood chisels. Jewelry-supply houses are another source of precision hand tools, from pliers to gravers. Small mills from tool-and-die supply houses become routing bits, and a machinist's depth gauge serves as a try square.

Measuring instruments vary with the degree of precision required by the project. Several high-quality 1-in. scale steel rules are available, marked off in scale increments of ¼ in., similar in function to the 1-in. architect's scale. Where finer measuring increments are required, scale dimensions are translated into decimal inches, and a machinist's 100th rule, dial caliper and micrometer are used. Unless your favorite form of masochism is the division of fractions, avoid the use of 1/16 scale in building miniatures. Given a scale dimension of 23½ in., for instance, it is much simpler to mark off the scale distance with a 1-in. scale instrument than to contend with a distance that is almost, but not exactly, 1⁶¹/₆₄ in. on a 1/16-in. rule. If greater precision is needed, the measured distance with a dial caliper is 1.9583 in.

Several tools required in the desk project illustrate the miniaturist's need to improvise. The basic problem in miniature projects is the need for precisely sized and thicknessed lumber. This desk called for scale lumber in the following sizes: ¼ in. (0.0208 in.), 5/16 in. (slightly undersize at 0.024 in. to fit the groove made with a 0.025 in. slotting saw), ½ in. (0.0416 in.), ¾ in. (0.0625 in.) and 1 in. (0.0833 in.). Short of investing in a planer that will work to these thicknesses, there are two alternative approaches. The more tedious and less satisfactory approach involves rough-sanding the lumber down to approximate thickness with a drum sander mounted against a 90° fence of a radial-arm saw. The semi-finished boards are then sanded down to final thickness with a flat disc mounted over a milling table in a Unimat drill press.

A better solution employs a thicknessing sander, as made by Jim Jedlicka *(The Scale Cabinetmaker* 4:4, Summer 1980). This tool, designed with the scale cabinetmaker in mind, employs an 8-in. tapered (2°) disc and is powered by a flea-market motor. In thicknessing 1½-in. wide boards, it is accurate to within 0.003 in. (edge to edge). In contrast with the chipping and splintering that often result with jointer knives on uneven or knotted grain, the disc grinds off the surface of thin stock without marring or chipping.

A second problem—cutting the system of tenons and grooves in the panel framing—I solved by using machinist's slotting saws. A 1½-in. dia. by 0.025-in. blade on a mandrel with a ⅜-in. arbor was mounted in a Unimat drill press over a table, which was in turn mounted to the lathe's cross slide. With a hardwood fence covering the blade, the height of the blade above the table could be controlled with the drill press and the depth of the cut with the longitudinal feed screw of

Photos: Don and Cindy Massie

the lathe. The setup produces joints that are crisp and precise. Blades are typically available in diameters ranging upward from ¾ in. and in thicknesses from 0.010 in. to 0.030 in.

The tambour curtain posed yet another problem. Because there is no commercial source for scale molding cutters, I had several options when special molding faces were required, as found on the beaded edges of the desk's stiles and rails or the S-profile of the tambours. Although some commercial moldings are available and can be adapted to a range of needs, these are typically supplied in basswood only. The desk moldings could have been cut with ball-and-cone dental burrs (as indeed the pencil shelves and drawers in the cubby unit were made), but hand-shaping of the finished profiles would have been required, destroying some of the crisp uniformity I wanted. So I chose another method. The needed molding profile is lathe-turned in mild steel. Flutes are milled on the end of the turned steel and dressed with pattern files, and then it is case-hardened. The resulting tool is not meant for production runs, but it does provide an adequate solution to a recurring problem in the craft.

Assembly always poses a variety of jigging and clamping difficulties, most of which are familiar to the full-scale woodworker. Sometimes the solution is unique to the particular piece being assembled. For that reason most miniaturists keep on hand an array of clamping tools—rubber bands, bulldog and alligator clips, C-clamps, spring clamps, handscrews, jeweler's ring clamps, clothespins and others. In assembling the desk base unit, for example, I often used two kinds of clamps—flat, magnetic holding jigs for clamping the flat panel sections, and violinmaker's clamps for holding the assembled pedestal. The jig consists of a flat, steel plate with pieces of 90° aluminum angle along two sides. Clamping is done with a number of small, square magnets, which hold the glued assembly in place. Violinmaker's clamps with their screw-tightened, cork-faced blocks provide a firm, but gentle, means of holding a carcase assembly during gluing.

The majority of miniaturists use either polyvinyl (white) or aliphatic resin (yellow) glue in assembly. Some of the high-viscosity, slow-set cyanoacrylates offer promise as general-purpose glues in modeling but are still relatively new. Regardless of the type of adhesive used, the woodworker's typical problem of pre-finish glue spotting is compounded in miniature cabinetry by the size of the workpiece. Pre-assembly sealing of the wood is a common solution, and excess glue is avoided. The desk was assembled with white glue, but a flexible polyvinyl fabric glue was used to attach the tambours to the linen back. The finish consists of a light wash of cherry stain and several light, rubbed coats of satin spray lacquer. Because the cherry will darken with age, the stain was optional. An equally desirable sealer might have been several coats of cut shellac (rubbed in). Sealer is used on a miniature to provide a finish without the type of surface buildup that will obscure the crispness of detail (or what one craftsman has called the appearance of "having been dipped in black molasses and drip-dried during a monsoon").

Had the function of the desk been only to fill out the illusion of an entire miniature setting, other design options could have been considered. The effect of the raised desk curtain could have been simulated with the application of only a few slats across the top of the open desk front. The structure of the pedestals could have been simulated through a system of flat, butt-joined boards to which fascia "rails" and "stiles"

Dovetail jig, patterned after its full-size counterpart and used in conjunction with a Dremel drill press and small tapered mills, cuts the joints for the drawers.

To cut moldings for limited runs, Dorsett equips his Dremel drill press with a shop-made cutter, left. To make a cutter, he turns the desired profile on a small bar of mild steel and then mills flutes in the sides. Once dressed and sharpened, the cutter is case-hardened.

For producing crisp and precise mortises, grooves and tenons, Dorsett uses a machinist's slotting saw mounted on a mandrel and driven by a horizontal miller. Fence and table register the stock.

would be glued. If carefully assembled and finished in this way, the joint lines could be made invisible and the appearance of the piece would be identical to that of the miniature employing mortises and tenons. Assuming that the miniature would never be subjected to the same stresses from use or changing humidity as would the full-sized desk, the simulated model should have proven quite durable and quite convincing. But I would have known the difference. □

Jim Dorsett is editor and publisher of The Scale Cabinetmaker, *a quarterly journal for miniaturists. For information on subscriptions, write Dorsett Publications, Box 2038, Christiansburg, Va. 24073.*

Index

FINE WOODWORKING
Editorial Staff, 1975-1985

Paul Bertorelli
Mary Blaylock
Dick Burrows
Jim Cummins
Katie de Koster
Ruth Dobsevage
Tage Frid
Roger Holmes
Cindy Howard
John Kelsey
Linda Kirk
Nancy-Lou Knapp
John Lively
Rick Mastelli
Nina Perry
Jim Richey
Paul Roman
David Sloan
Nancy Stabile
Laura Tringali
Linda D. Whipkey

FINE WOODWORKING
Art Staff, 1975-1985

Roger Barnes
Kathleen Creston
Deborah Fillion
Lee Hov
Betsy Levine
Lisa Long
E. Marino III
Karen Pease
Roland Wolf

FINE WOODWORKING
Production Staff, 1975-1985

Claudia Applegate
Barbara Bahr
Pat Byers
Deborah Cooper
Kathleen Davis
David DeFeo
Michelle Fryman
Mary Galpin
Dinah George
Barbara Hannah
Annette Hilty
Jenny Long
Johnette Luxeder
Gary Mancini
Laura Martin
Mary Eileen McCarthy
JoAnn Muir
Cynthia Lee Nyitray
Kathryn Olsen
Mary Ann Snieckus
Barbara Snyder

If you enjoyed this book, you're going to love our magazine.

A year's subscription to *Fine Woodworking* brings you the kind of practical, hands-on information you found in this book and much more. In issue after issue, you'll find projects that teach new skills, demonstrations of tools and techniques, new design· ideas, old-world traditions, shop tests, coverage of current woodworking events, and breathtaking examples of the woodworker's art for inspiration.

To subscribe, just fill out one of the attached subscription cards, or call us toll-free at 1-800-888-8286. As always, **we guarantee your satisfaction.**

Subscribe Today!

6 issues for just $25

The Taunton Press
63 S. Main Street, Box 5506, Newtown, CT 06470-5506
